Entrepreneur® MAGAZINE'S

startup

Start Your Own

SPECIALTY TRAVEL & TOUR BUSINESS

Your Step-by-Step Guide to Success

Rob and Terry Adams

EP
Entrepreneur. Press

Editorial Director: Jere L. Calmes
Managing Editor: Marla Markman
Cover Design: Beth Hansen-Winter
Production: Eliot House Productions
Composition: Ed Stevens

This publication is designed to provide accurate and authoritative information in regard to the subject matter covered. It is sold with the understanding that the publisher is not engaged in rendering legal, accounting, or other professional services. If legal advice or other expert assistance is required, the services of a competent professional person should be sought.

Library of Congress Cataloging-in-Publication Data

Adams, Rob, 1950–
    Start your own specialty travel and tour business/by Rob and Terry Adams.
      p.   cm.   —(Entrepreneur magazine's start up)
    Includes index.
    ISBN 1-891984-73-X
      1. Travel agents. 2. Small business—Management. 3. New business enterprises.
I. Adams, Terry, 1952– II. Entrepreneur (Irvine, Calif.) III. Title. IV. Series.

G154.A34 2003
338.4'791'068—dc21   2003046229

Printed in Canada

09 08 07 06 05 04   10 9 8 7 6 5 4 3 2

Contents

Tue wed

▲

Chapter 5

The Traveler's Trunk:
Business Structure and Location 57

Chapter 8

Daily Operations for the Tour Operator 111

Chapter 9

The Travel Kit: Your Business Equipment. 127

Preface

You're holding this book either in your hands, on your lap, or on your desk—probably dangerously near a spillable cup of coffee—because you're one of those people who likes to live on the edge. You're contemplating starting your own business.

This is one of the most exhilarating things you can do for yourself and your family. It's also one of the scariest.

Owning your own business means you are the boss, the big cheese, the head honcho. You make the rules. You lay down the law. It also means you can't call in sick (especially when you are the only employee) or let somebody else worry about making enough to cover payroll and expenses. And you can't defer that cranky client or intimidating IRS letter to a higher authority: You're it.

We're assuming you've picked up this particular book on starting and running a specialty travel business for one or more of the following reasons:

- You have a background in the travel field.
- You have wanderlust in your veins and a permanently packed suitcase in your hall closet, and you think the travel business would be fun and exciting.
- You have a background in speaking, training, or sales; and you like helping people learn new things about new places.
- You have no particular experience with speaking, training, or sales but believe you can sell travel or help people experience travel in an entertaining, informative fashion as a tour operator.
- You believe the specialty travel industry is an up-and-coming one, and you're willing to take a chance.

Which did you choose? (Didn't know it was a test, did you?) Well, you can relax because there is no wrong answer. Any of these responses is entirely correct, so long as you realize that *they all involve a lot of learning and a lot of hard work*. They can also involve a heck of a lot of fun, as well as a tremendous amount of personal and professional satisfaction. Our goal here is to tell you everything you need to know to:

- decide whether a specialty travel business is the right business for you;
- get your business started successfully;
- keep your business running successfully;
- make contacts and advertise your business successfully.

We've interviewed lots of people out there on the front lines of the industry, from all around the country, to find out how the specialty travel business really works and what makes it tick. And we've set aside lots of places for them to tell their own stories and give their hard-won advice and suggestions—a sort of virtual round-table discussion group, with you placed right in the thick of things. (For a listing of these successful business owners, see the Appendix.)

We've attempted to make this book as user-friendly as possible. We've broken our chapters into manageable sections on every aspect of start-up and operations, and we've left some space for your creativity to soar. Our pages are packed with helpful tips so you can get up and running on your new venture as quickly as possible. We've also provided an appendix crammed with contacts and resources.

So sit back—don't spill that coffee! Get reading, and get ready to become a specialty travel pro.

Pack
Your Bags!

Once upon a time, travel was only for the wealthy and the adventurous. It took a fair amount of capital, an inordinate amount of time and—unless you were going the luxury trans-Atlantic liner route on a first-class ticket—a willingness to accept discomfort as your due. Today, however, almost everybody travels, from backpack-toting students to

▲

briefcase-wielding corporate types, to retirees sporting group-tour name badges. Travel is a multibillion-dollar industry that has skyrocketed since the first trans-Atlantic commercial jet took to the air back in 1957.

And although we still tend to think of travel in terms of airline seats or trips in the family wagon, today's touring encompasses far more than coach class to St. Louis or an endless drive to Toon World spent squabbling in the back seat with your siblings. You can choose from among a staggering number of specialty tours—everything from a trip down the Amazon studying ethnobotany with local shamans to surf camp à la The Beach Boys to walking, biking, hiking, or chocolate-bingeing tours. There are specialty tours for gardeners, gourmet cooks, antiques lovers and art history buffs; and tours based on auto racing, agriculture, rafting adventures, wine-tasting, exploring the historic world of King Arthur, dog sledding, storm chasing, llama trekking, caving, cattle driving, and more—much more!

This chapter explores the flourishing travel business. It's a sort of in-your-lap TV-newsmagazine report without the commercials. We will delve into the steadily rising economic success of the field, dip into its secrets and—unlike any TV news-magazine—help you decide whether it's the business for you.

Splurging on Travel

At last count, domestic travelers and internationals journeying to the United States spent more than $495 billion on travel-related expenses in this country, says the Travel Industry Association of America. In the late '90s, that spending came in at $1.36 billion per day, $56.5 million per hour, $941,971 per minute and $15,700 per second.

Stat Fact
Thirty years ago, the average American went on vacation once a year and spent a leisurely two to three weeks off the job, says the United States Tour Operators Association. Today, people take shorter but more frequent vacations that average seven days to 10 days each.

Even better, the U.S. Bureau of Labor Statistics says the money people spend on travel is expected to increase significantly over the next decade. With the current employment boom, rising incomes, and smaller-sized families, funds that formerly had to be doled out for necessities can now go toward splurging on luxuries like travel. People are marrying later than they used to, which makes for a considerable population of young urban 20- and 30-somethings with money to spend, unfettered by family cares. And with an ever-increasing population of peppy elders, more and more Americans are expected to travel for fun—watch out for those boomers! In fact, according to the Bureau of Labor Statistics, many folks now take more than one vacation per year.

But not all travel is recreation-oriented; business travel is also expected to increase. The Bureau of Labor Statistics says the projected growth rate in employment for managerial, professional and sales types—the ones who do most of the business traveling—is hale and hearty.

Mists of History

The earliest tour operators have faded into the mists of history, unknown except as shadowy figures who might have organized groups of pilgrims for junkets to holy lands or to view ancient wonders like the Sphinx.

In the summer of 1841, however, a Baptist missionary named Thomas Cook decided to send a group of people round-trip from Leicester to Loughborough in England for a temperance meeting. He got the Midland Counties Railway Company to take on these passengers at a group rate of one shilling per person—and thus was officially born the modern tour operator.

From that modest beginning, Thomas Cook went on to fame and fortune. By 1851, he was arranging tours to the Great Exhibit in London, and in 1856, he organized a European grand tour. By the end of the 19th century, Thomas Cook & Son had blossomed into a major travel and tour operation that sent travelers around the world.

The Thomas Cook & Son firm had lots of emulators. According to the United States Tour Operators Association (USTOA), other budding tour operators probably got a jumpstart on the business while working as ticket agents for steamship lines and railways. Since the tour operators were already selling the journey itself in the form of tickets, it was only a small jump to the additional business of planning itineraries and booking hotels for their customers.

By the 1850s—courtesy of Thomas Cook and others—you could commonly buy a railway

FunFact

On August 25, 1919, Air Transport & Travel Ltd., the forerunner of British Overseas Airway Corporation, launched the world's first scheduled international airline with service between London and Paris. Its maiden flight boasted one passenger and a cargo of Devonshire cream, newspapers, and grouse. Air travel was definitely an adventure—according to the British Airways' Web site, one pilot took two days to make the two-hour flight, making 33 unscheduled stops along the way.

tour; and soon after World War I, you could also purchase a steamship tour package. By 1927, prior to the Great Depression, the tour industry was beginning to thrive. However, it didn't really soar until after World War II, when aviation technology made long-range commercial flights not only possible but also affordable. Since those heady days, the industry has continued to fly high. The USTOA estimates that, taken as a whole, its active members have logged more than 1,100 years in the travel business. If you imagine that number as a chronological dip backward in time, you can just make out, through the mists, an ancient tour operator booking his flock on a trip to Constantinople.

If It's Tuesday

Leisure travel has come a long way since the cattle-car version of packaged tours made famous—or maybe infamous—by the 1969 film, "If It's Tuesday, This Must Be Belgium." When the movie was first released, the USTOA says 95 percent of tour passengers were traveling on a passport for the very first time. Today, only 5 percent of tour and vacation passengers are passport newbies.

If you haven't seen "If It's Tuesday," you should. It's charming and funny; and it accurately depicts the quintessential escorted tour of the mid-20th century, in which an eclectic assortment of passengers is herded onto a bus for a whirlwind tour of about 14 European countries in 10 hectic days. But lest you think packaged tours are still like that—they're not!

Thirty years ago, says the USTOA, Western Europe was the destination of choice for most Americans, with few brave souls venturing anywhere else. Today, people are eager to visit far-flung outposts from China to the Antarctic to the Amazon. And while back in 1969, 80 percent of escorted tours were whirlwinds, featuring a dozen countries in as many days, 80 percent of escorted tours in the new millennium are going to be regional, concentrating on a single country or area.

Now, tourists are both more sophisticated and more adventurous. They want to *do* instead of just view—everything from rappelling down cliff faces to participating in archaeological digs to joining the locals at a Scottish *ceilidh* (a Highland dance party, pronounced kay-lee). And while new-millennium travelers are eager for new experiences and more than willing to sample the unusual, they're also more discerning and demanding. Instead of the dreary hostels accepted unquestioningly by yesterday's tourists, they want first-class accommodations in five-star hotels and gourmet restaurants.

Stat Fact
In 1969, only 2.3 million Americans traveled to Europe. In 1999, that figure swelled to 11.6 million. That's a lot of tourists!

Fulfilling Wanderlust

So what does all this mean to the travel and tour specialist? It means more opportunity, more money, room for growth, and plenty of scope for creative entrepreneurship. And let's not forget fun! Most people go into the travel and tour business because they have a strong case of wanderlust and love to hit the high road, the low road, and all those fascinating avenues beckoning in between.

Being a travel and tour specialist gives you terrific opportunities to do just that, for far less money than nonprofessionals pay. If you lead tours, of course, you're out there on the journey along with your customers. There is also all the travel you have to do to choose the right sights and sites for your packages. If you're a travel agent, you get lots of perks called *fam trips*. "Fam" is short for "familiarization." A fam trip is a freebie or discount offered to travel agents by tour operators, resorts, and attractions (from wax museums to glass-bottom boat trips to amusement parks) in hopes you'll fall in love with the

In the name of legitimate research, you can take advantage of all sorts of low- or no-cost travel adventures.

offering and sell it to your clients. So in the name of legitimate research, you can take advantage of all sorts of low- or no-cost travel adventures. What other business offers this kind of perk?

On the Job

Now you know why the travel and tour industry is hot and why—assuming you like to travel—it's fun. But what exactly does a travel and tour specialist do? Good question! As a travel and tour professional, you can operate in one of two modes:

1. *As a travel agent.* You'll book clients on various tours and occasionally arrange (but not write) tickets so they can shuffle off to Buffalo or any other chosen destination by plane, train, or ship.
2. *As a specialty tour operator.* You will design and implement the tours your travel agent colleagues will sell.

We're going to cover both of these modes in this book. Since they're basically two sides of the same ticket, requiring much the same knowledge and skills, we recommend that you read through everything—even if it doesn't seem at first glance to apply to the mode you may already have chosen.

The Travel Agent's World

The first thing you should know about the travel agent's world is that it has changed radically in the past few years. You might still think of travel agencies as retail cubicles, decorated with sheaves of Hawaiian cruise brochures and European vacation slicks, and tucked into downtown storefronts or out-of-the-way spaces at the local mall. Maybe you think customers find their way into one of these emporiums to purchase airline tickets, a Club Med holiday or one of the aforesaid traditional travel packages (called *products* in the business). Not anymore!

The new trend is toward homebased travel agencies that have no walk-in traffic, don't write airline tickets, and don't wait for wandering passers-by to come in and purchase vacations. Homebased or *independent* travel agencies instead tend to focus on a particular market niche, like disabled travelers, the senior set, or people interested in educational tours. And the reason they don't write airline tickets is that they're not allowed to, at least in the usual manner.

But we're getting ahead of ourselves. To explain the phenomenon of homebased travel agencies, let's step back in time, to the days before computers ran the world.

Dark-Age Ticketing

In those barely remembered days (pre-1970s) when people wrote things out by hand, if you wanted to purchase an airline ticket, you had to trot on over to your local Pan Am or other air carrier's ticket counter—assuming there *was* a local counter or office—and stand in line until it was your turn. Then you had to wait while the ticket agent looked up flights in a book and wrote out your ticket in longhand.

Or—and this was a big time and effort saver—you could call your travel agent. He would then look up all the information in guides packed with eye-crossing small print, call the airline's agency desk, reserve your flight and write the ticket by hand from a supply in his desk drawer. The agent didn't mind doing this because he got tidy commissions on all the fares he wrote.

As the World Turns

Then, in about 1975, the airline-ticketing world took a breathtaking turn with the introduction of the *Computerized Reservation System* or *CRS*. There are several CRS systems, each owned by a different airline or group of airlines; they all work in basically the same manner. Today, just about anybody with a home computer and Internet access can reserve their own airline tickets; but back in the Brady Bunch era, computerized reservations were a major innovation.

With this online system, travel agencies could bypass the agency desk, make the reservations themselves and then print out not only your ticket but even a boarding pass and itinerary. At first, this benefited every-one. The airlines were delighted because they no longer had to pay a union employee to work the agency desk, and the travel agents were thrilled because they could offer lightning-fast automated service to their customers.

Travel agencies trumpeted the fact that they could give customers airline prices with no additional fees and with instant ticketing. And since even calling the airlines cost money, because they didn't have toll-free numbers, customers rushed to take advantage of travel agency ticketing. It was so easy; everybody won.

Of course, it wasn't all quite that simple. At first, travel agencies had to qualify to get a CRS. If they didn't show enough revenue to warrant a system, no amount of begging and pleading would get them one. By the time the '80s rolled around, more than 16,000 travel agencies boasted CRS systems.

Another Development

Eventually, however, the bloom fell off the rose. The airlines decided they could spring for toll-free numbers to regain customers lost to travel agencies and put a halt to at least some of those agency commissions they were paying out. By the mid-1990s, customers had discovered that they could reserve their own tickets right from home with their personal computers, which took another notch out of travel agencies' commissionable sales.

Then, in 1995, the domestic airlines pulled the rug out from under the agencies by placing a cap on the standard 10 percent commission. This meant that instead of earning as much as $200 or more for each business or first-class flyer, agents now were restricted to $25 for one-way tickets and $50 for round-trip tickets. Adding insult to injury, the airlines then began cutting the standard 10 percent commission down to 8 percent in 1997. And that still wasn't the end. In October 1999, a number of air carriers dropped their commission rates to a dismal 5 percent.

Put in its simplest form, this means that it now *costs* a travel agent money to write that airline ticket. Travel agencies spent almost two decades persuading consumers to come to them for their ticketing needs; now they can't afford to perform the service.

Your Host

Of course, there is more to being a travel agent than writing airline tickets. And that's where the new trend toward independent agencies has come in. As we explained at the top of this section, homebased agents could not write tickets even if they wanted to. To do so, you have to have an *appointment* (which is sort of like a license) from the *Airlines Reporting Corporation*, familiarly known as the *ARC*. And the ARC doesn't hand out appointments to an agency unless it's housed in a commercial office space.

So why not just rent that commercial space and be done with it? Well, there's the overhead, for one thing. It's far less expensive to run your office from a room in your home, which costs you nothing in rent or additional utilities, than to go the commercial route and have to worry about monthly leasing fees and office utilities. Then there's the fact that, aside from the whims of the ARC, you really don't need a commercial office space. Today's independent travel agents conduct most of their business by phone and e-mail. They don't rely on random customers who may or may not wander in, lured by that poster in the window, so a formal retail office is an anachronism.

But how do you sell airline tickets if you can't get an ARC appointment? Most homebased travel agents affiliate themselves with a *host* agency, which is a traditional, commercially-based outfit with an ARC appointment. The homebaser acts as an independent contractor—sort of a freelance salesperson—finding and maintaining his own clients, selling travel products to them, and then splitting commissions with the host agency. When his clients need airline tickets, he makes all the arrangements but has the host agency do the actual ticket printing.

This is a terrific relationship that truly works well for everyone involved. The homebased agent does not need to worry about that elusive ARC appointment (the

---

The E-Ticket

Back in the days when the Mousketeers still ruled Disneyland, an e-ticket was the one that got you on the fanciest and scariest rides, like the Matterhorn. Today, though, an e-ticket is the one that gets you into your airline seat without a boarding pass, at least without a traditional paper one. The "e" in e-ticket refers to "electronic," and this sort of ticketless travel is one of the newest trends in the industry.

In 1996, all four major CRS (Computerized Reservation Systems, remember?) programs made adjustments to allow for ticketless travel, and the major airlines began developing programs to implement it. There are currently several variations on the theme, but the basic idea is the same. When you make a reservation, you get a confirmation number instead of a paper ticket and boarding pass. You take this confirmation number and your photo ID (driver's license, for example) to the airport, and you're in.

The beauty of this system for the passenger is that he doesn't have to wait for his ticket to be delivered, and he doesn't have to worry about losing his ticket. The beauty for the air carrier is that it saves money, reportedly up to $2 per ticket, which is a lot of money when you count the millions of tickets sold every year.

commissions from this aren't going to make him rich anyway), and the host agency gets additional profit with a minimum of extra work.

The real reason this relationship is a winner is that there are many more products that can be sold than airline tickets, and these products will pay much higher commissions. Tours and cruises of all sorts abound, and the companies that provide them pay commissions of 10 percent or more. Since many of these products are priced much higher than airline tickets, selling them is a lot more lucrative than selling seats on planes.

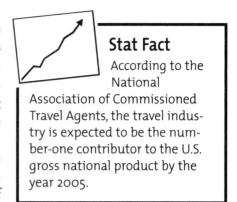

Stat Fact

According to the National Association of Commissioned Travel Agents, the travel industry is expected to be the number-one contributor to the U.S. gross national product by the year 2005.

What's the split between host agency and homebased agent? It depends on how the contract is negotiated. Most go for a 50/50 or 60/40 split, with the host agency taking the greater percentage (when there is one) as compensation for its ARC and other similar appointments. But this figure can fluctuate with the amount and type of business the independent agent brings in. We will explore this relationship in depth as we go through this book.

The Specialty Tour Operator's World

If you plan to go the specialty tour route, you won't have to develop a host relationship; but you will still work closely with many travel agencies, both the traditional, commercially-based ones and the independent types. Tour operators turn to travel agents to sell their products. They also sell their tours directly to consumers through magazines, direct mail, and by contacting associations and organizations that will be interested in their products. For instance, a tour operator would approach garden clubs to find consumers interested in tours of botanical gardens, or genealogy groups to find individuals interested in going on heritage tours. (We will dig into all the nooks and crannies of advertising and marketing in Chapters 11 and 12.)

If It's Tuesday, Revisited

Like travel agents, tour operators are carving out business from formerly unexplored territories, both in terms of geography and market niche. While the traditional tour once packaged tourists of all ages, interests and inclinations onto a bus and passed them lickety-split through Europe, smart travel marketers today are narrowing their sights and increasing their revenues. Some specialty travel firms focus on a specific interest or hobby such as bicycling, bird watching, art history, archaeology, or murder mysteries; and they organize tours designed specifically around them. Others hone in

Stat Fact

According to the United States Tour Operators Association, a 14-day, escorted first-class tour to China would have cost $1,782 in 1980—which in today's money would be $3,524. A similar tour now would cost $2,390.

on a particular region, like the Scottish Highlands or the Greek Islands, and give their clients the full flavor of the area in ways they could never experience on the old "If It's Tuesday" tour.

Specialty tours can range from the rugged to the relaxed. Everything from a strenuous mountain trek, with all the thrills of altitude sickness and incipient frostbite, to a luxurious stay at a secluded European villa can be offered.

Adventure travel is a popular ticket, and includes trips focusing on a variety of pursuits, from hiking to rafting to trekking to learning about the culture and wildlife of a particular country. Sometimes these tours are the *Rough Guide* version, where you sleep in tents and eat around campfires. Sometimes they offer the best of both adventure and elegance, as on safaris where guests traverse the bush during the day, spotting lions and rhinos, but spend their nights in first-class hotels.

The *ecotour* is another hot ticket, featuring trips to ecologically sensitive areas like the Amazon or the Antarctic, to study the flora and fauna and interact with native people—just like on The Discovery Channel or "National Geographic"!

For those who are more interested in "Lives of the Rich and Famous," there are also tours that let guests dine with European lords and ladies, and sleep in castles. These are by no means ecotours, but they still promote interaction with people of different cultures.

Specializing in Dracula

Besides just dreaming up adventure and romance, specialty tour operators need to be—or hire—experts in their target areas. You can't offer a tour of Dracula's Transylvania or Quaker Pennsylvania unless you or your guides know what and where you are talking about. And you certainly shouldn't offer white-water rafting adventures unless you or your guides are expert rafters.

When you plan your tours, you'll need to go on similar tours with existing operators to check out the competition and see how you can make yours different and better. You'll also need to locate top-notch guides who can be

Tip...

Smart Tip

Hard-adventure tours encompass high-energy, endorphin-rush activities like white-water rafting, cave diving, and mountain biking. Soft-adventure tours are more for the armchair-inclined and encompass activities such as antique hunting, cultural enrichment, gardening, and painting.

counted on to take your clients to fascinating places that aren't already swarming with tourists, and who will work for you as independent contractors until your business builds enough to hire them full time.

You may also need to locate outfitters and suppliers. This won't be necessary if you're doing tours of Des Moines After Dark, but will be a valid concern if you're doing African safaris or river running.

Stat Fact

The United States Tour Operators Association proudly proclaims that its members move more than 9 million passengers each year with total sales of more than $5 billion.

Now you know why specialty travel wasn't always hot, why it is now, and why it's likely to become an even hotter industry as we move into the 21st century. But there's more to it than just being hip. You also need to consider the weighty issues of how much you can expect in the way of start-up expenses, how much you can expect to earn, and whether you've got what it takes. So buckle up for the next exciting chapter—let's go!

Read All About It!

The written word is a powerful learning tool. One of your first steps in your new venture should be reading everything you can, not just about the specifics of specialty travel, but about starting a small business and about marketing and sales techniques. Blitz the bookstore. Make an assault on your public library.

Your own business library should contain a plethora of start-up tools. For starters, check out the following:

- ○ *Home-Based Travel Agent: How to Cash in on the Exciting New World of Travel Marketing*, by Kelly Monaghan, Intrepid Traveler
- ○ *How to Start a Home Based Travel Agency*, by Tom Ogg and Joanie Ogg, Tom Ogg & Associates
- ○ *Start and Run a Profitable Tour Guiding Business*, by Barbara Braidwood, Susan M. Boyce, and Richard Cropp, Self Counsel Press
- ○ *Conducting Tours: A Practical Guide*, by Marc Mancini, Delmar Publishers

Don't stop with these. Immerse yourself in the subject. The more you know, the better travel professional you'll be. Read all about it!

The Right
Stuff

As we discussed in our wind-up of Chapter 1, there's a lot more to being a travel specialist than just a love of travel or a desire to hop into a potentially lucrative industry. In this chapter, we'll explore the up-close and personal issues involved in starting a specialty travel business, including the skills you'll need, as well as the start-up expenses and profits you can expect.

Photo© PhotoDisc Inc.

Counting Your Coconuts

What can you expect to make as a specialty travel professional? The amount is up to you, depending only on how serious you are and how hard you want to work. As an independent travel agent, you can make $25,000 to $50,000 net annual income by selling low-end products, like Carnival cruises or trips to Hawaii, says Tom Ogg of the National Association of Commissioned Travel Agents. This income figure reflects part-time revenue, not a full-time effort. And while selling these low-end products is a fairly unsophisticated type of selling, according to Ogg, the income estimate is based on the efforts of serious and professional agents, not dabblers.

Full-time agents, working at their best, have the potential for much higher incomes. "I know outside agents who make $6,000 a year and some who make $70,000 a year," says Connie G., a travel agent with 21 years of experience in the industry, including seven years as an independent agent. "It depends on how hard and how smart they want to work.

"Building that up is really rough in the beginning," the Pennsylvania resident advises. "It's going to be tough on any commissioned salesperson in any industry. Sometimes outside agents just want to quit their full-time job and go into this, immediately take a salary and pay all their bills. That's rare. I really think they need to get a feel for the industry by working part time first. They need the support in the beginning of having a host agency. If they're dependent on that salary, they need to step into it slowly. The money's there to be made, but I really get upset when I talk to somebody who quit everything and figured all the business would come."

As a specialty tour operator, you can earn anywhere from almost nothing to revenue in the seven figures, depending on how hard you

want to work. But in this segment of the specialty travel industry, it can take a lot longer to realize a substantial income. Average annual gross revenue for the industry ranges from $50,000 to $150,000 and beyond. These figures can soar or plummet depending on many variables. A one-person operation that does half-day city walking tours will have a far different bottom line than a multi-employee company that runs 14-day European adventures.

As a start-up, you shouldn't expect to earn big bucks immediately. "It's high risk, low return," says Jerry Mallett of the Adventure Travel Society, a nonprofit association for adventure travel professionals. But it's also a lot of fun, according to Mallett, who says, "It's a lifestyle situation."

"It looks easy, like you can just put an ad in a magazine and develop the idea," says Barry S., a specialist in car race tours who's been in the business for 18 years, and whose company boasts revenue in the millions. "But it isn't easy. It's a matter of really sticking at it. After about seven years, I was at a point where I was doing $1.2 million and not making any real profits and wondering why I was doing it. But I loved it and continued, and then it started growing from there."

This is not to say that as a specialty tour operator you won't earn a living for years, but you should be prepared to grow your company by degrees rather than expect an overnight success. To make the most of your new company—be it independent travel agent or specialty tour operator—find out as much as you can from the start. This book is a good beginning. Its pages will guide you through every stage of starting your travel-oriented company. But keep in mind that researching the specific type of business you want to run, and following through, will be up to you.

Crank-Up Costs

One of the Catch-22s of being in business for yourself is that you need money to make money. In other words, you need start-up funds. For the specialty travel and tour business, these costs range from $5,000 to $25,000. You can start out homebased, which means you won't need to worry about leasing office space. Depending on how you choose to run your company, you may not need employees either, at least for starters. Your major outlays will be for a computer, software, a printer, a fax machine and Internet access (we'll come back to these in Chapter 9), which whittles down your other initial expenses to advertising and marketing.

Sounds good, and it is—except that direct-mail advertising (the best kind to do in this business) can carry a hefty price tag. This is not to say your start-up costs will be astronomical. You can start with a limited investment, but you'll have to go heavy on the creativity, and you'll have to try even harder than the next guy or gal to focus your energies on your specific target market. (We'll explore direct-mail advertising in Chapter 11.)

The Creativity Challenge

OK, you have decided that running a specialty travel business is potentially profitable. You are willing to invest not only the money but also the time it will take to learn the ropes and become established as a pro. What else should you consider? Personality.

Not everybody is cut out to be a specialty travel professional. This is not a career for the creatively challenged. It takes lots of foresight to figure out what will be a winning program, to design and construct it so that it turns a profit, and to promote it effectively. As a travel agent, you don't have to design tours, but you'll need the people skills to match clients with tours and make the sale. If you're one of those folks who'd rather undergo a root canal than have to come up with a peppy marketing plan, then you don't want to be in the tour business. And if you are a sales-challenged type who cringes at the thought of persuading people to buy a product, you might be happier doing something else.

This is also not a career for people lacking in the time-management department. Tours must be planned and organized months in advance, with everything from the tour guide to the motor coach to the dining reservations nailed down early on. As a travel agent, you must be aware of deadlines for ticket, tour, and hotel reservations and must be able to pull all the varied segments of a client's trip into a cohesive whole. If you're a star procrastinator who can't seem to get started on anything until the 11th hour, then you should definitely look elsewhere for entrepreneurial satisfaction. But if you delight in dreaming up sparkling programs and star-spangled advertising ideas, if you're an efficient time manager and organizer, and if you're a pro at helping other people have fun—this is *the* career for you.

Traits of the Trade

Hey, kids! Take this fun quiz and find out if you have what it takes to become a travel and tour specialist.

1. My idea of a fun evening is:
    a) watching five straight hours of the Travel Channel
    b) snuggling up with a hot toddy and a rough draft of my advertising copy
    c) cruising around town singing "Travelin' Man"

2. Here's how I usually send Christmas gifts to relatives who live out of state:
    a) wait until December 24th, stuff the gifts into old grocery bags with the addresses scribbled in crayon, then rush down to the post office and stand in a huge, snaky line with all the other procrastinators, and hope my gifts arrive in time and intact
    b) wrap my gifts carefully in specially selected packaging no later than December 10th, call my pre-designated FedEx or UPS courier (already checked to see which is cheaper and faster), and then follow up to make sure the gifts have arrived on time and intact
    c) hope no one notices I forgot to send gifts

3. Here's how I manage my library books:
    a) return them as soon as I receive the first overdue notice
    b) carefully note the due date and return them on or before then
    c) try to get them out from under the sofa when I get the collection letter from the city attorney's office

4. When out-of-town guests arrive at my home for a week, I:
    a) lock myself in the bedroom on the grounds that I have a chronic, contagious disease
    b) take them to several exciting local restaurants and drive them around town, showing them the sights, giving anecdotes about local features, and introducing them to interesting people
    c) leave a city map and some bus fare on the guest room night stand

5. I would best describe my self-motivational abilities as follows:
    a) get things done sooner or later
    b) love setting and meeting goals and accomplishing tasks
    c) have a self-starter that frequently gets stuck

Answers: If you chose (b) for each answer, then you passed with flying colors! You've got what it takes to become a specialty travel and tour pro. You're organized, an efficient time manager, and self-motivated.

Special Agents

Specialty travel professionals come from all walks of life. The travel agents we interviewed for this book had a variety of alternate careers, from police captain to full-time mom. The tip here is that each of these entrepreneurs figured out how to make their background and interests work for them in their new career in the specialty travel business.

Cruising for Fun

"Our love of cruising is how this whole thing got started," says Jim T., who with his wife Nancy runs a cruise-oriented travel agency in Dunkirk, Maryland. "We took our first Caribbean vacation to St. Thomas in 1989 and just absolutely fell in love with the area. We went back in 1990 on a cruise; and like the commercial about potato chips, we had one, and we were hooked."

Jim and Nancy both had high-stress careers, he as a police captain in greater metropolitan Washington, DC, and she in a county finance department. "Cruising was the perfect answer," Jim explains, "getting away and letting somebody take care of us for a week. We started doing a cruise a year as a vacation and escape form, and it got to the point where several of our friends were coming to us for advice about cruise lines and destinations. After our reviews, a couple of them said jokingly that maybe we should do this for a living."

Jim was nearing retirement from the police department, and the idea of dealing with cruise ships instead of bad guys who were cruising for trouble began to sound pretty good. After researching the industry, Jim enrolled at a local travel school, took a 15-week course in the evenings and on weekends, and obtained his travel agent certification.

"We decided that, rather than go to work for somebody else as we'd been doing all our careers, we'd be our own entity—no franchises, no working for anybody, just doing it on our own," Jim says. "And, in February 1996, we started the company." Jim and Nancy are still going strong on their own and are about to hit their five-year goal of $500,000 in annual gross sales.

"After almost 25 years in law enforcement," Jim explains, "I wanted to get into something where people were coming to you with a smile on their faces and were hopefully leaving the same way. The travel business has lived up to that reputation."

> **Fun Fact**
>
> The colossal 142,000-ton Royal Caribbean cruise ship *Voyager of the Seas* boasts a 1,350-seat theater, a vertical rock wall for climbing 200 feet above sea level, an inline skating track, an ice skating rink, a full-sized basketball court, a golf course and golf simulator, and the largest casino afloat to date.

Again, Mom?

Roberta E. also runs a cruise-oriented agency in Brayson, Georgia, just outside Atlanta; she too was hooked on cruises long before she opened her own company. Roberta, a full-time mom, took the helm when she found that cruise agencies were sloppy about returning calls—even when she wanted to purchase a cruise. So she decided to become her own agent, as well as an agent for other travelers, and enrolled in the Cruise Lines International Association (familiarly known as CLIA) certification program. This certification is similar to an ARC appointment in that it allows you to book cruises directly with the lines instead of going through a host agency.

> **Fun Fact**
> Celebrity Cruises is known in the industry for its posh suite-type staterooms, which include such high-falutin extras as 24-hour butler service, personalized stationery, and private portrait sittings.

The certification can take time, requiring that you visit five to ten different cruise ships and sail on two cruises, in addition to completing study courses and seminars. According to Roberta, it's a never-ending process. "I continually go to seminars and keep studying up on the industry," she says, after two years in the business. What about those mandatory cruises? "My husband and my kids always say the same thing," Roberta says with a smile. "Again, Mom?"

Boring—Not!

Connie G. has been a travel agent for 21 years. "I had a storefront ARC office for six years," the Glenolden, Pennsylvania, resident says. "About seven years ago, Northwest and American airlines got into a bit of a snit with each other, and the next thing I knew we were all in a half-fare war. It hit me when I was pulling 20 hour days—and ultimately losing money in airline tickets in that quarter—that the airlines had too much control over my business. I decided I wanted less dependence on airline tickets, so I'd have to forego the storefront. That's when I went homebased."

Connie's operation has been completely independent for the last four years. She specializes in tours and cruises for Christian and physically challenged travelers, and acts as a host agency for four other independent agents who are scattered throughout the country. "Our CLIA and other affiliations entitle the independent agents to take advantage of them without the expenses of having to pay these subscriptions and dues," Connie explains. "Our business relationship with our suppliers (tour operators, cruise lines, etc.) gives them the buying power they wouldn't have being on their own. Plus they have help, backup, marketing ideas, etc., with a host agency."

Connie delights in being an independent agent. "Ten or 12 years ago we were all selling the same thing," she says. "Now you can be creative, develop your interests, and

▲

deal with what you want. I've always hated issuing airline tickets—to me it was the most boring thing an agent did, other than filing brochures. Now selling travel is exciting."

The Other Side of the Coin

On the other side of the specialty travel coin are the tour operators. Like the travel agents we interviewed, the tour operators we spoke to have also come from varied backgrounds, and only one had any experience in tourism when starting out.

A Dream Come True

"I don't think I've done a tour or event where someone didn't ask 'How did you ever get started doing this?'" says Terry S., who runs city-walking tours and events in Seattle. "Most are just curious but occasionally someone would like to do the same thing themselves. I encourage them but try to explain that there is much more to it than just walking around. My sound bite answer is something like 'I lost my computer industry job and decided to try something different.' But there's more to it than that."

The "more to it" is that Terry had a very successful career in computer programming and product management until 1989, when his employer decided to drop out of the computer business. The company handed out pink slips to all 7,000 of the information systems employees on a single red-letter day. They also asked Terry to stay on and "wind down" operations, which he did.

Terry explains, "During the wind-down, I pursued computer industry jobs but found that 1) the best opportunities—and I had some great offers—required I move from Seattle, which was a no-no for me; and 2) locally they wanted Indians and not chiefs, and I didn't want to start at the bottom from whence I came. This circumstance caused me to think about what else I would like to do that I felt I could do well.

"I adopted the philosophy that there's more to life than computers and that I didn't need to make as much money as I had in the past. With this mindset, I reflected on the traveling I had done in the U.S. and around the world, both for business and on my own. When I got to a city, I would try to see as much as possible, often on a guided tour. And I would say to myself 'What a great job these tour guides have. I'd like to do that.' But then, like waking from a pleasant dream, I'd be back at my computer job. Now I had a real chance to act on my dream—the real inspiration for me behind my company."

And the dream came true. "I started in 1993, by putting brochures in hotels, getting listed in the AAA (Automobile Association of America) Tour Book, and joining the Seattle-King County Convention and Visitors Bureau," Terry says. "I made almost no money the first two years with just my walking tour. Then I created my Mystery & Scavenger Hunt and my Web site. Business picked up dramatically and continues so today."

Concorde Dreams

Further down the West Coast, in Southern California, Barry S. also started off on a wing and prayer. Barry decided to get into the travel business 18 years ago. "I worked for the Orange County Transit District," recalls the tour operator from Newport Beach. "We had a demand-responsive bus system with 70 to 80 buses out on the streets, running around like taxis, and a computer that crashed three times a day. At one stage I had 50 percent of my staff out on stress-related leave, and I thought 'This is crazy, living a life like this.'"

"I decided I had to do something for the rest of my life that I enjoyed doing," Barry explains. "It was really a matter of finding what I loved, which was car racing. So I went with the idea of doing car racing tours."

But it wasn't quite that simple. "There were other companies in other countries that were doing the same thing," Barry says. "I thought I'd copy what they were doing, but I had no experience in the travel industry. I spent a year and took in total sales of $20,000. If you can imagine, it was pretty disastrous because my expenses were something like $40,000. I wasn't working at it full time; I carried on with my job and ran the company on the side. My brother came over from England. He worked, and I didn't pay him anything—it was a way of getting started.

Happy Days

When you plan your tours, consider the amount of vacation time your clients are likely to have—unless you're targeting seniors, and then there are no such worries, mate! Tours that coincide with holidays are always popular because they can result in a few bonus vacation days. For instance, if July 4th falls on a Friday or Monday, your clients can tack that day onto the weekend for extra "free" time.

Most employers offer the same holiday calendar: New Year's, Memorial Day, Independence Day, Labor Day, Thanksgiving, and Christmas. Other popular days sometimes offered as holidays include Martin Luther King Jr. Day, Presidents Day, Good Friday, Columbus Day, and Veterans Day.

According to a survey by Hewitt Associates, a consulting firm in human resources management, only 1 percent of American businesses provides less than seven paid holidays in a year. About 30 percent of employers offer 10 paid holidays a year, and 16 percent offer between 12 and 12.5 paid holidays.

▲

Fun Fact

The first Paris to New York nonstop flight was made in early September 1930, when Dieudonné Coste and Maurice Bellonte set the record with a 37-hour stint in a Breguet biplane.

"The second year we went out and found some more money and did $18,000 worth of business. I was working full time at it then, but it still didn't make any money, so I had to go out and get more funding. This went on for a few years. It was a struggle."

But it was one that paid off. "I look back on it," Barry says, "and, fortunately, I was too old to quit and go back into a regular job. So I just kept at it. It was really a matter of doing it long enough to be recognized. It took probably 10 years to turn the company into something that I could see a real future in. We developed a name, a logo, and we're known as the leading tour operator of our kind throughout the country. We grow 20 percent to 30 percent a year."

Today, Barry's company employs a staff of 12 and earns revenue of $5.8 million per year. He's chartered a cruise ship to stand off the coast of Monaco with a private maitre d' to greet his guests by name and pour wine while they watch the races on shore. He's had English lords invite his clients for tea and multimillionaires personally show them their private car museums.

Barry's worked hard to earn those champagne rewards. "When I started, I imagined within two years I'd be chartering the Concorde to go over to Europe for races," the car enthusiast says. "Those dreams did come true. We did charter the Concorde a couple of times. But we certainly didn't do it in two years. We didn't suddenly jump into millions—it took us a long, long time."

The Fishing Aficionado

In the San Francisco Bay area, Harry G.'s favorite pursuit led him into a specialty tour career. "I was a client of various fishing tour operations," Harry says, "and I used to go to fishing trade shows. I'd walk around from booth to booth and try to ascertain if a particular trip was for me. Through the course of time, I determined that there were lots of credible operators and lots who probably believed a lot more in themselves than they should have. What they were saying at the table and what happened when you arrived at the fishing destination were two completely separate entities.

"So I decided 'Wouldn't it be great if I could put all this under one roof and offer trips

Smart Tip

Tip...

The terms *tour operator* and *outfitter* can be used more or less interchangeably, although an outfitter is generally an operator who also provides gear like river rafts and backpacks or bicycles.

for the budget-oriented client all the way to the exclusive? I'll have personal hands-on knowledge of all my destinations.'" And the former Shell Oil marketing representative ran with that idea. "I started out on a one-year letter-writing campaign in 1984 and received some good responses," says Harry. "We kind of hung out the shingle in 1985. We've been at it for some time."

"We" is Harry and his staff of four, who not only offer the company's specialty fishing tours around the world but act as representatives for hundreds of other fishing tour operators. Harry's own tours range from a one-week Alaskan steelhead expedition to a combo fishing/game-viewing safari in Africa to an Amazon adventure. "It's very interesting," Harry says. "Years ago I was able to make my hobby my profession, and it's given me the ability to travel around this planet of ours. I've done a lot of neat things, and I hope I have the opportunity to do a heck of a lot more."

Culinary Heaven

Like Harry, Judy E. has put a twist on the specialty tour operation. While Harry runs his own tours as well as representing other fishing outfitters, Judy acts solely as a representative for 17 cooking schools in France, Italy, England, and Brazil.

"These are week-long culinary experiences," Judy says. "You immerse yourself in the culture of the regions. Along with cooking classes, there are excursions—some [focus] on food, some on history or shopping. It's a fun kind of trip."

The Dallas resident and mother of seven segued into the travel field through her love of cooking. "Before I was a mother," Judy says, "I was a physical therapist. Then when I was a mother, I was a stay-at-home mom, totally devoted. But I loved to cook, so I ended up with a catering business—but I did it all at home. I had absolutely zero background to be in the travel business. It just happened. I've worked very hard at it, but I had no specific background for it."

How exactly did it "just happen"? Judy, who is a *cordon bleu* chef, was asked by a renowned Italian cooking instructor to come to her new culinary school in Tuscany and bring along a group. "I did," Judy remembers, "and then Lorenza asked me to be her agent and do all her bookings for her. I thought that would be a wonderful opportunity,

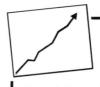

so I did. From that, I started visiting other cooking schools, mostly in France and Italy. I became their agent as well and started building the company."

That was 13 years ago, and the business is still going strong. "It's been very successful and a lot of fun," Judy says. "I don't personally meet all the clients I send over, but I talk with them a lot before they leave. And of course I've made friends of the Europeans I represent. It's a wonderful business."

The Doctor Is Touring

Dr. Phil S. was a high school social studies teacher for 12 years, until he turned his doctorate in history into a career leading walking tours of New York City. "I started five years ago, and I got into it accidentally," Phil says. "I was working as an intern to get a certificate in museum studies. Park rangers and private individuals would come in, and I'd tell them something about downtown Flushing, where I lived. I thought to myself 'Gee whiz, I could do this directly.'"

He developed tours—first of Queens, then Manhattan—and began working out the tricks of the trade. "I was improving my expertise so I wasn't a jack-of-all-trades, and gradually my reputation spread," Phil says. Assisted by three part-time guides, he now leads more than 20 different tours.

Leave the Worrying to Us

In Savannah, Georgia, Karen A., who had been a tour guide in the quaint and famously quirky Southern town for some years, decided along with several colleagues to take their experience in the field and strike out on their own.

"We have been in operation since December, 1997," Karen says. "We started by offering walking tours of Savannah's historic district, but they didn't generate enough revenue, and we've moved into other areas. We specialize in Savannah tours for Girl Scout troops; nature and birding package tours of the southeastern U.S. coast—Cape Hatteras to Cape Canaveral—for individuals; and assorted customized tours of Savannah and surrounding areas for school groups, meetings, and conventions, and motor coach groups." Their emphasis on offering special programs for Girl Scout troops is because Juliette Gordon Low, founder of Girl Scouts of America, was born in Savannah.

Stat Fact

According to the United States Tour Operators Association, the average age of the American tourist today is closer to 50 than 60.

"Our philosophy," Karen explains, "is to offer absolutely the best tours in a few specialized fields by designing excellent and unusual trips and supplying entertaining escorts. If someone has organized a tour for you, you are paying them to do the worrying, so the tour should be hassle-free, amusing and enlightening for the participant."

Karen and her partner, Beth, have yet to earn a living wage; they're still relying partly on their savings. But Karen delights in the five-person company—two partners and three part-time guides—that should turn its first real profit (estimated at $250,000) in 2000. "I think we're fairly typical in taking three years to become profitable," she says. "It takes that length of time to establish a reputation and make contacts with people who will become your customers."

Future Forecast

It's easy to see that all the travel and tour specialists interviewed for this book have put their own highly individual and creative stamp on their businesses, and that you can—and should—do the same. But in addition to personal background, creativity, start-up costs, and annual revenue, there's one more thing to take into consideration: the industry prognosis. Will the specialty travel business be around for years to come?

Consumer travel expenditures are on the rise and will continue to rise for the foreseeable future, according to industry experts. If you can sell, and in the case of specialty tour operators, also design products that will fulfill the needs and spark the

Weather Wonders

Weather can play an important and sometimes unpredictable part in tour operations. "Public walking tours are very weather dependent," advises Dr. Phil S., the operator who offers tours of New York City. "If it's a very mild rain, people will show up. If it's moderate, people will show up. And if it's an unusual topic and the weather's bad, they'll still show up."

But there's no way to be certain—of the weather or your crowd capacity. The first year Phil did his Brooklyn Bridge tour, he had 17 reservations for the New Year's walk. Then the weather took a serious, unexpected plunge. "I couldn't blame people for not showing up, but nobody called to cancel," he recalls. "One person who didn't have a reservation showed up, and we looked at each other like we were crazy. The second year, I had five people for the tour, and the third year I had excellent publicity. The tour became one of the top 10 things to do for [New Year's], and I had over 150 people.

imaginations of travelers, then you have a winning ticket to a successful business.

The risk factor for independent travel agents is moderate—less than opening a tofu taco restaurant but more than selling 10-cent coffees to caffeine-deprived commuters. If you're willing to learn everything you can about your business and then strenuously promote it, you should do well.

Fun Fact

Zehgram Tours, a well-known ecotourism firm, offers a week of real cosmonaut training at Star City in Moscow, including a session in simulated weightlessness.

For specialty tour operators, the risk factor is higher but not astronomical. The reason is that, although there's a strong market for travel of all kinds, you must be able to come up with the magic mix of factors. You have to match your clients' wants and needs with riveting programs, promoted with top-notch marketing skills and a strong sense of your bottom line. If you don't have the right mix, you will have a hard time making it. Don't worry, though. There's a method to finding that magic mix, and we'll show you how in Chapter 4.

Overall, the future of the industry looks bright. Barring a worldwide economic crisis—which industry experts do not currently foresee—would-be tourists and business travelers should have income to spend on gadding about for a long time to come. So stow that luggage, get out your travel journal, and let's hit the high road. Next up: Specialty Travel and Tours 101!

Bottle line .-u-doble.

At the Ready

Whether you decide to sell cruises, tours, or both, you should look into affiliation with the National Association of Commissioned Travel Agents, familiarly known as NACTA. The association was developed in 1983 specifically for homebased, cruise-oriented, independent travel agents and is now 1,700 members strong.

NACTA stands at the ready with all sorts of helpful hints and assistance for the independent agent, including—when you join—a handbook packed with sample contracts and agreements and press releases. Membership also grants you discounts on legal counsel and a variety of industry publications and software, as well as lots of cruise- and land-based fam trips.

The association also boasts 70 host agency members and acts as a sort of Better Business Bureau of travel agencies. Host agencies must meet a set of criteria; one complaint and they're off NACTA's list—which makes life easier for you!

3

Specialty Travel and Tours 101

You have decided to take on specialty travel and tours as your business. Good! The world is your oyster, with opportunities around every bend. But as with any business, you can't really be successful until you know what you're doing. So step into the hallowed halls of Travel and Tours 101, and let's begin learning about the industry.

Photo© PhotoDisc Inc.

Taking On Ticketing

One of the first things to know is that there's more to the travel world than agents and customers. There are also *suppliers*, without whom there would be nothing for agents to sell and customers to buy. Suppliers come in many forms—airlines, cruise lines, hotels, car rental agencies, and tour operators. Add to this mix a sprinkling of industry associations that—depending on your view—regulate, facilitate, or confuse issues among agents, suppliers, and customers.

You've already been introduced to one of these entities, the Airlines Reporting Corporation, commonly referred to as the ARC. The ARC is a closed corporation owned by a select group, all of whom are members of the Air Transport Association of America (aka the ATA), an industry group made up of the major domestic airlines. To qualify as an ARC shareholder, an airline must not only belong to the ATA but must be a passenger-carrying, scheduled airline. No offbeat, fly-by-night or no-questions-asked cargo planes to Colombia allowed. In other words, members of the ATA own the ARC. Got it? Good. But there's more.

Stat Fact
In the late '90s, the Airlines Reporting Corporation processed $70.5 billion in sales. That's a lot of travel!

Arguably, the ARC's chief job is as administrator of the *Standard Ticket and Area Settlement Plan*. This may sound like a weird melding of Disney World tickets with settling the Great Plains, but what it really does is ensure that both travel agents and suppliers get paid. As the "standard ticket" part of the plan suggests, the ARC standardizes tickets (or *traffic documents* as they are sometimes called). Standardized ticketing enables a customer who purchases a flight

Stat Fact

In the late '90s, the Airlines Reporting Corporation counted more than 45,542 accredited travel agency locations, 139 airlines, and three railroads in its system.

from Los Angeles to Tel Aviv to get from Los Angeles to New York on an American Airlines flight, from New York to Paris via TWA, and then from Paris to Tel Aviv on El Al Airlines—all on a single ticket.

But the part of the Plan that's vitally important to travel professionals is the "settlement plan" part—the portion that deals with doling out payments. Here's how it works. When an ARC-accredited travel agent sells an airline ticket or other ARC-affiliated product (like a tour), several pieces of information are transmitted to the ARC. These include the name of the airline or supplier, the price of the ticket or product, and the amount of the commission. The ARC then has the Herculean task of keeping track of this huge volume of data. Once a week, the ARC divvies everything up, sending payments to airlines and other suppliers, and commissions to travel agents.

Key Requirements

Don't forget that it takes more than moxie to become an ARC-accredited travel agency—and that you need that accreditation to print airline tickets. So what does it take to get this accreditation? The key requirement is that an agency has to have a commercial premise, by which we mean an office in a commercially-zoned building. It has to have a sign out front and be easily accessible to the public.

Another key requirement is that the agency has to post a sizable bond, a regulation that is designed to rule out flaky, seat-of-the-pants operators who might take customers' money and disappear without delivering the tickets. When an agency meets all the criteria and receives its ARC appointment, it also gets its very own eight-digit ARC number. In the manner of a social security or federal ID number, this identifies it in all ARC transactions.

If you decide to have a homebased business, you cannot be ARC-accredited. However, you can quite legally sell airline tickets—provided that you're affiliated with an ARC-appointed host agency that will print and issue them for you.

Fun with Photo ID

Now that you know all about the ARC, let's get up to speed on another travel industry association, the IATAN. This acronym is the shortened version of the International Airlines Travel Agent Network, which is a subsidiary of the IATA or International Air Transport Association. The IATA is the entity responsible for devising airport codes, like LAX for Los Angeles International and PNS for Pensacola, Florida—you know, the ones used on Weather Channel maps and on airline tickets. The IATA is also, for some obscure reason, responsible for the ARC numbers given to travel agents. Go figure!

Now that you have a few bits of trivia to wow (or bore) your friends with, let's get back to the IATAN and its chief importance for the travel specialist. Like the ARC, the IATAN disburses travel agency appointments. And, like the ARC, it has specific requirements that a travel agent hopeful must meet. (See the sidebar below.)

An IATAN appointment gives you credibility in the travel field. Like being an ASE-certified mechanic, it shows customers and suppliers that you've passed muster

---

IATAN Recognition

The IATAN recognizes two types of travel agencies: Airline Appointed and Travel Service Intermediary Agency. The Airline Appointed variety is very much like an Airlines Reporting Corporation (ARC) appointment. You have to have a commercial office with signage, a minimum of $25,000 in working capital, a minimum net worth of at least $30,000 and at least $1 million in errors and omissions insurance—or be accredited by the ARC with an ARC bond.

In addition, you must either have a safe in which to stash those valuable blank airline tickets or meet the ARC's security standards. And, of course, there's a pivotal requirement on which all this hinges: You have to have been authorized by some international air transport company to sell its seats.

You don't have to worry about getting an ARC or airline accreditation to get the IATAN's Travel Service Intermediary Agency appointment. But you do have to follow the rules, which include being in business for one year, providing proof that your company has at least $250,000 in annual gross sales, and carrying at least $1 million in errors and omissions insurance. Your business has to have its own bank account and show some form of advertising, even if it's a listing in the phone book. You'll also need to provide letters of recommendation from two travel suppliers and be a member of a nationally recognized travel association like the United States Tour Operators Association or the American Society of Travel Agents.

with a respected industry organization and your company is reputable. You can put your IATAN logo on your letterhead and advertising and marketing materials, and you get a cool sticker to put in your window if you have a storefront. But you also get—and this is a biggie—an IATAN photo ID card. If you want to obtain your own IATAN appointment, you can find out all the details by going to www.iatan.org on the Internet.

Getting Carded

This brings us to a major industry issue. There are lots of folks out there who call themselves travel agents, even though their only clients are themselves and their Aunt Mildred or Uncle Fred. The reason? Fam trips (familiarization trips, remember?) and other perks like hotel rooms and attractions, which supposedly can be had at sizable discounts by anyone with a card that proclaims them a travel agent.

If you're not careful, you might end up getting your "official travel agent photo ID card" by signing on with a host agency that is—truth be known—more interested in selling memberships than in selling travel. They require you to pay a fee (usually something like $495) for a package that includes various training manuals or videos, and of course, the ID card. They offer little in the way of commission splits and sometimes pay no commissions at all for products like hotels and car rentals.

These unscrupulous companies are known in the industry as card mills because of the way they hold out ID cards like carrots to prospective buyers. They are not the kind of host agency you want! You will find them popping up all over the Internet and advertising in various magazines, and you can recognize them chiefly by the fact that they spend more space touting the delights of "official agent" freebies than discussing actual business opportunities. You *can* sometimes get discounts with a card from one of these mills, but suppliers are becoming increasingly more stringent, offering fams only to those they recognize as true travel professionals.

Card mills give everyone in the industry a bad name, and they're one of the reasons the IATAN is so strict about who they appoint. They're striving to make sure that travel specialists—whether outside sales reps, traditional retail agencies or tour operators who also sell airline tickets—are reliable, reputable, and earn the respect of the public.

On the High Seas

We've talked a lot about ARC appointments, airline tickets, and airline seats. But what about sailing the high seas? The cruise industry is booming. New ships are being christened in ports all over the world, and cruise lines fishing for passengers are offering everything from three-day, no-frills packages to titanically sumptuous tours to voyages aboard authentic sailing vessels.

▲

Stat Fact

According to the Cruise Lines International Association, Certified Cruise Counsellors earn about 20 percent more cruise sales commissions than non-certified agents.

This is big business. The cruise industry, with sales of $8 billion per year, estimates that only seven percent of Americans have ever cruised, which leaves a whopping 93 percent that might be persuaded to board a ship soon. In anticipation, the industry is gearing up for an immediate 55 percent increase in ships and passenger capacity. And there are a growing number of travel specialists who have developed cruise-only or cruise-oriented businesses, selling cruises almost exclusively—as the name implies.

If this is where your particular interests float, you'll want to get in the swim with the Cruise Lines International Association (CLIA) and the National Association of Cruise Oriented Agencies, also known as NACOA. Most cruise-only companies hook up with an ARC host agency so that they can provide their clients with airline tickets between home and the embarkation port.

CLIA is a sort of cruise-world equivalent of the ARC, with the same sort of clout. A major difference between CLIA and the ARC, however, is that CLIA is perfectly happy to work with homebased agencies. It's a marketing association for cruise lines, and its mission is to convert the vast public to cruise enthusiasts. As part of this goal, it also assertively seeks to turn travel specialists into cruise-marketing mavens through a bevy of seminars, training manuals, videos, and other educational materials. You can join CLIA as a member agency, or you can affiliate with a CLIA-member host agency, and then become individually certified as either an *Accredited Cruise Counsellor (ACC)* or *Master Cruise Counsellor (MCC)*.

Lest you think going for CLIA counselor certification is boring—it's not! Sure, you've got to do the studying and exam thing (which you can do online if you choose). There are video versions of the training and exams, as well as cruise conferences that count as training. But to ensure that you have an up-close and personal knowledge of cruise products, you are required to take two cruises and conduct five to ten shipboard inspections. This is really tough duty!

There are four good reasons for spending the time and effort to get your certification:

1. The more you know, the better agent you will be and the more sales you will make.

2. Certification makes you more reputable—and thus your products a better buy—in the minds of prospective customers.

3. With CLIA certification, you don't need a host agency to sell CLIA-affiliated cruises.

4. CLIA certification gives you clout with hotels and suppliers.

Plus, you get goodies—a certificate to hang on your wall, a lapel pin, logos for your business cards and stationery, an ad and press release, and a listing on the association's Web site and in their direct mailing, *Cruise Vacation Planner*.

Buying Wholesale

Whether you're a cruise-oriented agent sending clients to Miami to board a ship for the Caribbean, or a tour operator sending clients to Paris for a wine-tasting adventure, you'll need to figure out how to get your clients from Point A (home) to Point B (where the trip or cruise begins). Which brings us back to the airlines. One way to accomplish this is via regularly scheduled flights—the kind even non travel specialists can reserve simply by calling air carriers. The other way is by using a *consolidator*.

A consolidator is a company that buys up chunks of airline reservations at wholesale prices and then turns around and sells them at a discount. Since air carriers live and breathe for the goal of having every seat on every flight filled every day, they're only too happy to give wholesale rates to consolidators who buy in bulk. The carriers can cool their jets and stop worrying about those particular seats! The bonus for you, of course, is that you can pass the savings along to your customers, which makes them happy and helps to make them repeat customers.

Are there any drawbacks to using consolidators? Yes, there are three:

1. Consolidators don't always have seats available when you need them.

Safe Sailing

If you're cruise-crazy, Cruise Lines International Association (CLIA) is not the only organization you should affiliate yourself with. There's also the National Association of Cruise Oriented Agencies (NACOA). This is the only travel agent association that focuses solely on the cruise world (CLIA is made up of cruise lines not cruise agents). You get a lot of the same perks, including public relations and advertising, and Accredited Cruise Counsellor and Master Cruise Counsellor accreditation points when you attend NACOA seminars and workshops.

You can also benefit from increased earnings by selling the association's SafeSail insurance program to your customers, as well as substantial discounts from NACOA-preferred suppliers. And then there's the quarterly newsletter packed with tips and trends, and the National Office Team for member support. Pretty shipshape!

---

2. Consolidators purchase international seats far more than domestic ones, so if you're sending clients from Burbank, California, to Albuquerque, New Mexico, you probably won't find a consolidator deal.

3. Since you're not buying directly from the airlines, you—and therefore your customers—don't get the benefits "regular" customers get in the event of glitches. For instance, if the flight is delayed or canceled, customers with seats purchased directly from the air carrier will be put up at a hotel or transferred to another carrier at the airline's expense. Passengers with consolidator-bought tickets are left to fend for themselves. Air carriers don't honor frequent flyer miles on some consolidator flights. And most consolidator tickets are neither refundable nor exchangeable. The best rule is to ask before you buy. And make sure you pass that rule along to your clients!

>
>
> **Smart Tip**
>
> Most tour operators design their packages with two prices—air-inclusive and land-only. As you can surmise, the former includes airfare to the tour origination city, while the latter is for the tour only so clients can make their own arrival arrangements.

Preferred Suppliers

When you think about selling travel, either as an agent or as a tour operator, you need to think about *preferred suppliers*. Suppliers, as you know, are the companies that provide travel products—cruise lines, tour packages, hotels, car rentals, and attractions. Preferred suppliers are those with whom you build a special relationship: you send business their way and they reward you with higher commissions, which are often called *overrides*.

We will explore this in depth in later chapters, but here's basically how it works. Let's say you discover a wonderfully romantic getaway in Transylvania, an absolutely perfect destination for upscale singles. You develop a marketing program aimed at singles, and you start sending bevies of them to the resort. Because you're sending scads of business its way, the resort decides to give you higher than average commissions. It's now one of your preferred suppliers.

If Joe's Travel Agency down the street—which doesn't have a preferred supplier relationship—sells a Transylvanian package, Joe gets the regular 10 percent commission. You, however, as a preferred agent of the preferred supplier get a 5 percent override on top of the commission, which adds up to a heftier 15 percent in your pocket.

Tours

Now that we've got your customers from home in Indiana (or Iowa or Oregon) to the take-off point for your "Ley Lines of Britain" tour, let's talk tours. You should know that today's travelers are fiends for in-depth, up-close and personal tours featuring specific regions and interests. But do you know why these trendy travelers still want their tours in group form?

To Host or Not to Host

One of the potentially confusing aspects of starting off as a homebased travel agent is deciding whether you need a host agency. If you're considering a host merely as a source for airline tickets, think again. You don't have to have one to put your clients on a plane.

Connie G., who specializes in travel for the physically challenged and for Christians, doesn't use a host at all. "We specialize in cruises and tour packages," the Pennsylvania travel agent explains. "We don't do airline tickets just for people going to see their grandchildren or flying to a conference." When Connie needs to get her clients in Philadelphia to a tour starting point in Paris, she has the tour operator handle the airfares or she issues them through a consolidator.

Jim and Nancy T., whose Maryland business is 98 percent cruises, don't use a host agency for airline ticketing either. "We're not an ARC [Airlines Reporting Corporation] agency, nor do we want to be," Jim explains. "We're not set up to sell airline tickets separately or your typical land type of vacation where you do land, air, hotel, and rental car separately. We're set up to do the package tours through major tour companies like Apple and Insight, which add air tickets as part of the package."

This doesn't mean that you should dismiss a host agency without a second thought. Industry experts recommend that you go the host route—at least initially—so that you've got somebody who knows the ropes to help with your learning curve. As you gain your sea (and land and air) legs, you can strike out on your own, just like Connie G. did. "The first couple of years, I booked everything through another agency," she says. "About four years ago, I set up my own CLIA [Cruise Lines International Association] agency and started working directly with suppliers."

Leave the Driving to Us

To paraphrase the Greyhound bus people, they want to leave the driving—and everything else—to the tour operator. Tourists can have a lot more fun when they let someone else:

Bright Idea

Some tour operators specialize in tours specifically for single women. Others organize coed singles tours—travel, companionship, maybe even wedding bells!

1. *Navigate around town.* There's no arguing with their spouse or significant other over why they said to turn left when the map clearly shows right!

2. *Make hotel and restaurant reservations.* There's no need to guess whether that word "quaint" in the description means "charming" or "last refurbished in 1947."

3. *Decide what's worth seeing and what can be skipped.* There's no fear of passing up the Smithsonian for Beezley's House of Wax.

4. *Develop entrees to people and places they might never find—or attempt—on their own.* No pub grub at Heathrow airport instead of champagne supper with Lord and Lady Hargreaves at their castle.

5. *Help them interface with the natives.* No worries, mate, about not speaking the language or making cultural faux pas, like showing up in shorts at an Arab mosque or ordering unsweetened ice tea in Mississippi.

6. *Provide guidance on everything from what to wear to what size tip to leave.* No shivering in T-shirts and shorts—the only outerwear they brought for summer in Michigan's Upper Peninsula.

The Buddy Factor

But these aren't the only reasons that group travel is a popular alternative to the lone wolf method. There is also the buddy factor. Most folks don't like to travel alone. It's scarier, and it's lonelier. If you go with a group, especially if you are a single female, you feel safer. Strange men and other foreign types are less likely to prey on a group of women than on one alone. And if you are mountain climbing, white-water rafting, bungee jumping, or even doing a walking tour, the buddy system is where it's at. Going it alone can be foolhardy.

Fun Fact

In the world of bus transportation, traveling by Greyhound is known as "riding the dog." Why? Because the motor coach company's logo, is of course, a dog.

Besides safety, there's also the friendship factor. In Victorian times, it was common for ladies of means to pay a companion to travel abroad with them, just to have a friendly face at tea and meals and to join in on carriage tours of local sights. When you take a group tour, you have a host of companions for the price of the tour. And since so many of today's tours are specialized, you're bound to have something in common with at least some of your fellow travelers.

Fun Fact

Pub grub is Brit for the sort of fare you get served at pubs—simple but filling stuff like stews and potpies.

Haunted Hollywood

Now that you know why group tours are popular, let's explore the types that are available.

- *Bus* (or as travel specialists prefer to call it, *motor coach*). This takes us back to the old "If It's Tuesday, This Must Be Belgium" model, except that these days motor coach tours are more leisurely than frenzied. These tours can encompass anything from a two-week trip through France to a two-hour jaunt through Kenosha, Wisconsin.

- *Rail*. The romance of the rails, once nearly extinct, is back in a big way. Travelers can choose super-luxury tours aboard the old Orient Express à la Agatha Christie (minus the murder), breathtaking journeys through Mexico's Copper Canyon or traipsing by train along coastal Nova Scotia, among a myriad of other offerings.

- *Your own wheels*. People with a penchant for motor homes, motorcycles, or off-road vehicles can take part in tours, which might more aptly be called caravans, organized around their favorite sets of wheels. Tour operators lead groups of RVs through Mexico, for instance, stopping at sights along the way just as you'd do in a motor coach, except that you have your own.

- *Adventure*. Here's the one where travelers climb Mt. Kilimanjaro, ski an Alaskan glacier, or go cave-diving in Kentucky. This type of tour is not for the faint of heart or flat of feet.

- *Ecotour*. This is the "National Geographic Special," where travelers take a river trip down the Amazon, meeting native flora,

Smart Tip

Tip...

An *inbound* tour operator brings tourists into her locality, while an *outbound* operator specializes in ferrying locals to someplace foreign. If you're based in San Antonio, for instance, and you are shepherding groups from Paris to the Alamo, you're an inbound operator. If you're based in San Antonio and you take an American group to the Eiffel Tower, you're acting as an outbound operator.

fauna, and folk; participate in archaeological digs in Guatemala; or traverse the Antarctic ice fields with penguins.

- *Theme.* This is the tour designed with a specific theme in mind, like "Beer Lover's Germany" or "Haunted Hollywood." Instead of just taking travelers to Germany or plain old Hollywood, each facet of the itinerary is planned around a theme.

- *City.* While most of the tours we've described last from several days to a couple of weeks, a city tour is a quickie that takes a few hours to one day. "Haunted Hollywood" is a good example, as is "Sherlock Holmes' London" or "Discover Detroit." You get the idea—this is a motor coach or walking tour that gives visitors the flavor of a town and a peek into its particular sights and sounds.

Planning Your Itinerary
Market Research

Every business needs consumers if its products or services are to "live long and prosper," as the Vulcans so eloquently put it. Now that you know what running a specialty travel business entails, you need to plan or target your market.

To do so, you'll need to determine who your potential clients are, what areas you'll draw from and what specific programs you'll offer to attract them.

This is an all-important phase in building your travel specialty. The proper market research can help boost your business into a true profit center. The more research you do before you officially send out your first materials or place that first ad, the less floundering you're likely to do. In this chapter, we'll home in on market research tips and techniques for the budding travel entrepreneur.

Defining Your Market

To be successful in the specialty travel business, you'll need to target your market carefully, deciding what sorts of products you'll specialize in and who your customers will be. Travel agents often run into difficulties selling their services because they fail to take this crucial step into consideration. Despite the fact that travel is much more accessible to the average Joe or Jane than it once was, it's still a relatively expensive proposition and is still considered by many—including some travel agents—to be a luxury instead of a necessity. What these agents fail to realize, however, is that travel is important to a lot of people who set aside part of their budget specifically for this purpose. There are those among us for whom travel is not a luxury but a requirement.

Choosing Your Clients

Let's start by looking at the types of travelers you might target. Choose from among this list of candidates:

- Business travelers
- Leisure travelers
- Adventure travelers
- Honeymooners
- High-income travelers
- Budget-conscious travelers
- Families
- Students
- Seniors
- Disabled travelers

You don't have to target one of these groups to the exclusion of all others, but the more you specialize, the better your earnings are likely to be. Why? One reason is that you develop a reputation—and therefore a clientele—as an expert in that field. Another is that, as you gain expertise in your market, you learn where the deals are so you can pass them along to your clients. And the more product you sell, the more overrides (extra commissions from preferred suppliers) and fam perks you get. So both you and your clients benefit!

The Business Traveler

Business travelers can mean big business for the travel agent, as well as for the tour operator. For the majority of business people, travel means shuttling back and forth between airport, hotel, and meeting site, in an exhausting round of suitcase and briefcase toting. They need somebody to make all those airline and hotel reservations. As you know, this is not where you as a travel agent earn much income; and as a tour operator, it probably doesn't sound interesting at all.

But commercial travelers often bring significant others along for the ride, and these folks need something to keep them occupied while hubby or wife is in a conference. A tour lasting an afternoon to a week can be just the ticket. Business travelers themselves often

Smart Tip

Tip...

Don't assume business travelers— even frequent flyer types— know what they want. They don't. Beyond the basics of "Cleveland" or "Curaçao," they usually have no idea of where to stay and what to see or even if there is anything to see.

Travel Consultant

8 - 10

As a travel agent, you're more than just a convenient link to the airline's reservation desk. You can save your clients a great deal of money by comparing schedules and prices on hotels, tours and other products, and airfares; and then by booking the ones that best fit their budgets and time frames.

But you're not merely a scheduler: You're a consultant. When people decide to spring for a spot of leisure travel, they often have no idea where they'd like to go or what they'd like to do. So your input is valuable. You know what's in, what's out, where there's a quiet haven for the businessperson frazzled by phones and e-mail, and where there's a great place to catch some swingin' nightlife. As a consultant, you can help your clients make the most of their travel dollars, by guiding them to products that suit their personalities as well as their pocketbooks.

Stat Fact

Business and fun do mix! Business travelers often take kids on their business trips, says the Travel Industry Association of America. In the late '90s, about 31.6 million business trips per year included a child—that's up 247 percent since the late '80s. And 28 percent of all business trips included some pleasure travel as well.

like to spend a morning or a day between appointments seeing the local sights. So business travel can be terrific business for the travel specialist. The airline reservations that you make as part of booking tours become the icing on the cake instead of a minuscule commission.

Since major corporations usually have large corporate agencies making their bookings, your best bet as a travel agent is to concentrate on smaller companies. They don't need or want the vast computerized networks of mega-chain agencies, like American Express. What they do want is precisely what you can provide: the personal attention and counseling they can get only from a small agency. That's you!

The Leisure Traveler

Most experts agree that the future of the small travel agency or tour operator lies in serving the leisure traveler—not the guy in that retro '70s leisure suit, but the person traveling for fun rather than business. Individuals and tour groups who hit the high or low road in the name of pleasure usually account for at least half of a traditional small agency's business. And unless you decide to focus on tours and other supplements for the small-business person, leisure travelers will probably account for all your business.

This is good. Leisure travelers want the same things small business travelers want: personalized service and individual counseling. These are the very things you as a travel agent can provide better than any monolithic chain agency. As a tour operator, you can also provide these same qualities, by giving clients tours designed around their interests and capabilities, and by treating them as individuals.

The Adventure Traveler

As you probably know, adventure and eco-tourism are growing travel specialties, but they're not the types of tour packages to develop if you're not an expert in the field. You can't very well take novices white-water rafting if you don't know an oar from a paddle. Likewise, you can't lead a trek through the Alaskan bush, if you yourself get lost going to the post office, or help people participate in an authentic archaeological dig, if you can't tell a

Smart Tip

Tourists interested in cultural and historic experiences tend to spend more, stay in hotels more often, visit more destinations, and be twice as likely to travel for entertainment purposes than other travelers, says the Travel Industry Association of America.

potsherd from a pebble. Most adventure and ecotour operators lead tours because of an overwhelming desire to share their experience and their love of the natural world with others. If this is you, then the adventure/ecotour traveler might just be the market to target—and not just as a tour operator. You can also target the adventure/ecotourist as a travel agent.

The Honeymooners

Newlyweds can be a big market for the travel agent. More than 2 million American couples tied the knot in 1998, and the numbers are expected to continue rising through 2012. Because many of these couples are marrying later than ever before—having spent years as working singles—they have the funds to splurge on a splashy honeymoon package.

The High Roller

How about targeting your agency or tour package toward the upper-crust types? These are the folks who take the posh Orient Express instead of plebian British Rail, and opt for tea with Lady Whosit instead of cocoa from a thermos. High-income travelers represent the minority, but you can realize a high profit margin, both as an agent and as a tour operator, by catering to this market.

Like the adventure/ecotour specialist, you have to know your target audience and the specifics of the product you're selling. If your idea of "really cool" is a pizza delivered to your motel room, then you may have a hard time knowing what your high-dollar clients will consider suitably sumptuous and where to find it.

The Budget Traveler

Volumes have been written about traveling on a shoestring—everything from *Cost Conscious Cruiser: Champagne Cruising on a Beer Budget*, by Mary Lin Pardey and Larry Pardey, to the immensely popular and well-written *Let's Go* series, published by St. Martin's Press. These books never fall out of fashion, for a very good reason. There are always budget-conscious travelers, people who long to

▲

Bright Idea

You might also consider marketing to ethnic or religious groups. Connie G., the travel specialist in Pennsylvania, for instance, sells lots of Christian pilgrimages and cruises.

see the world but whose pocketbooks run more toward peanut butter and jelly than pheasant under glass.

As a general rule, budget travel attracts lower-income families, students, and seniors. If you plan to target this market as a travel agent, be aware that although it's sizable as well as perennially popular, it pays the lowest commissions and takes the most time and effort to sell and service. Frugal travelers tend to ask more questions, have more changes of mind, and of course, have more problems with price. As a tour operator, you'll need to keep these caveats in mind when planning packages for this market.

Family Ties

Family vacations usually focus on destinations with plenty of kid-friendly activities so parents can retain a semblance of sanity. You know the drill: Disneyland, Disney World, Disney's Big Red Boat (which is a cruise), or Euro Disney. But there's a whole other world of fun for both big and little kids. There's everything from dolphin spotting along the crystalline sands of Panama City Beach, Florida, to biking through the Czech Republic. If you're a kid at heart, you can target this growing market, as either a travel agent or a tour operator, and do well.

In the late '90s, the quintessential family vacation accounted for 72 percent of all vacation trips, according to the Travel Industry Association of America. And this market may expand. The U.S. Census Bureau is projecting that by the year 2010, almost 80 million American families will sport children under age 18.

Targeting family reunions is another way to capture some of the family vacation market. Thirty-four percent of family vacationers attended a reunion in 1996, says the Travel Industry Association of America, accounting for about 32 million happy travelers. Suprisingly, Gen X travelers (the 18-to-34 crowd) are the most likely to attend a family reunion.

The Student Prince

Another (but vastly different) kid-type niche market is student travel, which is sort of a sub-category of budget travel, with a twist. If you've ever observed or been a participant in the rituals of Spring Break in Daytona Beach, Florida, or Cancun, Mexico, among other destinations, then you know the market is enormous and not particularly picky about accommodations. But in addition to the bikini-and-beer set, you can also market to high school and college kids and their parental units for graduation trips to Europe, surfing safaris to Costa Rica, and ski holidays to just about anywhere there's snow.

These trips are all geared toward kids old enough—and hopefully wise enough—to be let loose unattended. But there's yet another student market in the world of educational tours, the ones where a brave band of teachers and chaperones leads a group of kids on a tour of the "Wonders of Western Europe" or "Our Nation's Capital." These tours are aimed quite

Stat Fact

According to the U.S. Census Bureau, there will be almost 46 million Americans 60 years of age and over in 2001.

specifically at teachers, with the goal of having them sign up kids for the trips. Typically, the tour operator sends teachers a kit containing everything necessary to promote the package—invitational letters to parents, registration sheets, posters, videos, and even T-shirts. And some student-tour operators have special packages for home-schooled children so parents and kids can meet and learn with other home-scholars.

The biggest incentive by far, however, is that the teacher or "tour leader" gets a free trip for signing on a certain number of kids and then also receives a cash bonus for any additional students she signs up. Who could refuse?

Golden Girls and Guys

Today's seniors are hale and hearty, and tours aimed at them encompass everything from snowmobiling in Alaska to attending traditional weddings in Indonesia. Post-retirement seniors are free of the constraints of jobs and school-age kids that fetter the rest of us, so they have plenty of time in which to travel and plenty of enthusiasm. Karen A., the tour operator in Savannah, Georgia, says her best customer group,

A Bit of Speculation

Terry S., the Seattle tour operator, says his best customers for his walking tours are seniors, along with the 40- and 50-something set, professionals, convention groups and visitors to his fair city.

"I started my walking tours based on my observation that a) no one was doing such a tour in Seattle on a year-round basis (just van and bus tours), and b) my belief that there was a market for such a tour," says Terry. "A bit of speculation, but I was confident enough to give it a try. I did not conduct market research in the traditional sense. But I did informally ask a wide variety of individuals and organizations 'If there were such a tour, would you or your group be interested?' Most all said yes."

besides Girl Scout troops and school groups, is the older set, prosperous people in their 50s and 60s with money and time to spare for specialty package tours.

The Physically Challenged Traveler

Not so long ago, people with physical disabilities had to confine their travel adventures to Sunday drives in their own specially equipped vans. Today, however, disabled wanderlusters can roam the world thanks to tour operators who arrange wheelchair-accessible transport and seek out accessible sights. Even adventure travel is a can-do, with everything from skiing to horseback riding to canoeing to hand cycling on the menu. If you're familiar with the demands and quirks of getting about in a wheelchair or walker, you might find this a rewarding target market.

"My agency specializes in disabled travel, specifically for blind and deaf travelers, wheelchair users, and slow walkers," says Connie G., the travel agent based in Pennsylvania, who's been interested in sign language since she was a child. "I took sign language classes, which automatically [led to] working with deaf clients. The more involved I got in the travel industry and with deaf clients, the more I had people coming to me with other disabilities saying 'Why don't you handle us, too?' Most of it was friends saying 'If you can learn to work with a deaf client you can learn to work with a blind client or a wheelchair user.'"

Researching Your Market

When you have decided what sort of travel and tours you want to specialize in and who your participants will be, you might be tempted to stop there. But you are still not finished with your market research! Now you'll need to go directly to your potential customers to find out how they feel about the products you plan to offer. Would they buy? How much would they spend? How frequently would they use your services?

Calling All Attendees

One way to reach those potential customers is through telephone surveys. Some folks are delighted to answer questions. After all, it's always flattering to have somebody seek your opinion. Others in this era of caller ID are wary of unsolicited calls and don't want to squander valuable time on the telephone with strangers. Unless you've got thick skin, it can be difficult to make cold calls to people you don't know and

> **Tip...**
>
> **Smart Tip**
> Travelers in the 20-to-59 age range have the largest discretionary income because they are working. However, they also have limited amounts of time to spend on leisure travel.

Bright Idea

If telephone cold calling leaves you chilled to the bone, try hiring a college student. This age group is old enough to sound mature but young enough to bring enthusiasm to the job. Just make sure your ace assistant knows what questions to ask and why he's asking. And while you're at it, make sure he can take good, legible notes.

pick their brains. If you can concentrate on finding people in a specific audience that might be sympathetic to why you're calling—say adventure travelers, if you're going to sell white-water rafting tours—then you might have a better chance of getting relaxed responses.

What should you ask? Check out the sample "Focus Group Questionnaire" on page 48. Your queries will relate to your own target market and products, but you can use this as a starting point for what and how to ask.

Where do you get the phone numbers? If you belong to an association or organization, and it just happens to be affiliated with your target market—like an association that certifies scuba divers, if you want to target adventure travelers, or an alumni association, if you want to target student travelers—then you have it made. You may already have a directory packed with names and phone numbers at hand. If not, you may be able to beg, borrow, or buy a directory from the organization's main office. If your specialty is something more general, like senior travel, you might still start off with the members of your club or group. Your common membership will act as the proverbial foot in the door.

If you don't know anybody and you don't belong to any groups, how about a church roster or neighborhood association? Use your imagination!

Up Close and Personal

Another top technique for getting market research is to get up close and personal with a *focus group*. This is an informal gathering between you and a medley of potential travelers, usually five to 12 people. Try to hold several different focus groups. The more responses you have to work with, the better. You can invite family (though they may be biased on your behalf), friends, friends of friends, co-workers, and colleagues in clubs or organizations you belong to. Keep in mind, however, that your focus groups should be composed of people who will have some connection with your proposed products. For instance, when researching family travel, you should invite people who travel with their families regularly—your co-workers or those of your spouse or sibling, or people from a local business organization. Acquaintances whose only travel is taking the cross-town bus can be left out.

Bright Idea

Be sure to collect the names and addresses of all focus group participants. They'll be the seeds of your in-house mailing list, which you'll use for advertising and marketing.

Focus Group Questionnaire for
Family-Oriented Travel Agency

About Your Past Vacation Experiences

1. How many children are in your family?

   _____

2. What are their ages?

   _____

3. How many times a year do you travel with your kids?

   _____

4. Where do you usually vacation?

   _____

5. Where do you usually stay?

   _____

6. How long do your family vacations usually last?

   _____

7. What do you usually spend per family vacation?

   _____

About Future Vacations

1. Where would you like to vacation?

   _____

   _____

2. What types of activities does your family enjoy?

   _____

   _____

Focus Group Questionnaire, continued

3. Are you interested in the history of the areas you visit?

   _____

4. Are you interested in the art or music of the areas you visit?

   _____

5. If you could extend a business trip to include vacation travel, would you be interested?

   _____

6. Would you be interested in a destination that allows adult-only time by providing daily child care?

   _____

7. How many hours of child care per day would you consider reasonable?

   _____

8. What is your family income?

   _____

   (Keep in mind that some of your group participants may not be willing to share income information with you.)

About Business Names

1. Please comment on the name Fun-For-All Family Travel (love, like, dislike, or detest).

   _____

   _____

2. Please comment on the name Intrepid Family Adventures (love, like, dislike, or detest).

   _____

   _____

Once you have your focus group assembled, and you've distributed some sort of refreshment (always a nice touch), you essentially have a captive audience to respond to your most pressing market concerns. Hand out questionnaires, have plenty of pens and pencils on tap, and encourage discussion.

Delve into the sample Focus Group Questionnaire on page 48 for an idea of how to formulate your own question-and-answer sessions. Instead of family travel, you might be asking about New Age tours of Britain; honeymoon idylls in Australia and Alaska; or business travel programs for small office/home office types. Ask as many questions as you feel your group can comfortably handle. Keep your questions focused on your objective: finding out what potential clients will want to see and do, what they will pay and what travel products will draw them in.

Direct-Mail Dazzle

Direct mail is a terrific market research tool. You can use the same lists or directories you'd use in your telephone surveys, but don't attack the same people with both phone and mail questionnaires. Choose one form or the other.

What do you say in your mail survey? You can ask the same types of questions you've covered in your focus group questionnaire. But keep in mind that people are unlikely to return a mail survey unless you offer them an incentive. So get creative! Extend an invitation to be put on your regular mailing list, or give them a coupon for 10 percent off their first tour.

Just the Facts, Ma'am!

Besides going directly to your potential participants for market research, you'll also want to get some good statistical information—as Jack Webb on "Dragnet" would say, "Just the facts, ma'am." In other words, do you know how many families there are in the United States or how many there are in greater metropolitan Atlanta, for instance? How many retirees are there in the Midwest with sufficient income to travel? How many cooking enthusiasts are there in Anchorage, Alaska? The answers to questions like these will give you an idea of just how many potential participants there are for your products and if that number is large enough to be lucrative.

You can get this kind of information and much more from a variety of sources, as Karen A., the tour operator in Savannah, Georgia, did. "Several of us had been tour guides in Savannah for some years, so we knew something of the tourist industry here," she says. "We researched the information on tourism in Savannah collected by the Chamber of Commerce and the Convention and Visitors Bureau. From these statistics, we convinced ourselves that there was a living to be made offering walking tours of Savannah."

In addition to local chambers of commerce and visitors bureaus, check with the following sources for your own market research statistics:

- *The public library.* Reference librarians can be fantastically helpful with this sort of thing. All you have to do is call and tell the librarian that you need to know how many medical professionals, fly fisherman, or disabled children under age 14 there are in the United States. He'll look up the information and call you back with the answer. Or you can go into the library and dig through whole books of demographic statistics yourself, unearthing more facts and figures than you could use in a quadruple round of *Trivial Pursuit.*

- *The Internet.* A world library at your fingertips! If you are not yet Net-savvy, make becoming so a priority; you'll have access to all sorts of demographics without ever leaving your desk. For starters, check in with the U.S. Census Bureau at www.census.gov and the Department of Commerce at www.doc.gov (yes, they collect all that data for a reason—here's your chance to take advantage of it).

- *Organizations and associations.* What better places to go for information on your specific market? If you're targeting senior citizens, for example, you could contact the American Association of Retired Persons for a count of its members. To find out the number of high school teachers, you'd talk to the folks at state and regional teachers' associations.

Adding a Little Luxury

Carlson Wagonlit Travel boasts over 3,000 locations in 141 countries and more than $9.5 billion in annual sales. The company began in 1872, when Belgian entrepreneur Georges Nagelmackers decided to give travelers a little luxury by adding sleeping compartments (*wagons lits* in French) to existing European railways. After creating his new firm, not coincidentally called Wagon-Lits, Nagelmackers went on to found the world-famous Orient Express.

Meanwhile, in 1888, Ward G. Foster opened his travel company, Ask Mr. Foster, in St. Augustine, Florida. By 1900, it was clear that lots of people were "asking Mr. Foster"—he had 160 offices in Europe and North Africa, from which he sold train tickets and hotel rooms. In 1972, Peter Ueberroth (you remember him, the baseball commissioner who later brought the Olympics to Los Angeles) bought Ask Mr. Foster for a mere $1 million. Then in 1979, Ueberroth sold the company to Carlson, which merged with Wagon Lit Travel in 1997 to form the international firm of Carlson Wagonlit. And it all started with sleeping compartments.

Sizing Up the Competition

After you have decided on your target market, you'll need to find out what sort of competition you'll be up against. It's one thing to know that "Hey, there are 10 million potential clients out there." But it's another entirely to discover that there are already 200 companies serving those clients. So, you'll need to find out how many competitors you have, what their strengths and weaknesses are, and how you can compete with them successfully.

The Travel Agent's Competition

Sure, there are major travel agencies out there, ones who've seemingly been in the business forever. We're talking about the mega-corporations, like American Express and Carlson Wagonlit. While these giants do have name recognition working for them, they can't provide what you as a small company can; and that's personalized service.

As a specialized travel agency, you act as a sort of matchmaker between your clients and their dream vacations or business trips. You develop a rapport with your customers, learning their expectations, preferences, and quirks; and you can plan their journeys around those idiosyncrasies. When you make your clients feel special and pamper them with your own brand of personalized service, they will stick with you. You will not need to worry that another travel specialist—no matter how big or brassy—will steal them away.

> **B**ig companies can't provide what you as a small company can—personalized service.

Mega-companies often buy in bulk, which gives them volume discounts that they can pass along to their clients. But don't think this leaves you, the small agency, out in the Arctic. You can join consortiums and purchase through consolidators or buy through a larger host agency, all of which will give you the same volume edge.

Plus, as a specialized agency with a niche market, you have another edge—the creative one. With no giant-corporation clients to appease and no impersonal rules to stick to, you can develop relationships with individual suppliers who will reward you with handsome commissions. There are some carriers and suppliers who sell directly to the public, and they represent another source of competition, but not a big one. By and large, these companies really prefer to let travel agents like you sell their products, since you can do it far more efficiently and effectively.

The Tour Operator's Competition

As a tour operator, your competition will come primarily from existing firms that offer the types of specialty tours that you want to market. In a more general sense, however, you'll also face some competition from traditional tour packagers.

A traditional tour company arranges transportation for its clients, shows off the sights of a given city, provides an evening's entertainment (Hawaiians performing traditional Hawaiian hula dances) and arranges lodging in a hotel or motel. These companies usually buy transportation and accommodations at group rates, which means they're often getting bargain-basement prices that they can pass along to their customers.

While specialty tour operators technically have the ability to get the same deals, in actual operation it's difficult. Why? Because specialty tour packagers generally only purchase as much lodging and transportation as they need for the clients participating in a particular trip. Because the trip is more personalized, there are usually fewer travelers per journey. So specialty packagers don't buy in volume and don't get discounts to pass along to their clients.

To Boldly Go

The big-name operators may have more clout when it comes to finding ground suppliers and advertising dollars, but as a small specialty tour packager, you have your own oomph. You can offer the sort of intimate, personalized travel experiences the big guys can never hope to match. Because your groups are small and tightly focused, you can give each participant an exciting and rewarding vacation, one that will leave them eagerly awaiting your next offering.

As another bonus, your small groups can boldly go to spots that are often inaccessible to large groups. If you are river-rafting, a chosen few in a small craft can traverse narrow passages that would be impossible for the big-company bunch, crowded into a big tour boat. Plus, some wilderness areas are regulated by local governments that limit the number of visitors. So with a smaller band of travelers, you have a far better chance of gaining entry permits than the mega-company tours.

> You can offer the sort of intimate, personalized travel experiences the big guys can never hope to match.

The Road Less Traveled

So, we've narrowed your primary competition down to existing specialty tour operators. Since there are roughly 8,000 adventure travel companies in the United States alone, that's more than a smidgen of rivalry. Not to worry, though! You can succeed, but you need to carefully target your market and develop your own niche.

In the specialty tour business, going off the beaten track or taking the road less traveled is a strong selling point, especially when it comes to adventure tours. As we've already explored, these tours typically take small but hardy groups to remote areas. Unless you're talking Mars or the surface of the moon, though, really remote areas are harder and harder to come by.

The waters of the Amazon River, the steppes of the Russian Far East, and the slopes of the Himalayas are already on the books of a variety of tour operators. As expansive as these areas are, there may be a limit to the number of packagers that can run competing tours to them. You can't very well run an "exclusive" tour in a region overrun with a dozen other companies. And, as more visitors flood into remote locations, the less "unspoiled" they remain. So your challenge is to find unique and less crowded destinations.

Something Completely Different

One way to compete with existing operators is to offer something completely different. You could locate new or under-served destinations ("Midsummer Sahara Getaway!" or "Sing-Sing Like You've Never Seen It!"). Or you could offer a new twist on an already well-served destination, like "A Cook's Tour of Cook County," Illinois, featuring visits and lessons with famous Chicago-area chefs.

Offering a completely unique tour is probably the best way to compete with existing operators, but you can also vie for business by offering a tour fairly similar to those already on the market, if you can add something that distinguishes it from the others. Yours might differ through superior service; your personal knowledge of the terrain, people, culture, and history; or incomparable suppliers and outfitters.

Another approach is to cater to a different audience than the norm. While all around you operators are wooing young urban professionals or suburban seniors; you might ply your tours among 30-something singles, people with disabilities, or married-with-children types.

Fun Fact

There's more to see in North Dakota than you might imagine. This generally unsung area of the country boasts a bevy of oversized animals, scattered along the highways: a towering 40-foot sandhill crane; a massive Holstein cow, standing 38-feet tall; a buffalo weighing 60 tons; and a 36-foot tall gorilla. Who says you can't sightsee in even the most featureless landscape?

Shopping the Competition

A little competition is healthy. If you do your homework properly, research your suppliers and structure your company intelligently, you will shine despite—or because of—your rivals' lights.

As we have just explored, the time to scrutinize those rivals is during your market research phase. What are they doing that's absolutely perfect? What can you successfully emulate? What are they doing that you can do better? What can you offer that will draw customers away from them and to you?

How can you answer all these questions? Start by performing these research tasks:

- *Go ahead and shop!* The competition, that is. Find out what others are offering and what they charge. Take a few tours if you can afford them. Then study them. What works? What doesn't? And why?

- *Attend all the travel seminars and workshops you can.* Ask questions. Don't be shy!

- *Surf your competitors' Web sites.* Send for brochures—go ahead, flood your mailbox. Again, study what your rivals are doing. Explore what works and what doesn't work, and why.

The Traveler's Trunk
Business Structure and Location

OK, you've done your market research. You've decided on your target clients and your market niche. Terrific! Now, even though you may be living out of a suitcase for days at a time, you'll need to design a tight, sturdy "trunk" for your new company. A structure that will keep it not only looking good, but solid enough to weather anything life might dish out. In this chapter, we'll guide you through that process, from choosing a location for your office to deciding on a company name and a legal structure.

Name That Business

Every business, like every child, has to have a name. You should devote as much thought to choosing an appellation for your company as you would for your human offspring. After all, you plan to have your business baby around for a long time. You want a name you can be proud of, one that identifies it—and by extension, you—as worthy of your customers' confidence. You also want a name that gives your clients a clear portrait of who you are and what travel products you're selling.

Many travel specialists incorporate the name of the products they sell into their business moniker—for example, Amazon Adventure Tours or Pack Up The Kids Travel Agency. This idea can be a blessing, or it can backfire. The blessing part is that it easily identifies your product; anybody can tell at a glance what your specialty is. But, if you call your company Alaska Outback Tours, for instance, and you later decide to branch out and offer Australian walkabouts; you're going to run into difficulties because your name won't have anything to do with your new product. This will make you harder to identify as a supplier of that Australian tour, and it will also cost you credibility. (Prospects may think "What the heck does an Alaska tour operator know about Australia?")

The same goes for Pack Up The Kids Travel Agency. While prospective clients can identify it immediately as a family-oriented travel specialist, if the owner later decides to target honeymooners or seniors as well, she may run into identification difficulties. This doesn't mean you shouldn't use your products in your business name; it just means you'll need to think about your long-range goals before you choose.

If you'll be a travel agent, you might consider naming your company for a regional feature, like Sea Coast Travel if you live by the sea or Bluegrass Travel if you're in Kentucky. As a tour operator, this doesn't always work, though. Sea Coast Tours is fine if you're leading groups along the shore where you live; but if your real mission is taking tourists to Outer Mongolia, then Sea Coast Tours is dead wrong.

For some top-notch ideas on choosing your own business name, take a look at the specialty travel companies listed in the Appendix. You'll want to make yours as individual as you are, but these will get those creative gears turning.

Beware!
Your name not only has to look good; it has to sound good. Ellis Dee Tours for partners Ellis and Dee is fine on paper, but over the phone it will sound like LSD. This is not the kind of trip you want to sell!

Eminent Domain

If you plan on having a Web site, you'll need to register your *domain name*, that www.whatever.com address that people use to access your virtual office. There can be only one domain name per company, so you'll have to think up several versions of the name you want in case one's already been taken.

Here's what you do: Go into your Web browser and type www.networksolutions. com. You'll reach the Network Solutions Web site, which is very user-friendly. Follow the easy directions and check to see if the domain name you have chosen has been taken. If it has, choose another. When you find a permutation that's available, register online. The cost is $70 for two years of registration, or $119 for a two-year reservation (if you want to reserve a name but you don't plan to use it right away).

Laying Your Foundation

There's more to laying the foundation of your business than choosing a name. You'll need to decide on a legal structure, check into zoning regulations and insurance coverage, and line up an attorney and an accountant—all the nitty-gritty stuff that will give your company a solid base on which to build.

At First Glance

Your customers' first contact with your company will probably be virtual—either via direct-mail advertising or the Internet. This means that your visual image is vitally important to how they perceive you. Everything from the colors, graphics, and typefaces you choose for your Web site, to the stationery and brochures you send out, creates an impact. If your tours focus on kids, go all out for a logo that says children with bright primary colors and a bouncy, exuberant font style. If you're talking Europe, splash your materials with travel graphics— pictures of the Eiffel Tower or the Colosseum.

You can design just about anything with your trusty desktop-publishing program. But keep in mind that you're selling not only your special expertise, energy level, and ambience, but an image of soundness. You want potential clients to know they're in good hands when they hire you.

Have friends or family look over your designs before you commit to a print run. Do they see typos? Amateur quality? Or do they see the sparkle of a travel professional?

Beware!

Some cities, such as New York, Niagara Falls, Washington, DC, and Montreal, require tour guides to be licensed. Contact the business license department in your city to find out if your guides need to be licensed.

To keep those diligent IRS people happy, your business must have a structure. You can operate it as a sole proprietorship, a partnership, or a corporation with variations thereon. Many specialty travel start-ups go with the simplest version, the sole proprietorship. If you'll be starting out on your own, you may choose the same option. It's the least complicated and the least expensive. You can always switch to another format later on, if and when you take on partners and/or employees.

Home Zoned Home

If you plan to work from home, you'll want to check into zoning regulations. Since much of your business (except for actual tours) will be virtual—conducted by mail, phone and Web site—you won't need signs pinpointing your location. And since it's unlikely you'll have customers knocking at your door, you won't need to worry about parking restrictions. However, it's still a smart idea to play it safe.

Find out from your city government whether any permits are necessary, and if they are, file them. If you need a zoning variance, apply for that too. And while you're interfacing with your local authorities, be sure to ask about a business license. This generally consists of filling out a simple form and paying a nominal annual fee. Again, it's easier to get it upfront than to ignore it and have it nagging at the back of your brain. If you need advice, check with your attorney for all the general information you'll need about obtaining business licenses and permits.

Sign In Please

What other licenses and permits will you need? It depends. In most states, there are no licensing requirements to operate as a travel agency or tour operator. However, a few do insist that you have a license. As of this writing, according to the National Association of Commissioned Travel Agents (NACTA), these states include: California, Florida, Hawaii, Ohio, and Washington state. Some Canadian provinces also require licensing. This list, like many things governmental, is subject to change. Be sure to check with your own state or provincial attorney general's office or other

Smart Tip

If your first-choice domain name has been taken, get creative. But not so creative that your domain name has little or no relation to your company name. If your company is called Backwoods Tours, and there's already a www. backwoods.com; try something like www.goback woods.com or www. bwoods.com.

Tip...

business regulation authority to make sure you have the most current information. You should also be aware that most states that require licensing also require the posting of a surety bond (see section on page 63).

These laws, as they apply to independent agents working through a host agency, can be a tad murky. Some industry experts believe that if you're working through a host, you may be covered by its licensing; others do not. The bottom line is that it's up to you to check with your local governing body, your host agency and your attorney—do your homework!

The main idea behind these *Seller of Travel Laws* is to give consumers some sort of recourse if they bump up against an agent or tour operator who takes their money and runs. In California, for instance, travel promoters are required to pay into a statewide restitution fund from which scam-bitten consumers can be reimbursed. "Honest people bail out the crooks," says NACTA's Tom Ogg, "but it's a rock-hard consumer benefit."

Business Name Brainstorming

List three ideas based on the travel products you plan to provide (i.e., honeymoon packages, cruises, eco-adventures).

1. *Who-What and Why*
2. *Past · Present · Future*
3. *Historial · Cultural and Genealogy Exchange*
4. *USA - - Jamaica - Africa*

List three ideas combining a favorite theme with your planned products (i.e., cultural awareness, environmental awareness, kid-friendliness).

1. *Motherland Connection*
2. _____
3. _____

After you've decided which name you like best, have you:

❑ Tried it aloud to make sure it's easily understood and pronounced? (Has it passed muster with your family? Have you had a friend call to see how it sounds over the phone?)

❑ Checked your local Yellow Pages to make sure the same or similar name is not already listed?

❑ Checked with your local business name authority to make sure it's available?

Heritage tours + Legacy Travel

Wilderness Pursuit Permits

If you're planning on operating as a tour packager, government licensing issues can get even more complicated. If you run an in-bound business, your state may require that you employ state-licensed guides. If you act as an outfitter, you will probably need a license. You will most likely need to get permits for activities like fishing or hunting, not only for your company, but also for the members of your group.

And that's not all. Some wilderness areas require that you obtain a permit before venturing inside. You may already know about passes to enter national parks, for example. But you should also be aware that if you run a river-rafting adventure, you might need a license to access a particular river. Keep in mind that some states limit the number of enthusiasts allowed on the water.

How do you determine if these rules apply to your operation? Ask. Always check with local and state authorities before proceeding. If you don't need special permits, you can rest easy. If you do, you'll know upfront, before you've spent valuable time, effort, and money developing a tour.

> ## Smart Tip
> Tip...
>
> Check with the National Association of Commissioned Travel Agents or the American Society of Travel Agents, as well as your state attorney general, for the latest skinny on all things licensed.

Private Land

If you'll run tours on privately owned land, you will definitely need to get permission from the owner. If you're planning on including privately owned historic sites, like European castles, you'll need to contact the property owner and find out what his or her policies are regarding visitors. Ask these important questions:

- What are the property's hours of operation? *Phone – Web – Email – overnight mail*
- How far in advance do you need to make reservations? *3 months*
- How large a group can you bring? *8 – 10*
- How long can you stay? *1 wk*
- Are there any restrictions on activities while on the property?

Attorneys and Plumbers

Attorneys are like plumbers—you don't want to think about them until you need one. But as a business owner, you should have a good attorney on call, one that knows small business. You'll want her to check over any contracts you write with host agencies, suppliers, or outfitters and to advise you on the fine points of small business and tourism law. You won't need to call her every week, or even every month. But there's no point in waiting until you've got a problem to establish a relationship. Along with that on-call attorney, you'll want to look into hiring an accountant to fill out those tax returns and advise you of any special ways you can save money with your business structure.

And don't forget your insurance agent! He can be an invaluable source of information and expertise. If you'll be homebased, you will need to find out if your homeowners' package covers your business assets, inventory, and equipment, or if you need additional coverage. If you'll be based outside the home, you will need coverage for these same items, as well as your physical location. If you plan to hire employees, you may need workers' compensation insurance, too.

Then, there's routine liability insurance. This covers you for things like a client slipping on a banana peel (or more likely, black ice), tripping over a tree root in your yard, walking into a wall, or in any other way damaging him or herself on your property and suing you for bodily injury. As a tour operator, you may also be required to carry a specified amount of liability insurance to qualify for some wilderness area permits (for rafting expeditions on various rivers, for example).

Bondage

If you plan on going the travel agent route, you'll want to be bonded. In some states, you don't have a choice; you must be bonded. Your insurance agent can help you out here as well. Bonding tells clients and suppliers, as well as entities like the ARC and state regulatory agencies, that you have the financial wherewithal to meet your contractual obligations. In other words, if you or an employee manages to lose your clients' deposits for tours or other products, the fact that you're bonded means you have the funds to pay back the money.

The way it works is that you pay a fee, and the bonding company puts up the money. Bonding is not the same as insurance. If a claim has to be paid, the bonding firm hands over the money immediately and then turns to you to repay it within a time frame of generally 80 to 90 days. This means you'll most likely have to put up collateral to obtain the bond. Again, ask your insurance agent to help you find the best arrangement for you and your company.

Beware!

California's *Seller of Travel Law* requires even out-of-state travel sellers who sell to California consumers to register.

Oops Insurance

Because people in today's society can be alarmingly lawsuit-happy, you should also consider *errors and omissions insurance*. This is a bit like malpractice insurance in that it covers you for mistakes that you might make or that a hyperactive client might think you made. For example, if you send a client on a trip to Ireland, and he's injured by an IRA bomb while there, he could conceivably sue you for packing him off into dangerous territory. Or perhaps, despite your best efforts, that client gets bumped off a flight; misses his connection for a hot business meeting; and sues you because he loses a $50 million dollar account. Yes, it's ridiculous, but these things can happen.

You may be able to tap into your host agency's errors and omissions policy; you simply pay the additional charge for being tacked onto the existing coverage. Alternatively, you can shop around for your own coverage or purchase coverage from an industry association like NACTA and get a tidy discount.

Staying Healthy

If you will be doing specialty tours, you have yet another insurance concern to consider: your clients' health. Specialty tour companies usually have had their tour members sign liability waivers, which state that the clients accept responsibility for their own health and physical conditions. You'll want to do the same; have each client fill out a form describing his or her physical condition. This is very important in any type of trip, and is especially important for one that's physically demanding. Your clients should also provide statements signed by their doctors, asserting that the doctor knows and approves of the client's intended travel plans. And as a final safeguard, you

---

Know Before You Go

Don't forget that most foreign countries require both you and your tour members to have the appropriate visas before you can enter. Foreign locales may also require their own licenses and permits for fishing, hunting, or other activities. And in some countries, foreigners—that's you and your group—are limited in the amount of local currency they can carry into or out of the region.

Various regions of the world have their own customs, too, which are tantamount to laws if you try to ignore them. For instance, women are prohibited from entering some Middle Eastern religious sites. To know before you go, contact the American-based consulate of the country you plan to visit.

---

should have all clients sign a form releasing you from any liability incurred due to their own ill health.

Some outbound operators ask to be named as co-insured parties on riders to outfitters' insurance policies, if the operator charters transportation and support personnel from the outfitter. Then, if catastrophe strikes a client while on a chartered vehicle, the tour operator is protected under the outfitters' insurance. Which doesn't mean you should ignore insurance of your own—once again, check with your agent for the best coverage for your particular operation.

Contract Smarts

While we're working away at the worry bone, what about that contract with your host agency? You do need one; and it should spell out everything including commission splits, when they're paid, and how overrides and bonuses are handled and split. Your host agency may have a standard contract on hand. You can obtain sample contracts from professional associations like NACTA. Your friendly attorney can also put one together for you on her own or using one of these samples as a starting point.

> I n the case of contracts, a cup of foresight is worth an ocean of afterthought.

If you decide to go with somebody else's standard, make sure your attorney looks it over before you sign it. In the case of contracts, a cup of foresight is worth an ocean of afterthought.

Choosing a Location

As we've explained, one of the perks of running a travel business is that it lends itself ideally to the homebased entrepreneur. Specialty travel doesn't require a high-traffic or high-visibility location, so you don't need to set up shop in a trendy part of town. Because your business is virtual, you won't need a mahogany-paneled office with a lobby and conference room in order to impress or entertain clients. The only space requirement is an area large enough for your desk, your chair, your filing cabinets, and perhaps a bookshelf.

The home office is convenient: You couldn't get any closer to your work unless you slept with your computer and your telephone. It's economical: You don't need to spend money on leased space, extra utilities, transportation costs, or lunches down at the corner grill. Working at home is not, however, mandatory. You may want to leave your laundry, your dog, and your loving-but-noisy family at home while you go off to an office space that's quiet, clean, and yours alone.

The Home Office

You'll probably choose to be home-based; that's part of the joy of being an independent agent or tour operator. All of the travel agents we interviewed for this book have home offices, as do three of our tour operators. If you go the same route, you can locate your office workspace anywhere in the house that's convenient; but

ideally, you should have a dedicated office, a room that's reserved just for the business. You can locate this room in a den, a finished room over the garage, the garage itself, or a spare bedroom. Keep in mind that whatever space you choose will be your work station and command center. Use the worksheet on page 67 to evaluate possible locations for your home office.

"We decided not to take on the overhead of a storefront," says Jim T., the Maryland-based cruise specialist. "It's worked to our advantage as well as our clients' because they're not paying our overhead." Jim, with his wife and partner, Nancy, started off utilizing one room of their suburban home as a dedicated office and later built on a special office space.

If a dedicated office is not an option for you, you can also station yourself in a corner of the kitchen or at the dining room table. If you have a boisterous family, however, a cubby hole in your bedroom is liable to be much more conducive to quiet, clear thinking than a nook in the family room with the TV blaring at all hours. Also,

The Fine Print

Tour operators, like cruise lines, routinely include all sorts of rules and regulations for clients in their brochures. You'll find everything from how cancellations and refunds will be handled, to what the trip price does and does not include, to responsibility and release clauses, to trip insurance information. This is important stuff—as a tour operator you'll need to add a page of not-so-fine print to your catalog or brochure with these same caveats.

While studying the competition's brochures, take a careful look at their fine print, which is usually on a page called "General Information." Then decide on the modifications you might need to make for your operation and have your friendly attorney look over your materials.

The Home Office Worksheet

Use this handy worksheet to locate and design your home office.

Start by listing three possible locations in your home for your office, which should include a work area for you and enough space for your desk, computer and telephone.

1. _Basement_
2. _S.E. Bedroom_
3. _Attic_

Make a physical survey of each location

☑ Are phone and electrical outlets placed close enough to your equipment so they can be accessed easily? Or will you be faced with unsightly, unsafe cords snaking across the carpet?

☑ Measure your space. Will your current desk or table (or the one you have your eye on) fit?

☑ Do you have adequate lighting? If not, can you create or import it?

❑ Is there proper ventilation?

❑ What is the noise factor?

❑ Is there room to spread out your work?

❑ Optional: How close is it to the coffee maker? Refrigerator? (This can be either a plus or minus, depending on your current waistline and jitter factor.)

If you'll have equipment like backpacks, food storage containers, or bikes, list three possible home locations for this stuff.

1. _____
2. _____
3. _____

Take a survey of each:

❑ Is there adequate lighting, ventilation, and space for you to easily access your stuff?

❑ Will you need to construct special shelving or add other storage space? If so, make notes here.

_____

_____

_____

▲

Bright Idea

Some homes, especially older ones, have walk-in closets that are large enough to turn into a cozy little office—some even have windows. If you decide to turn your closet into an office, make sure it has adequate ventilation and light.

---

remember that yelling into the phone over cartoon *kerblams* and *pows* will not give your customers confidence in your company's soundness and reliability.

The Tax Man Speaketh

A big advantage to the home office is the ability to wear two hats, to be at home with your family and be at work at the same time. Another advantage is the ability to count your home business as a tax write-off. The IRS will graciously allow you to deduct money from your income taxes if you're using a portion of your home as your income-producing workspace. You can deduct a percentage of expenses equivalent to the percentage of space your home office occupies. For example, if you're using one room in an eight-room house, you can deduct one-eighth of your rent or mortgage plus one-eighth of your utility bills.

There is, of course, an "if" involved here. You can only use this deduction if you're using a space in your home solely as your office. If you've turned your spare bedroom into your office, and you don't use it for anything but conducting your business, then you qualify. However, if your office is tucked into a corner of the kitchen and you're still feeding people in there, you don't qualify for the home office deduction, unless you can convince the IRS that you order takeout every night and the refrigerator is actually a file cabinet.

Organized and Efficient

When you're working at home, it's important to remember that you're still a professional. Your work quarters, like yourself, should be organized and efficient. If at all possible, designate a separate room with four walls and a door. Aim for pleasant, quiet, well-lit surroundings. You're going to be spending a lot of time in this space, so you want it to be comfortable.

If you can't carve out a dedicated space, by all means take over a corner of another room but consider it your permanent office. Clearing your work materials off the dining room table before meals is a definite drag. Appropriate a desk or table large enough to hold your computer, keyboard, phone, pencil holder, and stapler; and be sure you'll have enough room left over to spread out your working papers. A charming 19th-century cherry wood secretary looks great, but probably won't allow enough space for your files, your computer, and you. Don't skimp on elbowroom.

Make sure you have enough space to neatly file client profiles and booking information, currently running ads, and ones you have already tried, as well as files for current and potential advertising venues, suppliers, ground operators, freelance tour guides, and outfitters. Whether you choose to use the fanciest hanging file folders in mahogany drawers or simple manila ones in cardboard boxes, you must be able to access this information quickly and easily. It's no fun digging through the back of the clothes closet or running out to the garage every time somebody calls with a question.

Then there are all those brochures and catalogs from cruise lines and tour operators. "I carry a lot of brochures," says Roberta E. in Georgia. "People will ask what a particular stateroom looks like or about the items on an itinerary, so I have an area filled with brochures for the various cruise lines." Don't forget your own catalogs, brochures, or other mail-out materials! You'll need easily accessible boxes or shelves where you can keep these items safe, clean, and tidy at all times.

The Commercial Office

Although the trend is definitely toward homebased travel businesses, it's not always the only way to go. In some instances, you can be successful with a commercial site, and for some tour operations a "storefront" can be an even better alternative. Whether homebased or commercially based, it seems that most new travel entrepreneurs are not buying existing businesses, but rather starting their own from scratch.

Travel Agent's Base

As a travel agent, your best bet is a homebased location. You can, of course, go the commercial route if you like, with an office in a downtown high-rise or uptown shopping center. But industry experts these days don't recommend this approach. Sure, you meet one of the ARC's major approval requirements, which means you can write your own airline tickets; but with the multitude of host agencies and consolidators available, this just isn't necessary for the start-up travel agent. "Technology has made the homebased office so very, very feasible," says Dr. Robert W. Joselyn, CTC (Certified Traveler Counselor), president of Joselyn, Tepper & Associates, an industry consulting firm in Scottsdale, Arizona. "It's cheap and convenient."

Joselyn explains that, since 98 percent of a travel agent's business is conducted by phone and e-mail, there's no need to base yourself outside the home. Business clients just one floor away will still call rather than come in, which puts the kibosh on the high-rise location. As for that shopping center, Joselyn advises it's the worst location. You'll face constant interruptions from looky-loos who have no intention of buying your products. In addition, the cost of space in shopping centers can be astronomical.

Tour Operator's Base

If you're looking at the homebased vs. commercial site question from the tour operator's point of view, things are a bit different. You may want to go the homebased

Beware!

Be sure to print and file hard copies of all e-mail correspondence sent to you and all missives you send to others. Keeping everything on your computer's hard drive may seem like a swell paper-saving idea. However, if your computer crashes, you'll lose everything including, temporarily, your mind. The same goes for computerized databases of clients, suppliers, and the like.

route if you're doing tours that don't require much in the way of equipment or personnel—at least for starters—because it's by far the least expensive alternative. On the other hand, if you decide to run an operation like white-water rafting expeditions—where you'll have rafts, oars, life jackets, ice chests, tents, and sleeping bags to contend with—you might do far better with a commercial space where you can stash all your equipment. You can use this same space for meeting, greeting, and checking in your clients. A commercial space is also better for displaying and selling peripheral goodies like T-shirts, sweatshirts, coffee mugs, and caps emblazoned with your company name.

Of course, equipment storage doesn't have to be your only reason for taking on a commercial space. As your company grows, you will also need room for employees. Barry S., the car race tour operator, houses his 12-employee company in 1,500 square feet of office space. Barry contracts the space within the offices of another tour operation that owns 20 percent of his company. He says, "Cost is below general market prices, and it is located in Newport Beach, California—a great address."

In Savannah, Georgia, Karen A. chose an office for her five-person tour company on the basis of price and location as well. "We have a gorgeous office," Karen says, "an 800-square-foot, two-room space in an 1824 stucco building. As additional space, we get a private corridor, a walk-in closet, and a large, private, rooftop patio. The main office has 14-foot ceilings, fireplaces, and huge windows. We chose it purely on price and location: $500 a month, right in the middle of the historic district. It fits our needs beautifully in that the location is perfect, the price is right, we have congenial neighbors, and lots of space to divide it into a dozen or so cubicles when we need more privacy for more office employees."

Outfitting the Commercial Space

Your office may be situated in an historic building, an upscale shopping plaza, a downtown office, or a barn by the river; nevertheless, you'll need the same basic setup as in a home office. Have a look at the worksheet provided for planning your commercial office (see page 71).

You'll need plenty of room for all those files, plus your desk, chair, a few pieces of visitors' furniture, as well as desks and chairs for any employees you may hire. Whether in a home or commercial office, your computer should occupy a place of

The Commercial Office Worksheet

Use this worksheet to help you plan your commercial office.

Start by listing three possible locations for your office based on your niche market. For an adventure travel agency, you could locate your office in a trendy shopping area next to a bookstore with a large travel section. For walking tours, you could have an office in an historical district. For rafting expeditions, you might want to locate yourself near the headwaters of a river.

1. _____

2. _____

3. _____

Make a physical survey of each location's exterior and environs

❑ Can clients find the location easily? Or is it on an obscure back street or cow path that takes exceptional navigational skills to locate?

❑ Can clients easily access the space? Or will they have to cross several lanes of heavy traffic or make unsafe or illegal U-turns?

❑ Is there adequate parking?

❑ Do local business people, shoppers, and passersby conform to your niche market? Or will you be an apple mixed in among oranges?

❑ Is signage a problem? Check with landlords and local zoning authorities to make sure the sign you have in mind will be accepted.

Make a physical survey of each location's interior office space. Make sure there is adequate room for work areas for you and your employees.

❑ Is there enough room for desks, computers, and telephones for you and for employees who may need their own units?

❑ Are phone and electrical outlets easily accessible at potential workstations?

❑ Is there adequate lighting and proper ventilation?

❑ Is there adequate storage space for equipment?

If you'll conduct some sort of retail sales, like T-shirts and ball caps, list three possible spots to display and sell these items. You may want to consider a cash register, cash box, or electronic credit card machine as well.

1. _____

2. _____

3. _____

▲

honor, away from dirt, drafts, and blinding sunlight. The same goes for your printer and fax machine.

In a commercial tour operation office, you may want a display area or counter for any retail products like T-shirts or tote bags, as well as a cash box or electronic credit card terminal for taking payments. You should also consider that altarpiece of American offices, the coffee maker. And of course, if you've got gear to stash—whether it be bungee cords, bicycles, or boat oars—you'll need sufficient storage space.

6

Currency Exchange
Figuring Your Finances

That old refrain, "The best things in life are free," does not quite apply when you are starting a new business. This chapter dips into the murky waters of budgeting, financing, and operating costs, and clears them up.

Photo© PhotoDisc Inc.

Start-Up Costs

One of the many nifty things about the specialty travel business is that its start-up costs are comparatively low. You have the advantage of homebased ability, which cuts office lease expenses down to nothing. Except for any merchandise you might choose to develop (like T-shirts or tote bags emblazoned with your company name), you have no inventory. And even if you have inventory, you won't need fancy display cabinets or trendy décor. Your major financial outlay will go toward office equipment, marketing, and promotion. And you've probably already got the most expensive piece of office equipment—a computer system.

But let's take it from the top. The following is a breakdown of everything that you'll need to get up and running, from heavy investment pieces to flyweight items:

- Education/certification *500.00*
- Consortia fees—for travel agencies only (Tour operators don't need to add this one.)
- Professional association fees
- Computer system with modem and printer
- Fax machine

- Electronic credit card terminal
- Internet/e-mail service *60.*
- Web site design — *120.*
- Marketing materials (brochures, mailing lists, etc.) *200.*
- Software *300.*
- Reference materials *150.*
- Phone and voice mail; answering machine or answering service *70.*
- Stationery and office supplies *120.*
- Postage *100.*
- Add rent and utilities if you go the commercial office route *X*

You can add all kinds of goodies with varying degrees of necessity to this list. We'll cover them all in Chapter 9, which features a sort of shopping bonanza. For example, a copier is a plus. It's also nice to have bona fide office furniture: a swiveling, rolling, leather-upholstered chair with lumbar support; shiny new filing cabinets that really lock; and real oak bookshelves.

But let's consider that you're starting from absolute scratch. You can always set up your computer on your kitchen table or on a card table in a corner of the bedroom. You can stash files in cardboard boxes. It's not glamorous, but it'll suffice until you get your business steaming ahead. The wisest way to go is to spend thrifty, buying what's necessary but using brains, barter, and bargaining to get the rest.

> **You can add all kinds of goodies with varying degrees of necessity to this list.**

"Our start-up expenses have consisted largely of paying operating expenses until we produce a profit," says Karen A., the tour operator in Savannah, Georgia. "This is because we didn't buy any office equipment; we moved our home office furniture, computers, scanner, etc., to our office downtown. Fax machine, printer, and various other bits and pieces were donated by friends. We had minor start-up expenses: domain [Web site] name; incorporation; deposits on office rent; monthly phone service; copier lease; insurance; and wages and salaries, the toughest expense of all to cover. We have put $66,000 into the company, and that will rise to about $75,000 before we become profitable in 2000," she explains. "We shall then try to borrow money to grow the company more rapidly."

Karen feels a three-year run before achieving a profitable bottom line is an industry norm. She also feels hindsight is better than foresight. "Had we known profitability would take so long," she says, "we would have spent less on start-up costs. For instance, we spent $10,000 on advertising in our first year of operation, and then discovered most of our first-year revenues of $25,000 resulted from other types of marketing."

Get Certifiable

To sell cruises, you need to be certified by the Cruise Lines International Association (CLIA). And while obtaining your CLIA certification definitely counts as fun, it doesn't come cheap. You've got to spring for cruises as well as travel to attend seminars and visit home ports on ship inspections. If you plan to add that spiffy CTA (Certified Travel Agent) credential, as Jim T. in Maryland did,

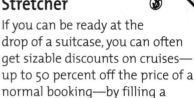

Dollar Stretcher

If you can be ready at the drop of a suitcase, you can often get sizable discounts on cruises— up to 50 percent off the price of a normal booking—by filling a ship's last-minute vacancy. Call the cruise lines and ask.

or go on to a CTC (Certified Travel Counselor) credential from the Institute of Certified Travel Agents; that's another expense to add.

These credentials are well-worth the time, effort, and cost. "The people with the most education make the most money," says Gracie Hiett, CTC and educational advisor with the Institute of Certified Travel Agents. "The key to success is to be a specialist." Travel consumers are more sophisticated these days; and when they set out to buy travel products, they want their agent to be a specialist. Just as people want to purchase stocks from an expert like Charles Schwab, Gracie explains, they want their travel agent to be an educated pro as well. According to a recent survey by *Travel Counselor* magazine, CTC-certified agents racked up significantly more sales than their noncertified counterparts.

Consortia Fees

A consortium is a group of suppliers that provides higher commissions in exchange for doing a specific volume of business with them. Joining a consortium or two can add to your commission structure as a travel agent. But since most consortia charge sign-up fees, you have another start-up expense to add to your list.

For a good idea of what makes a consortium so useful, check out Vacation.com. "I can easily recommend them," says Jim T. in Maryland. "They have been very helpful to us, and we anticipate good things from Vacation.com as they continue to establish and grow."

Connie G. also recommends Vacation. com, as well as Cruise Shoppes of America. You will find contact information on both of these companies listed in the Appendix.

Get Professional

Professional associations like NACTA (National Association of Certified Travel Agents, remember?), National Association of Cruise-Oriented Agents (NACOA) and the Adventure Travel Society (ATS) can be valuable resources for any travel specialist.

(See the Appendix for a listing of professional associations for the travel business.) But they also represent a source of membership fees, so add these costs to your start-up list.

ARC Again

If you really want to consider that ARC accreditation, you can expect a set-up fee of $850. You'll have to purchase an ARC-approved safe (which will cost in the range of $1,500); a minimum $20,000 bond (for which you'll spend $200 to $2,000 per year); and the cost of blank tickets after you use up your initial "freebie" set ($16 to $50 per box of 1,000). In addition, you'll bear all the costs of a commercial site.

Reference This

Because the travel world changes so fast, you'll need a lot of reference materials as well. And there are lots available—from in-depth travel almanacs, in the form of online subscription services, to online reports on consolidators, to a host of hard-copy tour directories and magazines. How many you'll need for starters depends on what type of operation you'll run and what your focus will be. We'll explore the possibilities in Chapter 9, but for now you can pencil in about $85.

Computer Candidate

Buying a computer system heads the list of in-house start-up expenses. For a basic system—hard drive, monitor, mouse, modem, and printer—you should allocate about $2,000 to $4,500, depending on how fancy you want to get. We'll go over the various permutations in Chapter 9, but this will give you a figure to pencil in for starters.

"I spent about $5,000 for my computer and software," says Terry, the tour operator in Seattle. "I do much of my business via e-mail, and I created and maintain my own Web site. Computer prices have come down [since his 1993 start-up] so it would be less now—say $3,000."

The Software Skinny

Although your computer will fill that silent partner/co-pilot slot with panache, it needs software to give it all those brains. You'll need a good word processing program, a desktop publishing program, a database program for tracking clients, and an accounting program. Again, this is a subject we'll discuss in depth in Chapter 9. For start-up purposes, let's say that you'll want to allocate about $400.

Dollar Stretcher

When you purchase your new computer, you can often buy it pre-loaded with word processing and accounting programs that will suit your needs. If you negotiate wisely, you might save valuable software dollars.

Go Anywhere

A good Internet and e-mail service is a must for the travel specialist. With the power of the World Wide Web at your command, you can go anywhere on the globe instantly, all from the comfort of your own desktop. You can research your market, communicate with clients and suppliers, and even create bookings. And it's cheap! Most Internet service providers, or ISPs, charge about $20 to $25 per month and give you unlimited Web and e-mail access.

Dollar Stretcher

Use that e-mail service to contact suppliers abroad. Why place a pricey international call when you can send an e-mail message virtually for free?

Internet Explosion

All the travel professionals we talked with for this book either have their own Web site or are in the process of getting one. The cost of putting up and maintaining a company Web site can vary considerably. If you're lucky enough to have a computer brain in the family, or if you take the time to become your own computer expert, you can pencil in a zero under Web site design and construction costs.

Smart Tip

Tip...

Web site design and hosting fees may be higher in large urban areas. Shop around. It doesn't matter if you're in Atlanta, Chicago, or Los Angeles; you can hire a webmaster in Pipsqueak, South Dakota, and work with the person as easily as if he or she was next door.

Judy, the culinary school representative from Dallas, has an on-call webmaster, her son Craig, who also happens to be a computer techie at the local university. It was Craig who suggested the company go online, and then he designed and installed the Web site. "It saved me a bundle of money," Judy says.

What can you expect to pay if you out-source your Web site construction? You can pencil in about $300 to $500 for hands-on help from a Web site designer. Or, if you have the talent, the temperament, and the aptitude, you can set up a site yourself. You will need to learn HTML (that's *hypertext markup language*), which usually takes several weeks of brain power; but once you have it, you can make all the changes you like whenever you like, without having to rely on an outside source. As a third option, you may be lucky enough to have a friend or relative who'll put up your site in exchange for lawn mowing, baby-sitting, or a steady supply of home-baked cookies.

Fax Facts

Although technically you don't *have* to have a fax machine, your life as a travel specialist will run much more smoothly with one. Having a fax machine allows you to communicate quickly with clients, suppliers, and your host agency, instead of waiting on the U.S. postal service. You can purchase a basic plain-paper fax machine for as little as $250, or a fancy, multifunctional model for up to $700.

Electronic Money

An electronic credit card terminal can be a major boon to your business. You can take credit card payments, either over the phone or from faxed information, for the products advertised on your Web site. More and more merchant card service firms are springing up that cater specifically to the small office/home office and Internet entrepreneur. Shop around, especially on the Web, and you'll find a variety to choose from.

What can you expect to pay for an electronic terminal? Fees depend on several factors, including the company you go with and your personal credit history. Take a look at the "Electronic Card Terminal Fees" chart on page 80 to get an idea, but also keep in mind that this is an industry that's growing rapidly with better deals all the time. You can lease or purchase the terminal itself from the merchant bank, or you can go the bargain hunter route and buy a used (but still serviceable) machine from a company that's gone out of business or has upgraded their unit.

Phone Fun

We'll assume that you already have a telephone, in which case you already know all about phone bills. You should install at least two separate, dedicated lines for your business. You'll want one line for handling phone calls and another for your fax machine and ISP, unless you plan to transmit all your information and conduct all your research late at night or in the wee hours of the morning. Computers and fax machines use phones the way teenagers do; when they're transmitting, no one else can possibly get through. So unless you want to risk having callers receive a busy signal or an empty ring, which is fatal for a business that takes telephone orders, you'll need to have a separate line.

Of course, costs vary with the number of fun features you add to your telephone service, and which local and long distance carriers you go with; but for the purposes of start-up budgeting, let's say you should allocate about $25 per line. You'll also need to add the phone company's installation fee, which should be in the range of $40. Check with your local phone company to determine exactly what these costs are in your area.

Electronic Card Terminal Fees

Item	Fees (swiped*)	Fees (mail, phone or Internet order)
Discount rate (multiply each transaction by this rate, i.e., $200 ticket fee x 1.59% =$3.18 that the bank charges you to process the transaction)	1.50% to 1.59%	2.09% to 2.50%
Transaction fee (another fee the bank adds on for each transaction processed)	$0.20	$0.25 to $ 0.30
Monthly minimum (if your monthly sales are less than this amount, you pay this amount)	$10 to $20	$10 to $20
Monthly statement fee	$5 to $10	$5 to $15
Application fee	$0 to $75	$0 to $75
Programming fee	usually free with equipment lease or purchase	usually free with equipment lease or purchase
Electronic card terminal	$300 to $600 purchase or $19 to $72/month lease option	$300 to $600 purchase $19 to $62/month lease option

*Merchant card services charge higher discount rates for orders taken by mail, Internet, or phone than for those handled in person or swiped through the credit card terminal. Why? Because if a customer signs for your products while he's standing there, you and the merchant service run less risk of a charge-back where the customer refuses to pay the charge.

**In addition to the fees shown here, you may be charged an AVS or address verification fee per transaction, a daily batchout fee to send charges from the electronic terminal to the merchant service in batches or chunks, and an annual membership fee. Be sure to ask and negotiate before you sign up!

The Mechanical Receptionist

You will not always be available to answer your phone. So, other than having the phone surgically attached to your ear, what can you do? You have three ways to go here: the trusty answering machine, the phone company's exciting voice mail service, or a *call center* to answer your phone and process your orders.

All three phone options have pros and cons, which we'll discuss in Chapter 9. For estimating start-up costs, let's figure in a basic answering machine at about $40, and voice mail at about $6 per month.

My Calling Card

Company stationery is as important to your specialty travel image as a well-answered phone. Even though your customers may see only a Web site or specially designed direct-mail piece, you'll still need stationery for your dealings with suppliers, manufacturers, and bankers. To help build that solid, established identity that will make other businesses eager to work with you, you'll need professional-quality letterhead, envelopes, and business cards.

You can purchase blank stationery, including business cards, and print everything up by yourself using a desktop publishing program. Or you can have a set of stationery and business cards printed for you at a copy center like Kinko's or Office Depot. Either way, you should allocate about $200.

Floating Pencils

Don't forget about basic office supplies: pens, pencils, and paper clips, plus a stapler, a letter opener, tape, and those all-important printer cartridges. You'll also need blank paper for designing ads and for printing out invoices, receipts, and other forms. If you figure that you're purchasing all of this brand-new for the business (as if you didn't have scads of pens and pencils floating around the house), you can write in about $150.

All That Jazz

Other expenses you'll need to plug into your start-up expense chart include business licenses, business insurance, legal advice, and all that jazz—the costs intrinsic to any company's beginning. If you plan to go with a commercial site, you'll also need to consider rent, utilities, and signage; and if you'll hire employees, you'll have to add in payroll and

Smart Tip
Remember that if your state requires that you post a surety bond, you'll need to figure it into your start-up costs.

Start-Up Costs: Independent Travel Agents

Costs	Merry Makers Travel	After the Wedding
Education/certification	$345	$14,000
Rent & security deposits	0	2,400
Utility deposits	0	150
Signage	0	1,500
Consortia	375	425
Professional associations	145	544
Office set-up expenses (see chart on page 89)	2,217	8,567
Licenses	150	150
Bonding	200	0
Phone (installation/line charges)	90	90
Grand opening	100	500
Legal services	375	375
Miscellaneous postage	50	50
Internet service provider	20	20
Web site design and marketing	0	500
Insurance	500	500
Employee payroll	0	2,000
Workers' compensation insurance	0	225
Miscellaneous expenses (Add roughly 10% of total)	465	320
Total Start-up Costs	**$5,032**	**$32,316**

Note 1: After The Wedding's education/certification costs include cruises and travel taken to gain CLIA certification.

Note 2: After The Wedding receives surety bonding at no charge by virtue of its CLIA certification.

Start-Up Costs: Tour Operators

Costs	Magic Bay Adventures	Mysterious Journeys
Education/certification	$345	$345
Professional associations	145	395
Rent & security deposits	0	2,000
Utility deposits	0	150
Signage	0	75
Office set-up expenses (see chart on page 90)	3,107	7,996
Licenses	150	250
Bonding	200	2,500
Phone (installation/line charges)	90	90
Grand opening	100	500
Legal services	375	375
Postage	50	100
Internet service provider	20	20
Web site design and marketing	0	500
Insurance	500	500
Employee payroll	0	2,000
Workers' compensation insurance	0	225
Special equipment (i.e., food storage chests, pirate's chest)	500	0
For-sale products (T-shirts, etc.)	600	0
Miscellaneous expenses (Add roughly 10% of total)	63	193
Total Start-up Costs	**$6,245**	**$18,214**

workers compensation fees. To give you an idea of what to budget for, we have provided start-up costs and projected monthly income statements (which include operating costs) for four hypothetical companies. You can compare two travel agencies on page 82 and two specialty tour operators on page 83.

Meet our hypothetical start-ups—first the travel agents. Homebased Merry Makers will target seniors with an emphasis on land-based tours and will go through a host agency. After The Wedding is also homebased, and will use a host agency, too. This business will target honeymooners and sell both land-based tours and cruises, with the administrative assistance of one full-time employee.

As you peruse the start-up costs and income statements (page 89), you'll notice significant differences in some of the items. In our sample start-up costs, for instance, you'll see that After The Wedding is paying a lot more for office set-up than Merry Makers. The reason? One is that After The Wedding has an employee. The owner expects that she will be great as far as productivity; but she will need a desk to work at, an ergonomic chair to sit on, a computer, and a phone. All of these will add considerably to the cash register tape at the office supply warehouse. Another reason is that After The Wedding's owner is also buying all new, top-of-the-line equipment for herself.

> **Work up several options, compare them all, and decide which will be the best for you.**

The owner of Merry Makers, on the other hand, is going solo and plans to use the equipment already in his home; so his office set-up costs are far lower. You'll notice that Merry Makers is paying for bonding while After The Wedding is not. The reason here is that After The Wedding receives surety bonding at no charge through its CLIA certification, while Merry Makers—which isn't CLIA certified—must purchase its own bond.

Now meet our hypothetical tour operators. Homebased Magic Bay Adventures will provide half-day and one-day nature and historic tours of its owner's Gulf Coast hometown. Mysterious Journeys, which will make its base in a downtown loft, will start with tours of ancient and arcane Britain. Its owner will lead the tours, while her sole employee holds down the office.

Again, you'll notice some significant differences between our lower and higher range companies. Magic Bay, for instance, which will concentrate solely on local tours, has chosen to join only a few professional associations; while Mysterious Journeys, which plans to range farther afield, has opted for more affiliations. As a result, the costs are higher for Mysterious Journeys.

Like its travel agency counterpart, After The Wedding, Mysterious Journey's office set-up expenses are higher because it is outfitting not just the owner, but her employee as well. Because Mysterious Journeys will charge a great deal more for its

Start-Up Costs

Costs

Education/certification	$ _____
Professional associations	$ _____
Rent and security deposits	$ _____
Utility deposits	$ _____
Signage	$ _____
✝ Office set-up (see the checklist on pages 136 and 137)	$ _____
Licenses	$ _____
Bonding	$ _____
Phone (installation/line charges)	$ _____
Grand opening	$ _____
Legal services	$ _____
Postage	$ _____
Internet service provider	$ _____
Web site design and marketing	$ _____
Insurance	$ _____
Employee payroll	$ _____
Workers' compensation insurance	$ _____
Special equipment	$ _____
For-sale products	$ _____
Miscellaneous expenses (Add roughly 10% of total)	$ _____
Your Total Start-Up Costs	$ _____

tours than Magic Bay, it has chosen to purchase a larger bond (meaning its bonding costs are higher). Its phone costs are higher as well, because it has additional phone lines with voice mail, in a commercial location. In addition, Mysterious Journeys is paying an outside source to handle its Web site design and marketing, while Magic Bay's owner will handle his own Web tasks.

Finally, Mysterious Journey's license costs are higher than Magic Bay's because it is paying not only for general business licenses, but also for special licenses that allow it to guide tours in specific cities. These costs vary with the licensor; check with cities, historic sites, and other venues in your targeted field to find out what your costs may be, if any.

Having looked over the start-up costs for these sample businesses, now go to the "Start-Up Costs" worksheet on page 85 to begin drawing up a list of your own start-up costs. If you make a few extra copies of this sheet, you can work up several options, compare them all, and decide which will be the best for you.

Operating Expenses

These are the various and sundry costs that make up the backbone of every travel professional's operation. Subtracted from your projected gross profits, these operating expenses will tell the true tale of how much you'll be making. Since tour operators expense out each tour (as you'll see in Chapter 13) to determine costs and net profits per program, operating expenses for tour operators and travel agents are about the same.

So here we go. We're going to assume once again that you'll be homebased, and won't have to worry about expenses for office rent or utilities. We do, however, need to consider the following expenses:

- Phone
- Postage
- Web hosting (so your Web site has a server to keep it up and running)
- Reference materials
- Stationery and office supplies
- ISP (Internet service provider)
- Loan repayment

As with your start-up costs, you'll also need to consider rent and utilities if you'll go with a commercial site, as well as payroll and workers' compensation if you hire help.

Beware!
If you will be traveling frequently to check up on clients, as Judy E., the culinary representative does five or six times a year, you may need to count airfare as an operating expense.

Olé! Online Service

What praises have we not already sung for the Internet service provider? As we've said repeatedly, this is a must for the travel specialist. It's also in most cases a fixed expense. ISPs generally charge a flat rate of $20 to $25 for unlimited monthly service, which gives you access to the World Wide Web and to e-mail.

Web Host

If you get a Web site (and it is advisable that you do), you'll need a Web host. This is not a dapper chap in a tuxedo standing at the door with a tray of champagne cocktails, but rather the computer or computers that handle all your customer traffic. A Web host can be likened to an Internet service provider such as American Online or CompuServe. While you can manipulate your Web site all you want from your computer, it takes a much, much larger server to handle the complexities and size of Web traffic; and that's why you need a host. Expect to pay in the range of $30 to $50 per month for your Web host. The best way to find a Web host is to shop from among the hundreds available online, using a search engine. Be sure to comparison shop prices, and don't forget to ask for—and investigate—references from current customers. You can also ask businesspeople with sites similar in size to yours for a referral to their Web host.

Phone Home

As we discussed in the start-up section of this chapter, phone service is a must in the travel business. Start with a base rate of $25 per line—one for your business, separate from your home phone, and one for your fax machine and e-mail. Then, add in estimated long-distance charges based on where your clients and customers will be located; how often you expect to call them; and what sort of rate you've negotiated with your long distance carrier. You'll probably also want to invest in a toll-free number so clients can call you at your cost instead of theirs. This can run $300 or more per month; but if the number of customers you'll nab increases exponentially, it's probably worth it.

Dollar Stretcher

Be environmentally and economically smart. Reuse that printer paper. Instead of practicing hoop shots into the trash with all those versions of letters, evaluation sheets, and other printed materials that you decided you didn't like; set the pages aside. When you've compiled a tidy stack, load them back into your printer and print on the blank side. Save your "good" paper for the final draft that goes out in the mail.

Bloomin' Postage

As your company grows, your postage expenses will bloom, too; but for your first year of operation you should be able to keep it to a minimum. If you figure on an average of two pieces of mail per day at the first-class rate of 33 cents per piece, you can pencil in about $20 per month. Keep in mind, however, that what we're talking about here is your postage to mail various and sundry bills and invoices. Your costs for direct-mail advertising (which we'll explore in Chapters 11 and 12) will be a great deal higher than this.

Paper Tiger

Once you've made your initial outlay for office supplies and stationery, your fixed expenses in this category should be fairly low. Staples last a long time; you can reuse paper clips; and unless you're planning some violent activity with your letter opener and scissors, for which the police will bag them as evidence, you shouldn't have to buy another set.

Your main expense will be paper: paper for your printer and fax machine, fine-quality paper for stationery, and envelopes. You can refer to the "Office Equipment Checklist" (see pages 136 and 137 in Chapter 9) for supplies you'll need.

Paying the Piper

We've set aside a fixed expense called loan repayment. If you don't borrow money to start your business, you won't need to bother with this one. If, however, you finance your start-up costs through any means, you'll need to repay the piper. Here's where you pencil in whatever your monthly fee is.

Putting It Together

See the worksheets on pages 89 and 90 for a look at the income and operating expenses of our hypothetical travel agents and tour operators. Then, use the "Projected Income/Operating Expenses" work sheet on page 91 to pencil in your own income and expense figures and determine your new company's monthly bottom line. If some of these items won't apply to you—like rent if you'll be homebased or employees and workers' compensation if you'll start out solo—then you can bypass them. And don't forget to add in any additional income from sale items, like T-shirts!

> **Tip...**
>
> ### Smart Tip
> For the best possible impression on your banker, assemble your start-up materials in a professional looking folder, along with your desktop-published brochure or price lists. The more businesslike your company looks the better.

Projected Income/Operating Expenses: Independent Travel Agents

	Merry Makers Travel	After the Wedding
Projected Monthly Income	$2,500	$9,833
Projected Monthly Operating Expenses		
Rent	0	1,000
Utilities	0	125
Phone	75	250
License renewals	13	33
Electronic terminal	31	45
Employee payroll	0	2,000
Legal services	30	30
Accounting services	25	40
Reference materials/subscriptions	50	52
Bonding	17	0
Postage	20	40
Web hosting	30	50
Internet service provider	20	20
Advertising/promotions	235	500
Travel	200	400
Loan repayment	0	200
Stationery/office supplies	10	50
Insurance	90	90
Miscellaneous (Add roughly 10% of total)	82	530
Total Expenses	$928	$5,455
Projected Net Monthly Income	$1,572	$4,378

Projected Income/Operating Expenses: Tour Operators

	Magic Bay Adventures	Mysterious Journeys
Projected Monthly Income		
Income from tours	$3,632	$12,250
Income from product sales (T-shirts, etc.)	$240	$0
Total Monthly Income	**$3,872**	**$12,250**
Projected Monthly Operating Expenses		
Rent	0	1,000
Utilities		125
Phone	75	250
License renewals	13	33
Electronic terminal	31	45
Employee payroll	0	2,000
Workers' compensation insurance	0	50
Legal services	30	30
Accounting services	25	40
Reference materials/subscriptions	19	40
Bonding	17	208
Postage	20	80
Web hosting	30	50
Internet service provider	20	20
Advertising/promotions	235	1,000
Travel	0	250
Loan repayment	0	200
Stationery/office supplies	10	50
Insurance	90	90
For-sale products	120	0
Miscellaneous (Add roughly 10% of total)	58	556
Total Expenses	**$793**	**$6,117**
Projected Net Monthly Income	**$3,079**	**$6,133**

Projected Income/Operating Expenses

Projected Monthly Income

Monthly income from tours $_____

Monthly income from product sales $_____

Total Projected Monthly Income $_____

Projected Monthly Operating Expenses

Rent $_____

Utilities $_____

Phone $_____

License renewals $_____

Electronic terminal $_____

Employee payroll $_____

Workers' compensation insurance $_____

Legal services $_____

Accounting services $_____

Reference materials/subscription renewals $_____

Bonding—annual renewal $_____

Postage $_____

Web hosting $_____

Internet service provider $_____

Advertising/promotions $_____

Travel $_____

Loan repayment $_____

Stationery/office supplies $_____

Insurance $_____

For-sale products $_____

Miscellaneous $_____

Total Projected Monthly Expenses $_____

Projected Net Monthly Income $_____

Romancing the Bank

Now that you've done all the arithmetic, you can determine just how much capital you'll need to get your business up and running. And as a bonus, you can show all these beautifully executed figures to your borrower to show him or her that your business is a good risk and that you'll be able to repay the loan without difficulty.

You might want to consider financing through your bank or credit union. In this case, your start-up costs and income figures are extremely important. The bank will want to see all of this, neatly laid out and carefully calculated. You will also want to show them all the statistics you can gather about the bright future of the travel industry.

In Your Pocket

Most entrepreneurs use a very exclusive source to finance their start-up expenses—family and friends. You may choose to go this route yourself. You will have a lot less paperwork to fill out, and you can let your financier share in the excitement as your business takes off. But remember that you will still need to figure the repayment of borrowed funds into your costs, and that you should treat your repayment agreement as seriously as you would any bank loan.

Another route many entrepreneurs take to obtain financing is through an entity as close as your back pocket: the credit card. Before you choose this option, though, take a look at your available credit balance and especially the annual percentage rate. Card companies frequently offer low, low rates as an incentive to sign up or to use their service; eventually, these rates go up. Go with the one that offers the best rate for the longest period.

There are many other start-up financing avenues you can use besides those which we have already explored.

The Travel Agent's Daily Operations

By this time, you're probably wondering what exactly an independent travel agent does all day. Will you spend a few hours on the phone or Internet telling people how much fun they'll have on that Caribbean cruise; then sit back, sip piña coladas and count up the commissions? Or will you spend all day with your ear glued to the phone, hunting for a motor coach tour that will accommodate your client, her granddaughter, her grand-daughter's legendary motion sickness, and her poodle. In this chapter, we peer into the tasks that travel agents deal with daily.

Selling the Cruise

Here's the scenario. You have hung out your independent agent shingle and you're ready for action. The phone rings. It's your brother's golfing buddy, who wants to book a cruise. Your first potential client! Now what do you do? Follow these steps:

- Help your clients design a wish list.
- Find out how much your clients are willing to spend.
- Choose a cruise.
- Book the cruise.
- Make the sail, er, sale.
- Pay the cruise line.
- Get travel documents to your client.
- Collect your commission!

Now let's back up and take each of these steps one at a time so you can see exactly what you do and how you do it.

The House Call

First you set up an appointment to meet with the potential client at his home or office, which in itself makes a great impression. Most people are used to the traditional brick-and-mortar travel agency routine: they have to make the trek to the mall or strip center (or wherever it's commercially located) during office hours and sit in an uncomfortable office chair in front of somebody's desk to thumb through brochures.

As an independent agent, however, you can bring your "office" directly to the client. He doesn't have to abandon all those important e-mails and faxes at his own office to come to yours. And if he prefers, he can have you make an evening house call and relax in the cozy depths of his own living room recliner while he makes that cruise choice, along with his wife and their golfing buddies who want to cruise along, too.

Your first meeting with your new client is the time to find out all the nitty-gritty you can about his travel habits and preferences, as well as personal information. Take a look at the Preferred Client Profile on page 98, and you'll see what we mean. This may seem a bit like the old name, rank, and serial number routine; but it will give you valuable insight into your client's travel wants and needs. Anniversary dates give you the chance to suggest romantic destinations for a rekindled honeymoon. Club memberships and hobbies give you the chance to suggest group travel or special tours. When a client contacts you, their profile will be at your fingertips to help you give them the kind of personalized service they want and a trip they will love.

The Wish List

The major key to success in this business is personalized service. In this case, it means helping your clients design a wish list of the perfect products for them. They might not know a thing about cruises except that "My wife's sister's cousin went on one and had a ball." This won't be a problem for you, though. As a specialty travel professional, you'll get started by going over these wish points with your clients:

- *Destination decision.* Your clients may have been hooked by a TV commercial for a Caribbean cruise. Or maybe they've simply had enough of February in Des Moines and think that they'll become permanent Popsicles if they don't escape to a warm place. In any case, your first mission is to find out if your clients have a destination in mind.

- *Cruise newbie or old salt.* People who have never cruised before usually have no idea what to expect or even what

Smart Tip

Tip...

Ask your old-pro clients—those who've cruised before—what they liked and didn't like about past voyages. More clues to help you narrow down the choices!

Go, Go Gigi!

If you say "GG," it sounds like you're referring to the character Leslie Caron played in the movie, "GiGi," the sweet young French girl serenaded by Maurice Chevalier and Louis Jourdan. But in cruising parlance, GG rates mean guaranteed group rates. When a cruise line offers GG rates to a consortium or travel agency chain, it's putting another feather in its preferred supplier cap by giving that consortium or chain the same bargain prices for Joe and Jan Golfer, the couple, as it gives to large groups.

If you know you're a part of a GG rate consortium, be sure to mention this when you make your clients' bookings. If you don't know, ask anyway. You might just get it. And imagine how happy your clients will be when you get back to them with a lower price than your original quote!

▲

Brochure Dazzle

Cruise line brochures can be terrific teaching and selling aids, especially when you're dealing with clients who haven't cruised before. These glossy books contain photos of the ships in the line, as well as deck plans that show the layout of a typical cabin and where the various categories (or price ranges) of cabins are located on each deck. They also come complete with maps of each passage, with lines drawn from port to port, just like the maps showing Indiana Jones' travel routes in the movies.

Start building and studying your brochure library now. Then, when it's time to show your clients the difference between inside and outside cabins, or demonstrate the route from Athens to Istanbul, you'll have all the tools at hand.

they want in a cruise ship, so you will need to be their guide. If clients have been on cruises before, they often fall in love with that line and wed themselves to it. They're great candidates for a different product, but they want to stick with that line. More adventurous types, however, will like to experience several different lines.

- *Shore excursions or deck-lolling.* Some voyagers want more time at sea, while others are more interested in cruises that offer shore time at intriguing ports of call.

- *Learn or sunburn.* Some cruises offer educational or cultural experiences, like history lectures on the ports visited, cooking classes, or wine-tasting lessons. Others—like the flashy ones advertised on TV—specialize in giving passengers a floating-hotel experience featuring nightclub type revues, casinos, bars, and decadent days of sunbathing with nothing to do but unwind.

- *Time travel.* Unless you know the secrets of making time elastic, you can't send a person on a round-the-world junket if he only has three days to spend (including travel to and from the cruise ship). Likewise, a client with two glorious weeks of vacation before her won't be

> **Tip...**
>
> **Smart Tip**
>
> If your clients choose the cruise-only package, you'll need to make sure their route to the ship is accounted for. If the ship sails from Miami and they live in Baltimore, find out if they plan a leisurely drive down with stops to visit relatives along the way, or if they need some sort of transport from home to embarkation port.

happy with that two-day quickie to the Bahamas. Most cruises are three- to seven-day events; but there are many time variations, so ask your clients how long they want to be out.

- *Party of five.* You'll need to know how many people will be going with the client. A retired couple out for a second honeymoon (or that first one they never took) would want an entirely different product than Grams and Gramps planning a fun cruise with the grandkids. People also often take cruises with a group of friends, from a trio of couples to a gang of 20.

- *The cost factor.* Pitching a black-tie, champagne-and-caviar cruise to a client who has a margaritas-and-chips budget isn't going to do either of you any good. Neither is touting a four-day cruise to Fort Meyers, Florida, when your client is the type who likes Monaco and the Mediterranean. So you'll need to determine what the client can afford or wants to spend.

- *Make a date.* One of the most important things you'll need to know is when your clients want to travel. Some people like to reserve cruises months in advance, which makes booking easier for you. Other more disorganized types decide at the last minute that they have to sail or go insane.

- *Sleeping on it.* Some cruise customers prefer the posh treatment, which is usually an outside cabin with ocean view or a luxury suite. Others are perfectly happy with less expensive inside cabins. Different ships have different cabin configurations—double beds with a third berth disguised as a sofa, twin bed, or bunk bed. Especially when you have a group of travelers, you'll need to know who wants what configuration, and who sleeps with whom.

- *Alternate dates or cabin preferences.* Like airline seats, cruise cabins are often sold out or at least reserved surprisingly far in advance. So you and your clients will need to brace for a bit of jockeying for dates and cabin categories. For example, say your client wants an A category cabin on a cruise that embarks April 6, but all the A cabins are already sold. The client, with your help, will have to decide if he'd rather have a B cabin on the April 6 sailing, or go for an A cabin on the May 14 sailing.

You may want to discuss scenarios like this with your client ahead of time, or you can wait until you make the reservation and see what happens. As your business grows, you'll develop your own style, and learn to read clients to determine whether they are the type that wants to tackle all the contingencies at once or be fed them in small doses.

- *Dining decisions.* Larger cruise ships deal with the logistics of serving hundreds of meals by dividing the dinner crowd into seatings, or what they called lunch periods in high school. Usually, the first seating chows down at 6 P.M. and the second seating at 8 P.M. So you'll want to ascertain whether your clients are the starved-before-sunset types or Continental, dinner-at-eight diners. That's not all. Some ships also ask passengers to decide whether they want assigned or

Preferred Client Profile

Personal Information

Name: _____

Home address: _____

_____

Office address: _____

_____

Home telephone: _____

Office telephone: _____

Fax: _____

E-mail address:_____

Spouse or significant other: _____

Birth dates: _____

Anniversary date:_____

Honeymoon haven: _____

Children's names: _____

Birth dates: _____

Household income: _____

Any special health or diet considerations? _____

For which family member(s)? _____

Family interests:_____

Club and organization memberships: _____

Business Travel

No. trips per year average: _____

Average length: _____

Usual destinations: _____

Would you like to take your family along if you could? _____

Are your business trips paid by company or paid by you and reimbursed?

_____

Must business trips be made through an employer-approved agency?

Yes ❏ No ❏

Preferred Client Profile, continued

Leisure Travel

What times of year do you usually travel? _____

How many vacations do you average in a year? _____

Length of average trip: _____

Favorite destinations: _____

Dream destinations: _____

Do you prefer:

Independent touring ❑   Escorted tours ❑   All-inclusive resorts ❑   Cruises ❑

Airlines

Preferred airlines and frequent flyer numbers: _____

_____

Seating preference: _____

Car Rentals

Preferred companies and frequent renter numbers: _____

_____

Car preference: _____

Hotels

Preferred hotels and frequent lodger numbers: _____

_____

Room preference: _____

Suite ❑   Smoking ❑   Non-Smoking ❑   King ❑   Twin ❑

Cruises

Preferred cruise lines: _____

_____

Favorite ship style:

Large ❑ Medium ❑ Small ❑ Sailing Vessel ❑

Cabin category preference:

Upper ❑   Mid ❑   Lower deck ❑   Suite ❑   Outside ❑   Inside ❑

Meal seating preference: _____

Additional comments:

_____

general seating, so you should ask your clients this one, too.

- *Special needs.* While you're discussing food, find out if anyone in the party has special dietary needs (diabetic, kosher, vegetarian, or kibble) or any disabilities that might require special attention.

Dollar Stretcher

You may be able to beat the cruise line's air-inclusive price by shopping around for airfares on your own, then booking your clients on a cruise-only price.

- *Add-on attractions.* If the ship or cruise offers extra amenities, like revitalizing spa massages, beauty makeovers, or pre-paid shore excursions, find out which ones your clients want to spring for.

- *Paying the piper.* You'll need to know whether your client will be paying by check or credit card. And in cases of group travel, you'll also need to know who's paying for what. Will each person or couple pay their own way, or will the group issue a single check?

Choose a Cruise

Once you've gathered together the elements of your client's wish list and budget, it's time to choose a cruise. You have lots of resources to help you make the right choice. There's the wish list itself, which you'll use to make a match. Then there are all those brochures you've been amassing busily. You also have your own cruise experience to fall back on; and you can check into a bounty of industry references, which we'll explore in Chapter 9. And don't forget any preferred suppliers that might fill the bill! Your clients get the benefit of a great cruise and you get that terrific override.

Jim and Nancy T., the cruise-oriented travel agents in Dunkirk, Maryland, use preferred suppliers. "The cruising industry is growing by such leaps and bounds," Jim says, "that you'd drive yourself crazy trying to speak knowledgeably about every cruise line and every ship within it. Even though cruising is a small segment of the travel industry, there's a lot to know within that segment. So we try to focus on our preferred suppliers," the former police captain explains. "We've culled out those in several different areas, be it your value market, your mass market, your premium and then your luxury market. We can keep the variety there so we can accommodate any taste you may have or any budget you may bring to the table."

Beware!

Some countries, like Bali, will refuse entry to visitors whose passports are even six months from expiration. Make sure your clients' passports are travel-ready.

Book the Cruise

You've found the perfect cruise for your brother's golfing buddy and his wife. They're excited about it (and so are you). Now what do you do? You book the cruise! Which means you call the cruise line and make a reservation for Joe and Jan Golfer. Here's how:

- *Introduce yourself.* Give the reservation agent your name and your company name. If the cruise line is a preferred supplier, be sure to say so—if you don't, this important fact can slip away like a bowling ball on a tilting deck, with the end result that you lose that override commission. Try something like, "Hi there, this is Cassidy Cathcart with Happy Wanderer Travel. We're a Castle Consortium member and you're one our preferred suppliers. You have us down for a 15 percent commission. Could you confirm that?"

- *Order the cruise.* Give the reservation agent the particulars of what your clients want: the name of the ship and cruise, the sailing date, and the cabin category. As we explored earlier, be prepared to have to change dates or cabin classes— or both. As with airline tickets, when in doubt, pick your best alternate and reserve it. You can go back to your client afterward and say, "The A cabins on the April 6 sailing were all booked up. Since I know this is the only time you can take a vacation, I went ahead and reserved a B cabin for you. Will that work?" If your clients don't go for it, you can change or cancel the reservation. Which is better by far than not making a reservation, waiting to ask them first, and then discovering that all the B cabins are already sold, too.

- *Introduce your passengers.* Give the reservation agent your passengers' names, ages, and nationalities. The reason for giving names is obvious—so they can be identified on travel documents—but why the rest? Some cruise lines are interested in the age factor because they don't allow teens or kiddies to berth in a cabin unattended by an adult. (Sorry, parents—no escape this way!) Nationality is important for passport or visa purposes, especially for ships visiting foreign ports or foreigners cruising American waterways.

- *Give payment particulars.* Let the reservation agent know which clients will pay for which cabins and by which method (check or credit card).

- *Choose dining options.* Relay your clients' choices about first or second seating and general or assigned seating.

- *Get price points.* Once you have made the reservation, you need to get some important information for your clients. They will need to know exactly how much the cruise will cost, including port charges and any add-ons like shore excursions or those revitalizing spa sessions.

- *Go over payment schedules.* Cruise lines all have their own schedules for deposits and final payments, and these are tied to elements like the length of the cruise and how early or late the reservation is made. There can also be fees for making changes or (horrors!) cancellations. Although these rules are spelled out in the cruise lines' brochures, it never hurts to go over them with the reservation agent.

- *Write down confirmations.* Even if you have a group of 12, most cruise lines handle each cabin as a separate reservation with its own confirmation number. You'll use this number each time you call the line with any questions or changes, so be sure to copy it (or them) down correctly.

- *Find out cabin assignments.* Some cruise lines make their cabin assignments TBA (to be assigned at a later date), but others give you the cabin number when you make the reservation. Find out which is the modus operandi for the cruise line you'll use, and get your clients' cabin assignments if available.

- *Figure out flying.* If you're making an air-inclusive booking, get all the air travel information like who your clients will be flying with and when. You'll also need to ask about the cruise lines' plans for getting passengers from airport to ship.

- *Confirm ticket delivery.* Find out when the travel documents—air and cruise tickets and any vouchers for extra goodies—will be delivered. Cruise lines usually send these off from 14 to 30 days before sailing, not to the passengers but to you or your host agency.

- *Sign off.* Repeat your name and your travel agency name; and give the reservation agent the ARC, IATA, or CLIA number of your agency or your host's agency. It doesn't hurt to reiterate the part about the consortium-level commission, either. It's also a good idea to take down the name of the reservation agent so you have somebody to reference as the source for all the material you've just given and received.

Make the Sale

After you've booked that perfect cruise at a fabulous price, you still have to get your clients to pay for it. Some travel agents ask for the deposit when they make the booking. Others wait and present the booking, and the brochure with the clients' cabin numbers enticingly circled on the deck plan, before asking for that check or credit card number.

The Protection Racket

How do you know, after you spend many happy moments with your ear glued to the phone booking a cruise for your clients, that they won't find another agent who negotiates a lower price and then abandon you and your booking? You don't. Unless you ask the cruise line to protect your booking.

What this means is that the cruise line will let you match any price a competitor may negotiate for Joe and Jan Golfer. Say, for instance, you book the Golfers on a Santorini Starlight sailing for $2,550, and That Other Agency Down The Street manages to book the Golfers on the same sailing for $2,150. The cruise line will morph your Golfer booking to $2,150 so you can keep the Golfers and the commission. Pretty cool, huh?

Of course, not all cruise lines will go for this maneuver. But it's smart business to ask. And when the reservation agent does agree, remember to get his or her name so you have backup for your claim.

"We normally book the cruise prior to getting the deposit," says Jim T. in Maryland. "This accomplishes two things—it gives the client further incentive to go through with the booking because there's something tangible there, and it locks in the price quoted. Provided you book a reasonable time in advance, the cruise lines will give you a seven-day hold on a booking to get the deposit in."

You can handle this in any order that works for you and your particular clients. Just make sure you get the deposit so you can pass it along to your host agency or directly to the cruise line.

Either way, you'll need to go over the following points with your clients:

- *Payment.* Review the payment arrangements that are spelled out in each cruise lines' brochure. Be sure your clients know exactly when the final payment is due and how much it will cost them to change their minds in mid-stream.

- *Cancellation.* Make your clients aware of the penalties for canceling the cruise— not being made to walk the plank, but having to pay as much as 100 percent of the full fare. Not to panic, though! Remind your clients that for a minimal charge they can purchase trip cancellation insurance (see page 109 of this chapter).

- *Travel documents.* Let your clients know when they can expect their airline and cruise tickets. Make sure they review the passports of everyone in the group to check that they're a) accessible and not hidden at the bottom of the

Smart Tip

FIT for travel! In travel lingo, a FIT is not something you throw if things don't go your way, but a foreign independent tour, or one in which the tourist explores on his own instead of with a group.

drawer under those hopelessly outdated argyle knee socks, and b) not expired or near expiration.

Pay the Cruise Line

Once you have your client's check or credit card number, you pay the cruise line. "In the case of a check," Jim T. says, "we deposit the client's check [into the agency account], then write a company check—minus the commission—to the cruise line. In the case of a credit card payment, we let the cruise line handle it. We have chosen not to be a credit card agency, so we give the client's information to the cruise line, they process the charge and then mail us a commission check."

It's a simple process, but it's also one where—in the case of credit cards—things have the potential to get a bit sticky. As a travel agent, you're acting as a sort of intermediary between your client and the supplier. When that client buys a package tour, for instance, he gives you his credit card number, and you give it to the cruise line or tour operator.

Now, problems can arise if the client turns around at some point down the line, after he gets his bill from his credit card company, and decides not to pay for the cruise. All he has to do is call his Friendly Bank customer service department and claim that he never authorized the charge. Friendly Bank will then take the client's money back from the cruise line. This is called a chargeback, and it's no retailer's idea of fun. So the cruise line will turn around and try to get the money from your host agency, and your host agency will then try to get it from you—which is definitely not fun.

That's why it's important to make sure you have some sort of proof that the client actually authorized the charge. "The only real way to protect yourself," says Connie G. in Glenolden, Pennsylvania, "is to actually have an imprint of the card and the client's signature."

But since travel agents are handling so much business by phone and e-mail, and particularly off the Internet, this poses a problem. "We homebased agents 'see' even fewer of our clients," Connie explains, "making the imprint and signature impossible. Well, possible if you have the luxury of time to mail a credit card form, hope the client has access to a validator

Beware!

Try to get a feel for how serious your prospect is before you commit too much counseling time. If the person is a vacation looky-loo (and you'll learn the signs as you grow), you can send him politely on his way with a few brochures. If he gets serious later, he can call on you again.

[the machine you run the card through], or is good about using the side of a pen to rub an imprint on the form, signing it and returning it. Which is not a very viable option.

"Instead, we accept credit cards over the phone from established clients. For new clients, we require that they fax a letter authorizing use of their credit cards, including what we're charging for, the amount, their address, account number, expiration date, and cardholder's name and signature. In a couple of cases, I've required them to include a photocopy of their driver's license." You might also ask for a photocopy of the credit card.

Selling the Tour

Selling a tour is about the same as selling a cruise. You need to find out what your clients want, what they can afford, when they plan to travel and who (if anyone) will be traveling with them.

A lot of your leisure travel sales will be simple—sending Grams, Gramps, and the grandkids to Orlando for Disney World and related adventures, or packing that cute

The Do-It-Yourself Package

An alternative to the pre-packaged tour is to design a custom tour for your clients. This requires a lot more work and a lot more experience than selling the packaged tour. What you're doing in essence is acting as a tour operator by quilting together various suppliers' products (tours, hotels, airline seats) to form your own product.

You might decide to give this a shot if you have a client who doesn't quite fit into any pre-packaged niche. You may have booked him for a tour of England, including London, Cornwall, and Bath. This is great, except that he's decided he also wants to visit the ancestral castle in Scotland. In this case, you have several potential options:

○ Find out if the tour operator has another package to the proper part of Scotland that you can book your client on, in addition to the tour of England.

○ Find another tour operator with a package going to Scotland at a time that coincides with the tour of England.

○ Arrange airfare to Scotland, line up a rental car and a hotel, and send your client off on his own—a DIY FIT (do-it-yourself foreign independent tour) mini-package.

▲

young honeymoon couple off on the Club Med getaway they've been saving for since college. But you'll also encounter lots of clients who have no idea what they want, which puts you in the position of dream vacation counselor.

Your first mission is to get them talking about what they think they want—a week in Hawaii or a fortnight in the Hebrides? As your consultation progresses, you can start steering them into what's best for them and for you. What do they want out of life or at least this trip? Do they want to meet people? Do they want to expand their cultural horizons? Do they want to get away from it all, as in Beach Club Jamaica, or *really* get away from it all, as in grass huts in Borneo? Do they plan to mix business and pleasure? What are their time constraints, their financial limits and their physical stamina?

The Big Difference

The big difference between selling a tour and selling a cruise is that on a cruise there's only one mode of transportation and a limited number of shore excursions to worry about. (Passengers have to be back before the captain sets sail for the next port!) There's also the fact that cruises are more or less self-defined. They might last one weekend or several months, but the format consists of your clients filing up the gangway and letting the captain and crew do the driving.

Land-based tours, on the other hand, can take any form or combination of forms that a client or tour operator can dream up. A tour can be a simple fly-drive package, in which you book your clients an airline ticket to Kansas City, a rental car, and a hotel room for two nights. Or it can be a three-month blow-out to a foreign country, comprised of various air, train, and boat trips; hotels, villas, and campgrounds; and escorted tours or self-drive adventures. So besides determining what clients want as far as education or decadence, you'll also need to find out if they're the hardcore adventure hiker/biker/skier/rafter types or if they are adventurous enough to drive a rental car through Rome during rush-hour.

Beware!
There are a zillion tour operators out there, and not all of them are in the best financial shape. As a travel agent, it's your responsibility to be as certain as possible that these businesses won't collapse, taking your clients' money and vacation plans along with them. As always, do your homework and keep abreast of industry news. You'll often read about those on shaky ground long before they hit the dirt.

Tour Shopping

With so many dazzling tour choices, how do you help your clients decide on the one that's perfect for them? As with choosing a cruise, you let the client's wish list be your starting point. If she's the type that likes to sip cocoa in a cozy inn, then a hiking adventure across the frozen tundra won't work and vice versa. So first look at your clients' personalities. Then, as with cruises, start shopping your preferred suppliers. This has two advantages:

1. Your host agency and/or consortium has undoubtedly sold the supplier's tours a great many times already and can (hopefully) give the operator good reviews.

2. You get the commission override when you sell the tour.

What if your client has her heart set on a tour of Transylvania for Halloween, and none of your preferred suppliers operates within 400 miles of Count Vlad's castle? Do your homework and find a tour operator that does. You can look up specialty tours in the *Official Tour Directory*, within the pages of *Travel Weekly* and *JAX FAX*, or use the *Weissman's Report*. (We will thumb through all of these in Chapter 9, so don't worry on this page if you've never heard of them.)

Then, there's your own memory banks from those fam tours you'll take (half the fun of being a travel agent), and all those brochures you'll amass from trade shows and seminars.

Optional Adventures

Once you've chosen a tour that your client falls in love with, you book the tour basically the same way you book a cruise. Then you're on to the next step, which is making the sale. Review the elements in the cruise section, and you'll know just how to go about this—with one exception. When you go on a cruise, it's a self-contained world with just about everything included: meals, between-meal munchies, and entertainment. But a land-based tour can encompass all sorts of variable elements that may or may not be included.

Make sure you clue your clients in on the following:

- *Dinner in the diner—or not.* Tour operators will often design their programs around a MAP, which is not a street or topographic map, but the Modified American Plan. With the MAP, tourists are fed two out of three meals a day (usually breakfast and dinner) as part of the tour price. So your clients should be prepared to pay for lunch from their own pockets.

- *Optional adventures.* Sometimes tour brochures can be a bit misleading. If that Transylvania package has a line like,

Smart Tip *Tip...*

Tour company luggage tags and stickers aren't just "team spirit." They're also used to help ground operators identify tour members' bags in a sea of airport baggage. So make sure your clients stick those stickers on their stuff!

"Day 3 includes a scenic mountain drive to the quaint village of Igor Abbey, location of the famous Vampire's Kiss Winery," it doesn't necessarily mean that a winery tour is included. Make sure your client understands this subtlety. Then suggest the winery tour—it's added fun for her and can be an added commission for you!

Beware!
Some states have rules about who can sell insurance, including travel agents who offer it to their clients through an independent insurance agent. Be sure to check with your host agency, your state's regulatory body, or both, before proceeding.

- *Extra perks.* Tour operators often add extra perks to make the tour a special experience. If the package includes goodies like dinner with a celebrity ("Count Vlad at your table!"), be sure your client knows about this, too. Anticipation is part of the fun.

Guidebooks and Goodies

After you've gone over all these elements with your client, and she's cheerfully paid the deposit and then the final payment, the travel documents will be delivered to you on your client's behalf. What should you expect to receive?

- *Airline tickets.* Review them to make sure they're imprinted with the correct name (or names if you have multiple travelers) and that all the information is correct, including times, dates, and departure and arrival cities.

- *Coupons or vouchers.* These can encompass rental cars, champagne or cocktail welcomes, side excursions (like that winery tour), and meals. Again, check to make sure everything's in order with the proper number of vouchers marked with the right names, dates, and destinations.

- *Itinerary and instructions.* This is the "menu" of where the tour goes and on what days. It also has the drill on what special clothes or equipment to bring, what sort of shape the client may need to be in (couch potato or NASA-prepped astronaut), and any rules of the road about interacting with native peoples.

- *Guidebooks and goodies.* Some tour companies—especially the ones oriented toward cultural enrichment—may send homework in the form of guidebooks or other learn-before-you-leap materials. Tour operators may also send promotional treats like tote bags and luggage tags in the tour colors and logo.

Tripping out on Cancellations

Cruise lines and tour operators will demand exorbitant fees when people cancel trips that are already booked. And they'll make you pay that cancellation fee, even if you cancel for a good reason, like because you broke three teeth, one arm, and both legs; your grandmother died; you came down with galloping pneumonia; and your house was torpedoed by a nearby military base. Depending on how close to the departure date you bow out, you can be liable for up to 100 percent of the price of the cruise or tour.

That's why it's extremely important to discuss *trip cancellation insurance* with your clients. They may not go for it, but as a travel agent you need to alert them to the dangers of not purchasing it. And since some suit-happy types can get nasty and claim you didn't tell them they'd be liable for those stiff cancellation fees, you should also have them sign a disclosure or waiver if they refuse the insurance.

You can and probably should discuss other types of travel insurance with your clients, too. These include insurance for:

- Medical emergencies
- Baggage damage, loss, or delay
- Flight insurance
- Legal difficulties

Tour operators and cruise lines often offer travel insurance, especially trip cancellation coverage, for an additional fee.

You can also offer your clients travel insurance through various independent insurance companies, as Jim and Nancy T. do. "We sell insurance through both means," Jim says, "and we highly recommend that everyone take some form of insurance. We have every client sign a waiver form indicating we've discussed insurance with them and what their decision is—Decline, Cruise Line, or Independent. We always suggest that the independent is the best form of insurance because it will provide default protection against the cruise and airlines. Insurance from the cruise line will not." The best part of offering your clients travel insurance, besides peace of mind for both them and you, is that it's commissionable, which is pretty rewarding for you.

Daily Operations for the Tour Operator

W e've investigated the daily life of the

independent travel agent. Now, what's your day going to be like

as a specialty tour operator? Do you put the phone on voice

mail, lock up the office and spend the day out on the river or

exploring the city with your clients? Do you spend all day on the

phone trying to line up a ground operator who'll pick up your group at the airport at 3 A.M.? Or is your time taken up designing tours that will tempt people to sign on?

All of these scenarios are realistic, plus many more. In this chapter, we'll give you an overview of the daily life of a tour specialist and explore the ins and outs of tour operations.

Designing the Tour

One of the most important aspects of a winning tour—the one that garners rave reviews and keeps clients coming back for new offerings—is its design. You can take tourists to the Taj Mahal and bore them silly or to downtown Ozona, Texas, and get oohs of approval, depending on how you structure your program.

You want your tours to give your clients new and intriguing sights, sounds, and scents; but you also want to make sure they reflect the personalities and desires of your target market. A home-schooling group, made up of 10 ten-year-olds and their parents, will want to whiz through the cathedral of Notre Dame in 10 minutes; while a group of 10 art historians can happily spend an entire day poring over ceilings and floors. Seniors tend to want more handholding on a tour than Gen Xers. More affluent tourists from sophisticated areas like New York or San Francisco may need less coaching on travel etiquette, like how to tip a hotel bellman, than tourists coming from rural regions.

Practice, Practice

Your tours should also reflect your own personality. There's no need to hit people over the head with your comic timing or your encyclopedic knowledge of Roman history, but your interests and enthusiasm will contribute a great deal to your clients' sense of fulfillment and fun. "It's not what you know, it's how you come across," Dr. Phil S. in New York advises. "If you come across as a friendly, caring person and tell some wonderful anecdotes, people will think you give a wonderful tour."

Which is not to say that leading a tour is a no-brainer, so long as you have charm. Phil spends a lot of time practicing and refining each of his more than 20 tours; these include such eclectic offerings as the Jewish gangster tour, a murder and mystery tour, and a Chinatown at twilight tour. He starts each one based on information found in guidebooks and gradually develops a specific theme or approach. "From there you can find out what works and what doesn't," he says. And that includes pacing. The original version of Phil's East Village tour covered a three-mile area in two-and-a-half hours—a hike that the history professor soon whittled down to just one mile. "It's not a marathon any more," he says with a smile.

The Mystery Tour

Your tours can be as creative as you are. Don't be afraid to break the mold and try something different, as Terry S. did in Seattle. Terry started his business giving walking tours—now he has four different themes to choose from, and each is a result of requests from groups that took his original tour.

But about two years into running his business, the former computer programmer realized that walking tours were just not going to attract a certain demographic group—namely Gen Xers and local corporate groups. "So I created an alternative way to see the city," Terry explains, "a competitive event that I call Mystery & Scavenger Hunt.

"These sleuthing contests are great morale events, social mixers, team builders, and entertainment for large or small groups," says Terry "They are conducted in Seattle with chauffeured limousines or on foot—the Inspector Clouseaus types vs. the Dirty Harrys. This is the most successful part of my business. Corporate and other groups use it as a morale event, and my most frequent customer is Microsoft."

Full Moons and Rainy Seasons

Another element that will make your tours shine is your special knowledge of your market niche. Your clients will return year after year because of your expertise in your field—just as Harry G.'s do for his fishing smarts.

"In the fishing game," Harry says, "we're concerned about full moons, when certain species of fish happen to be running and when they're not, about rainy seasons and dry seasons. There's so much involved in a trip—the time of year, the species of fish. We have spin fishermen, fly fishermen, and guys and gals who use other techniques. So many folks like doing things so many different ways that we have to be ready to answer any questions.

"Somebody might call me," the former oil company representative explains, "and say he wants to go fishing in Alaska and catch a king salmon. But the guy can't go until September, and the salmon come in June and July, and by September there's none left. So we need to be truly up on everything, familiar with the geography of the particular state, country, and province as to their seasons and when the runs start."

Serendipity

Barry, the car race tour operator, also uses his expertise in his chosen field to give his clients a unique experience. "We may have a driver spend some time with people," he says. "We may have a race commentator give them special information. We'll put on theme parties—we did one in Canada for a thousand people. We may have an auction of car parts in which the money goes to charity. We do many different things in these areas. If we're charging a premium, there has to be a reason for somebody to go on our tours."

Some of Barry's tours are hosted by celebrities, and sometimes the celebs put in a surprise appearance. "Things will happen that you don't envisage," he explains. "You can't tell clients that this or that will happen. Somebody invites you where you never expected to go, as when an English lord invites a tour group for tea or the owner of a museum personally shows you his magnificent cars."

It sounds like serendipity, and it is. But these unexpected delights also happen because Barry has developed a friendship and rapport with the people involved—the windfalls of which he's able to pass along to his lucky clients.

Debrief and Distill

"*Specialize*," advises Karen A., the tour operator in Savannah, Georgia. "Whether your customers are Girl Scouts or…music students, whether your tours are bird watching or gambling, you will never get *really* good at giving a tour unless you give the same kind of tour to the same kind of people over and over and iron out the kinks. If you get really *good* at it, people will spread the word; and you'll get much of your new business from return customers and by word of mouth.

"Hold debriefing meetings after every tour and distill what you have learned into *policies* that will make the next tour run more smoothly. Our favorite saying," Karen says, "is 'I don't want to know whose fault it was. I want to know what policy we need to institute to prevent it happening again.'"

> ### Tip...
> **Smart Tip**
> "The whole goal in running a tour," says car race tour promoter Barry S., "is to give people something they can't do on their own. If you can do something that's impossible for people to achieve alone, then you have them as customers."

Structural Elements

You've determined what the theme of your tour will be and how you'll use your knowledge and expertise to make it special. Now how do you give it a structure? Take a look at the following elements, for starters.

Dream Dates

Choose your dream dates. These are not Julia Roberts or Antonio Banderas, but times your prospective clients will perceive as perfect for going on a tour. You might schedule a "Fifth Avenue Shop 'til You Drop" tour for women during Super Bowl weekend, but a "Basketball Mania" tour for men during the same weekend would bomb. Make sure you take the following into consideration:

- *Holiday rambling.* Decide what the best time of year is for your particular tour. As Harry, the fishing aficionado, points out, some activities—like king salmon fishing in September—insist on their own time frames. Some types of clients, too, are time-sensitive. Family vacations play better during school

Brownies and Cub Scouts

Leading a tour is a bit like being a master psychologist. You've got to take all sorts of personalities into consideration, and people's personalities can undergo subtle (or not-so-subtle) changes when they're under your guidance. Especially when they're in a foreign country and feeling insecure with alien cultures and languages, your clients can seem to revert to a sort of junior Brownie or Cub Scout status, relying on you to be the den mother or dad and handle every transaction for them.

And just like Brownies or Cub Scouts, clients on tour will sometimes start displaying such juniorish traits as vying wildly for your attention and accusing each other of playing up for favoritism. One way to overcome this sort of problem is to be sure you don't play favorites. If you'll be in and out of a motor coach or minivan for days at a time, you might make a practice of rotating seats. That way no one gets to sit by you, or by the window, or in the front or wherever, to the exclusion of somebody else. Follow a similar practice when it comes to seating in restaurants or at attractions.

Another way to keep your flock under control and happy is to make a habit of "reading" your clients as you go along, something Dr. Phil S., the New York City tour guide, learned the hard way. His worst walking tour, he says—out of many, many bests—was one made up of a group of seniors that he led on a rainy day. "I wasn't paying attention for feedback," the history professor explains, "thinking they were young people like me. I was pushing them when they didn't want to be pushed." The result was a miserable group, but a wonderful lesson learned.

and work holiday periods, traditionally summer vacations and short-hop holidays like Memorial Day and Labor Day. Big-time family holidays like Easter and Christmas, however, usually don't sell well because people prefer to stay at home with their relatives than go off to see the world.

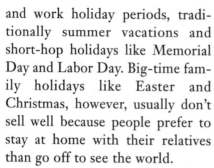

Bright Idea

If you'll target a particular professional organization, try scheduling a short tour right before or after your target tourists' national convention. People who'll be in town to attend the big meeting can add in your tour without adding in extra travel expenses or significantly more time away from work.

- *Eight days a week.* Working world travelers like an eight-day tour that starts and ends on a Saturday. This way they only lose one work week (Monday through Friday) and get to tack on an extra three days of vacation fun. On the other hand, if your clients are retired seniors, you might want to start your tour midweek, say on a Tuesday, Wednesday, or Thursday, when airfares are significantly lower.

- *Paint the town.* Unless a special event is the focus of your tour, make sure your program doesn't coincide with paint-the-town-red events. These would be events like the Olympics; Mardi Gras; Le Mans; the running of the bulls at Pamplona; or other feasts, festivals, and general mayhem that can tie up traffic and hotel rooms—and make the latter much more expensive.

- *Red flags.* Think about the red-letter events on your clients' calendars. If your target clients are artists and crafters, for instance, don't plan your tour for the same weeks as major gift shows. If your potential participants will be high school teachers, don't schedule your tour during finals, when your clients will want to be at their posts, looming over students. And if you're aiming for New Age types, make sure you don't plan your gig at the same time as the harmonic convergence over Sedona, Arizona.

- *Weather wrinkles.* In some parts of the world, brutal weather can make a big difference. It's hard to conduct a tour during blizzard conditions in the Midwest or Northeast, or during monsoon season in India. You can't know precisely when some of these weather events will occur, but you can definitely take them into consideration.

- *Time redux.* One more timing element to take into consideration is the length of your tour. A half-day tour of Apalachicola, Florida, is probably long enough to see all there is in this small fishing town, but you can easily schedule a full week in San Francisco and environs. Think about what you want to show off, what your clients will be interested in, and what their attention spans are likely to be.

High Concept

Give your tours a high-concept title. In Hollywood terms, this means a title that paints an immediate and intriguing picture. "Midnight, Moonlight, and Magnolias" sounds far more interesting than "The Charleston, Beaufort, and Savannah Tour." Think of your products in terms of how they'll sound in a brochure and the romance or excitement (or both) they'll conjure up in potential clients' minds.

Keep these high-concept pointers in mind as you design your tours:

- *Stick with the program.* Don't wander away from that unique concept. If your theme is "Midnight, Moonlight, and Magnolias," and you're packaging seafront cities of the Old South, you can't suddenly throw in Chicago as well–even if your clients will be changing planes there en route to Charleston.

- *Do the splits.* If you're planning a tour designed for a special interest group, say baseball fans, you might also plan activities for the non-baseball-aholic part of the family. While Pops and Brother are touring the dugouts, for instance, you can send Mom and Sis off to view historic homes. Arranging for alternate activities on the same day is called a split itinerary.

- *Act smart.* Planning a tour is like writing a three- or four-act play. You need to give it a kicky start, an exciting end, and not let it fall somewhere in the middle. Plan an itinerary that's full of surprises but that also has enough pleasant lulls to keep your clients from feeling overwhelmed. A two-week trip—as well as a two-hour walking tour—should be stimulating but also allow time for relaxation.

Supplier Smarts

Once you've decided on your tour's theme, length, and itinerary; you'll need to make arrangements with hotels, attractions, and ground operators. This gets easier as your business and expertise grow. "We have ground operators we've been working with for many years," says Harry G., the fishing pro. "They know our idiosyncrasies and our whims and wishes, so everything goes very smoothly."

As a travel professional, you'll have to start from ground zero in finding the right folks. One way to start is by feeling out suppliers on your scouting trips. For instance, when you travel to Vienna to research your "Mozart and Major

> ## Smart Tip
> *Tip...*
>
> Be sure to explain facets of foreign cultures to your clients before they encounter certain situations—everything from the fact that you can't always get unsweetened ice tea in Southern restaurants, to the fact that bowing in Japan is common courtesy. It makes for a more interesting tour and also reduces their insecurity factor.

▲

Chocolate" tour, talk to hoteliers, restaurateurs, and other suppliers whose products appeal to you. Sound them out on prices and commissions. Talking to people face to face is often the very best way to negotiate.

"Hotels demand deposits for group reservations and payment in full before the group arrives," advises Karen A. in Savannah, Georgia. "Motor coach owners also require deposits. In theory, so do many other attractions. Everything, however, is negotiable, and the reputation of the tour operator is all-important. (One Savannah tour operator has been banned from a Savannah museum for paying their bills too slowly and booking in too many no-show groups.) In practice, we pay hotels in full a couple of weeks in advance. In our second year, we paid some of the more prosperous restaurants by invoice after the event and most other restaurants and attractions at the time of the tour. In our third year, with a reputation for paying our bills, we are being billed after the event by nearly all our vendors except hotels."

Lodging Logistics

Your choice of lodgings will play a large part in how your clients view your tour. Your choices can range from a quaint bed and breakfast in the country to a suite at the

---

Cooking Up Bookings

The smart tour operator makes hotel arrangements as far in advance as possible, ideally six months or more. Rooms will be at a premium during paint-the-town events, and you'll need to book them as much as a year in advance. Barry S., the car race tour promoter, began to make hotel arrangements in June 1999 for the U.S. Grand Prix in September 2000. This can be pricey—hotels were asking for a 50 percent deposit on rooms they'd marked up about four times the regular or rack rate.

Once you've booked those rooms, it's important to make sure you can fill them. "We have a computer program," Barry says, "that calculates if we're going to hit the number of rooms we said we'd take. If not, we need to cut back very early, maybe six months out, or three months at the very least, to allow the hotel to sell the rooms to somebody else. Otherwise you're going to pay for them."

"We're very careful about this," Barry explains, "because with this business we always go to the same cities. We need to be on good terms with the hotels or we're not going to be able to do business with them the following year." Barry says that you get better rates once you build a relationship with the hotels and they trust you to fill the rooms you take.

Paying You, the Piper

When you run a multiday tour to foreign climes, you ask for 50 percent of the tour price when your clients make their bookings and the balance prior to the departure. But how do you handle deposits and payments with a half-day walking tour?

Quite simply, you take clients' payments at the start of the tour. You can request that people pay cash, which means you don't need to fuss with out-of-state checks that might bounce or take forever to clear the bank. And you don't need to worry about any sort of credit card processing. (Don't forget, however, that just because it's cash doesn't mean you don't report it to Uncle Sam!)

You can handle group or private tours a little differently. When they call ahead to make reservations, you can ask that they seal the deal by mailing a check. Or you can let the group leader hand over a check at the start of the tour. Experience will teach you what works best with which sorts of groups.

Terry S., the Seattle walking tour pro, gives pre-arranged group tours first dibs on his services. "First priority goes to reservations made by pre-arranged groups—walking tours or scavenger hunts," he explains, "with a $200 minimum. These may be conducted on any day. Second priority goes to the Seattle walking tour for individual walkers—reservations for a total of six people are required before this tour is conducted on any given day. I always ask folks if there are any other days they could go on a tour in case of a schedule conflict with the pre-arranged group affairs, or if we have less than a minimum of six reservations. Otherwise this tour is available Tuesday through Saturday, except for major holidays."

Ritz. Naturally, one's going to be pricier than the other, but one will also appeal to different clients more than the other. So how do you choose?

First, realize that your hotel price will be built into the price of your tour, as we explained previously. This means you're not actually "paying" for the hotel all on your own; although, you will have to pay a deposit upfront.

Even though you build lodging into the cost of your tours, you still have a lot of decisions to make. Do you go with the hotel that's a downtown dowager or with one that's new and classy but out in the burbs? Or do you forego the traditional hotel altogether and choose a resort that's out in the country?

Take a look at these tips for making the right decision:

- *Compatibility.* Choose a hotel that's a good match with your clients and your subject matter. If you're doing a tour for business executives, you might choose a snazzy, modern hotel near the airport or in a fashionable, upscale semi-burb like Beverly Hills. These are the types of environments the suit-crowd feels comfortable in and considers worth its time and money. On the other hand, if your market niche is the paranormal, you might seek out an old downtown hotel with an ambiance of emanations and possibly even a resident ghost or two. One more example: If your topic is "Lush Landscaping of Louisiana" and

> **Smart Tip** Tip...
>
> Always make sure to get all the hotel arrangements confirmed in writing. Then call to reconfirm a month and then a week before your tour will arrive. Don't leave lodgings to chance.

your clients will be seniors or landscape architect students on a budget, a mid-priced hotel near a park might be the perfect place. But if your topic is "Lush Landscaping of Louisiana" and your clients are professional landscape architects on a two-day tour/workshop, a conference center in an upscale resort area would be more the thing.

- *Bad rap burgs.* Your choice for where to house your clients is not relegated only to the hotel itself but also to the part of the city or region in which it's located. Some burgs have a bad rap: people would rather stay in Malibu or Newport Beach than in Watts or Garden Grove, even though they are all within the greater L.A. metropolis. The first two cities sound trendy and glamorous while the latter two do not. For New Jersey, say Trenton or Princeton and see which people choose!

- *Pack it in.* Most travelers are not enamored of packing and unpacking every night (which is one of the selling points of a cruise—that you don't have to). So if your tour will encompass several cities or regions, it's a good idea to check clients into a centrally-located hotel and plan day trips for the surrounding areas. For example, you might choose a hotel in Dana Point, California, and take minivan excursions to Los Angeles, San Diego, and Ensenada, Mexico, instead of shuttling people to three different hotels.

The Lodging Wish List

Once you've chosen your ideal lodging, it's time to talk price with the sales manager. Hotels—especially larger properties that are used to dealing with seminars, conventions, weddings, and other groups—tend to operate something like car dealers, fully expecting that in any negotiations they'll come out ahead. Therefore, they may (and probably will) quote rates that are higher than they actually need to turn a profit, insist that they can't help with certain requests because it's not "hotel policy," and otherwise drag their feet.

Your part in dealing with hotels is to realize that hostelries love groups—which is what you're bringing them. They get lots of rooms filled in one fell swoop, along with the stellar opportunity to have you bring groups back over and over again. So stick to your guns in the negotiating process. Don't be rude or aggressive; you're trying to win long-time contacts. But do be prepared to bargain.

First, you need to know what you want. Take a look at this lodging wish list:

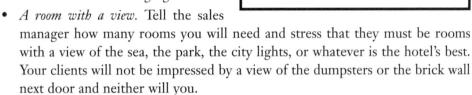

Dollar Stretcher

Don't forget that airlines, hotels, attractions, and many other suppliers offer senior discounts. If you'll have seniors on your tour, negotiate this into your costs.

- *A room with a view.* Tell the sales manager how many rooms you will need and stress that they must be rooms with a view of the sea, the park, the city lights, or whatever is the hotel's best. Your clients will not be impressed by a view of the dumpsters or the brick wall next door and neither will you.

- *Dining delights.* Find out if the hotel will include breakfast as part of the room rate. Then make sure you're negotiating for either a continental breakfast, which is the European version with just coffee and rolls; a full dining room meal of bacon and eggs; or a special room in the basement for a buffet-type breakfast.

- *Dining delights part deux.* If the hotel won't go for complimentary breakfasts, make sure it does have a dining room or that there's a breakfast eatery somewhere nearby so that your clients can eat before departing for the day's activity. Ditto this for evening meals, unless you will arrange for them to eat out as part of the program.

- *Meeting room.* You may want a sizable room if your tour will include any sort of workshop or seminar. Discuss this with the hotel well in advance.

- *Party.* If you will include a welcome reception or farewell bash, you will want the hotel to spring for eats and drinks (at a reasonable cost), as well as a provide an appointed room in which to hold the affair.

- *Cool comps.* Ask for *comps*, which are complimentary, i.e. freebie rooms, for your coach driver and tour guide.

Diner Decisions

For most people, dining out is one of the major perks of traveling. As a result, you'll need to factor a certain number of food experiences into your itinerary. You can choose to give your clients breakfasts as an inclusive part of your tour, especially since you'll probably get morning meals included in the room cost.

Most tour operators also give clients a certain number of lunches and dinners as part of the scheduled activities, like a dinner with native dancing as entertainment or lunch on an intimate island. But you'll want to leave some meals for people to enjoy on their own and pay for on their own.

Negotiate with restaurateurs in basically the same way you bargain with hoteliers. Let them know that you'll bring groups back again and again, if treated well. This is great for them as well as for you. But keep these points in mind when choosing eateries:

- *The numbers game.* Not all restaurants are set up to deal with groups. That quaint or trendy little café you found may be overwhelmed dealing with a party larger than ten. So if you'll have a large group, make sure you give the restaurant a visual check-out and then also discuss the situation with the manager.

- *Group grub.* Some large restaurants make a point of catering to large groups—and in many cases, the grub is your basic rubber chicken dinner. Don't take "great group joint" recommendations for granted. Ask for a sample meal.

- *All-inclusive eats.* You may be able to negotiate an all-inclusive meal for your clients that will cover the meal, beverage, tax, and tip. Of course, this usually means that everybody has to eat the same thing, which may be a drawback unless the restaurant is famous for something in particular. And keep in mind that if the restaurant is famous for roast beast, you may have vegetarian types to accommodate, too.

Bright Idea

Dr. Phil S., in New York City, has his walking tours meet at a local restaurant. This way early birds can get in out of the weather, and if he's late for some unavoidable reason, he can call the restaurateur and ask him to explain to the walkers that their guide is on the way. As an added do-good bonus, this practice leads to extra customers for the restaurant!

Infatuated Attraction

An *attraction* can be anything from Disney World to a 14th-century castle to a canoe trip down a lazy river. And unless you want to keep your tourists on that motor coach or minivan forever—or biking down that long, dusty road—you'll want to build in a few attractions as part of your itinerary. As with your other suppliers, you'll want to find out the details ahead of time. Check out these caveats:

- *Discount please.* Most attractions will cheerfully hand out group discounts. Find out what size pod of people in each case constitutes a discountable group and negotiate if you can. Sometimes extra seasonal discounts or surcharges are added in, so be sure to ask.

- *Advance warning.* Some attractions insist on advance notice before they'll allow a group discount; others will offer it at the gate. And some attractions will grant a deeper discount if you book in advance.
- *Free for me.* Most attractions offer free admission to the tour leader—either you or your appointed tour guide.
- *Outfitting.* If the attraction involves outfitting, with canoes or ice skates or snorkels, find out if the gear is included in the price. If the price is not, try negotiating a deal.

Motor Coach Madness

What about the perennial favorite of the tour operator, the motor coach? Those big bus companies and smaller local sightseeing firms operate in basically the same manner. Unlike hotels, they're delighted to work with you. Prices can vary considerably, so it pays to get bids from several competitors.

Keep these tips in mind while you're price shopping:

- *Copacetic capacity.* Make sure you specify the bus size. You won't want a double-decker, 100-passenger behemoth when you have a cozy group of 10 people, and vice versa.

> **G**uides are usually paid an hourly or daily rate, or they are paid per passenger.

- *Rate rules.* Bus companies generally quote rates by the day, while local sightseeing companies (even if they provide a giant motor coach) quote by the half day or full day or even per passenger. The price usually includes fuel, cleaning of the vehicle while on the trip, and the driver's pay. There are also additional fees not quoted, for which you will be responsible. These include road tolls, parking fees, and the driver's hotel room (remember, you may be able to get this comped). And if you start your coach tour in one city and end it in another, you'll have to pay for the day or however long it takes for the driver to take the empty bus back to the origination city—this is called deadheading.
- *Step-on smarts.* The guides (called step-on guides) who pop aboard to give commentary on local sights don't always work for the motor coach company; sometimes you have to arrange for them

Tip...

Smart Tip
The coach or sightseeing company will invoice you after the tour for tolls, parking fees, driver's hotel room, and other extras not included in its price quote.

Smart Tip

Tip...

Some airline con-
solidators quote *net
fares,* meaning the actual cost of
the tickets to you. Others quote
commissionable fares that
include a commission of usually
10 percent to 15 percent that the
consolidator rebates to you.

separately. You can ask for the company to recommend a step-on guide or find referrals from
local chambers of commerce and tourist
bureaus. Guides are usually paid an hourly or
daily rate, or they are paid per passenger.

Airline Appeal

Now that we've negotiated and booked
everything from the hotel to the attractions,
what about getting your clients to that foreign destination and home again? Unless
you'll be doing city walking tours or other short, local tours, you'll need to think about
that bane of the travel professional's world—airline seats.

Some specialty tour operators skip this step altogether. Judy E., the culinary school
representative, doesn't do airline reservations at all. "I let everyone who comes to me
use their own travel agent," she explains, "or I refer them to a travel agent. I wanted a
niche market—I didn't want to worry about the rest of the travel." A lot of Judy's clients
are already in Europe as part of a larger vacation and tack on the one-week culinary
adventure as an adjunct to their trip. This would make scheduling air fares for each one
a logistic headache. And since so many travelers today get around courtesy of their frequent flyer miles, Judy says, it's easier to let them handle their own tickets.

Many specialty tour operators do as Judy does and farm out airline ticket requests
to travel agents, or they go the consolidator route. "I'm able to get bulk rates into
Latin America and the South Pacific from various bulk air operators because we do a
lot of business there," says Harry G., the fishing pro. "On domestic tickets, I have two
travel agencies that do all the ticketing for my clients—not host agencies, just people
we farm out to, who are specializing in what they do best."

The Airline Den

If you decide to go ahead and brave the lion's den by purchasing tickets for your
clients directly from airlines, try these tips:

- *Dealing with the desk.* Airlines, like hotels, believe they hold all the cards when
  it comes to price quotes. Unfortunately, to some extent they do. You can and
  should get bids from a variety of air carriers, then go with the best one. Or even
  better, use one airline's quote as an incentive for the next one to come down in
  price. It doesn't always work, but it doesn't hurt to try, either. Ask to talk to the
  airline's group reservations desk—you can get the number by calling the toll-
  free numbers you find in your local Yellow Pages.

- *Commissions and overrides.* If you have a host agency you can process the tickets through, ask for these perks. If not, ask the airline to come down in price to compensate for the commissions they don't have to pay.

- *Another free for me.* Air carriers frequently give one free ticket for each 15 passengers in your group. You can use the freebie for yourself or your tour guide. If you have got a large group and you have several free tickets, you could give one as a gift or a charity giveaway, or save it for a later research trip on your own.

Beware!
In some states, you cannot use clients' deposits for your tour to make deposits to hotels or other suppliers—which is not a good idea in any case. Use your own funds and you, your clients, and any travel agents you sell through will feel much more secure.

Trial and Error

To give you an idea of how all these elements actually fit together to make up a tour, let's look at how Karen A.'s Savannah, Georgia, company sets up a program. "Tour design is a complicated matter of trial and error because so many things interact," Karen says. "For instance, Museum A is closed on Mondays; Tybee Lighthouse is closed on Tuesdays; Okefenokee Swamp is swarming with school children in April; Restaurant A will not take groups larger than 75 or smaller than 15; Hotel B does not include breakfast in its price, etc. In addition, the prices we pay are a movable feast. Vendors tend to increase (and decrease) prices without telling us (and the price you get may depend upon who answers the phone), but conversely, they give us better prices and conditions as we work with them for longer.

Smart Tip
Don't forget the rambunctious factor. Although lots of tours are designed with families in mind, there are also lots of tour operators who prohibit children under the age of 12, especially those whose programs involve long motor coach trips.

"For the package nature tours," explains Karen, the expert on Savannah and its environs, "a local travel agent acts as our associate and arranges air transportation. For the customized group tours, we send the customer a proposal (itinerary plus price). When this has been massaged to everyone's satisfaction, they sign a sales agreement and send us a deposit. Then we book hotels, meals, transportation, museums, cruises, etc. Customers pay for tours 30 days before the tour, so collecting accounts receivable is one (perhaps the only!) problem that most businesses have and tour companies don't.

Karen and her staff have carefully fine-tuned their tour operations. "During a tour," she explains, "[our guides]" use mobile phones to keep in touch. One office worker is designated the 'dispatcher' for each tour and any decisions that force a deviation from the written itinerary are referred to the dispatcher (such as what to do about a thunderstorm or a no-show cruise boat). We have found that it is better *not* to have the escort make such decisions because there is someone in every group who doesn't like whatever decision is made; it is better if they can blame some distant office worker instead of the escort with whom they are spending their time. We instituted a number of policies of this kind as a result of problems that arose during our first few months of group tours. We find that they make an enormous difference to customer satisfaction and the smooth running of a tour. It is vital to have such policies written down in an employee manual and to go over them at a staff meeting every six months or so."

The Travel Kit
Your Business Equipment

Even though you will spend a fair amount of time traveling the world, you will need an office—a sort of non-mobile travel kit. This will be your command center, the heart of your business, so stocking it with the proper equipment is vital to your success. Some of these items are geared more toward the travel agent than the tour operator. Others are tools you will want whichever route you take. As with every other chapter in this book, be sure to read through it all, then choose the elements that will apply to your company.

We've provided a handy checklist (see pages 136 and 137) to help you determine what you will need and what you already have on hand. Die-hard shoppers may want to rush out and buy every item brand-new; but don't be too quick a draw with the old credit card, at least not until you've finished this chapter.

As you read it through, run down the checklist and evaluate your stock. Is your computer travel-operations ready, or is it an antique that won't be able to keep up the pace? Does your answering machine take and receive clearly audible messages, or does it tend to garble crucial information? How about that printer? Can it produce professional-looking materials in short order, or does it take ages to spit out a solitary, quavery page? With your checklist in hand, let's take a whirlwind virtual shopping spree.

Office Equipment

First up, let's take a look at your office equipment, the tools of the trade that will get your operation off to a good start and keep it going efficiently. Keep in mind that there's always the buy of a lifetime, and there's always the ultimate tiptop of the line. What we're looking for here are the low- and middle-of-the-road models. You can trade up to the Rolls Royce of computers and other equipment after your business is up-and-running, and you're able to pay for its upgrades.

Computer Glitterati

Your computer will be the command center of your office setup, coordinating your invoicing, accounting, word processing, database, and desktop publishing activities; not to mention co-starring in all Web site activities and e-mail correspondence. Aside from semi-tangible items like cruise tickets for that CLIA certification, your computer may be your most important start-up purchase. If you already own a computer, you'll want to make sure it's capable of handling the tasks you'll assign it.

Now, while it's technically possible to start off without a computer system, you're asking to do things the old-fashioned—and really hard—way if you opt for this method. All the entrepreneurs we talked with have at least one computer, which they rely on to perform a variety of tasks.

> ### Smart Tip
> *Tip...*
>
> Monitors are often sold separately. You'll want an SVGA high resolution color display and a screen large enough to make long-term viewing comfortable—17 inches and up. Remember that a few extra dollars spent upfront will save hours of squinting in the long haul. You can expect to dish out $300 to $400 for a solid, mid-range model.

Stress-Buster

Unless you plan to walk or bicycle to the post office every time you have a package or promotional materials going out, a postage meter is a good idea. Depending on how snazzy you choose to go from among the various models available, not only can you stamp your mail; but you can also fold, staple, insert, seal, label, weigh, sort, stack, and wrap it. Phew! The fancier and faster the machine, the more expensive it will be to rent, lease, or purchase.

It used to be that you'd have to lug your postage meter down to the post office and stand in line to get it reset. Not any more! Now you reset them via phone or computer. What's the cost for all this technology? It depends on what you get; but as a ballpark figure, you can expect to rent a postage meter/electronic scale combo for about $24 to $117 per month.

With a good system as your silent partner, you can single-handedly perform more functions than you might believe possible. Just for starters, you can:

- Create your own brochures, display ads, and other direct-mail pieces
- Generate stationery, invoices, client profiles, and booking forms
- Perform accounting functions and generate financial reports
- Maintain databases of repeat and potential clients
- Access research materials and other resources online
- Sell via an online or "virtual" brochure
- Communicate with repeat and potential clients, your host agency, other travel agents, and preferred suppliers via e-mail

Your new computer should be a Pentium with a Windows-based operating system since this is what all but clunker, found-at-garage-sale software packages are geared for. To run your software properly, you'll need at least 64 MB RAM, plus at least an 8GB to 10GB hard drive, a CD-ROM drive, and a 56K modem. You can expect to pay from $1,500 to $3,500 for a good name-brand computer, with prices increasing as you add on goodies.

General Software

A dazzling array of software lines the shelves of most office supply stores, ready to help you perform every business task—design and print your own checks, develop professional-quality marketing materials, make mailing lists and labels, even act as your own attorney and accountant.

Most new computers come pre-loaded with all the software you'll need for basic office procedures. If yours doesn't, or if you've lucked into a stripped-down hand-me-down, you may want to look into the following programs. You'll need a word processing program, with which you can write correspondence, contracts, sales reports, and whatever else strikes your fancy. A good basic program such as Microsoft Word or Corel WordPerfect can be had for $60 to $220. For a similar price, you may want to consider a spreadsheet program such as Microsoft Excel or a database program such as Microsoft Access to keep track of your clients and contacts.

> ### Bright Idea
> Consider having your tour participants provide their own bikes or backpacks. It's less strain on your budget and allows people to tackle the trip using equipment they're familiar with.

You may also want an accounting program such as Intuit QuickBooks or Microsoft Money to track your business finances. These are a sort of checkbook on a CD and make record keeping a breeze. You assign categories such as office supplies and business travel to the checks you write, and at tax time you print out a report showing how much you spent for what. Your accountant not only thanks you but gives you a discount for not having to wade through all your receipts. You can expect to pay $49 to $199 for your cyberspace checkbook.

For those polished marketing materials, you'll want a desktop publishing program. Jim and Nancy T. use Microsoft Publisher for their newsletters and flyers although they'll be upgrading to Adobe PageMaker on the advice of daughter Angela, a college student and the company desktop publishing guru. PageMaker, considered the Cadillac of desktop publishing programs, runs about $500; Publisher, a nice starter program with a shorter learning curve, tallies in at about $100.

> ### Beware!
> Remember that you can't scan anything somebody else holds a copyright on, including graphics, artworks, and text. Make sure the material you scan into your own work is copyright-free, or in the case of other company's brochures, that you have permission to use the material before you import it.

For those mailing lists you're developing of past and potential participants, you'll also want to purchase a list management program like Parsons Technology's Ultimate Mail Manager—which includes U.S. Postal Service certified technology for ZIP Code accuracy. This will run you about $60.

Shot Through Gauze

If you plan on producing your own Web site, or your own advertising materials, or both, you'll definitely want a digital camera. With one of these wondrous tools, you simply snap those breathtaking photos of majestic scenery, or your tour participants having a ball; hook the camera up to your computer; move your mouse around a bit—and presto! You have the picture right in your desktop publisher. Expect to pay from $400 to $700 for a good-quality digital camera.

Once the photo is in your computer, you can manipulate it in all sorts of interesting ways, acting as your own photo finishing expert. You can crop it; expand it; zoom in or out on various features; blur the edges for that shot-through-gauze look (helpful if you're taking a picture of yourself with wrinkles or zits); make it look like a watercolor, pastel, or oil painting, ad infinitum. This stuff is not only great for business purpose, it's a heck of a lot of fun! Some digital cameras, like Kodak, come complete with this software. Or you can purchase any number of programs, from Broderbund's Print Shop Deluxe, priced at about $50, to Adobe's Photoshop, which costs about $600.

You may also want to consider a scanner, a nifty gadget that imports or "pastes" graphics from just about any printed medium—books, photographs, brochures, original art, or postcards—into your desktop publishing program. You can pick up a basic scanner for about $150 to $300; expect to pay more for higher resolution models.

Purring Printers

A good printer is a must. You'll want to produce all sorts of promotional materials, booking and information forms, mailing labels, thank you notes, contracts, statements, and sundry other materials; and they all need to look polished and professional. The materials you produce will be a direct reflection on your company. Shaky, faint dot-matrix printing looks amateurish. Sharp, bold graphics and print give your business an aura of confidence and success.

You'll also want a printer that's fast. There's nothing quite like the frustration of waiting for material to trickle out of a slow-going printer. One page per minute can seem like one page per hour. Fortunately, really hotshot printers are much less expensive now than ever before. You can purchase an LED, which simulates the higher-ticket laser printer, or an inkjet, many of which can produce all the wonderful colors of commercial artwork. Color-capable models print more slowly than their black-and-white colleagues; but if you'll be doing lots of marketing materials like brochures and newsletters, then color should be a consideration. You can expect to pay from $200 to $1,000 for a color inkjet or laser printer.

Bright Idea

Why not print out reports on various intriguing destinations—featuring your company logo and contact info, of course—and drop them off at the hair stylist, dentist, doctor's office, or other shop around the corner where folks have lag time to fill? They can take the place of all those tattered, months-old magazines and give people a reason to call you. (Be sure to get the merchants' permission first.)

Electronic Credit Card Terminal

The electronic credit card terminal is also becoming a must-have for the small office/home office and can be a bonus for the specialty travel business. People who might balk at spending cold cash on pricey travel products won't feel as bad when they can put that major purchase on plastic and defer the costs. But you can also use your terminal in the field, taking credit card payments for local city tours or for impulse goodies like T-shirts and ball caps.

As we explained in Chapter 6, you can lease or purchase the terminal itself from the merchant bank. Alternatively, you can go the bargain hunter route and buy a used but still serviceable machine from a company that's gone out of business or upgraded their unit. For an idea of just how much you can expect to spend, take another look at the chart on page 80.

Just the Fax

The fax machine is a must for anybody in business these days. Along with e-mail, it's the method of choice for communicating quickly and clearly with clients, host agencies, travel agencies, and suppliers. Many clients like to fax information back and forth, and as a savvy marketer, you want to oblige. After all, the easier you make communications, the easier it will be for people to book with you. And don't forget faxing lunch orders to that deli down the street! You can expect to pay in the range of $200 to $400 for a plain paper fax, and about $400 to $700 for a multifunction machine.

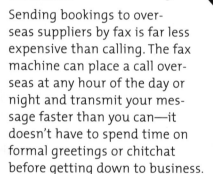

Dollar Stretcher

Sending bookings to overseas suppliers by fax is far less expensive than calling. The fax machine can place a call overseas at any hour of the day or night and transmit your message faster than you can—it doesn't have to spend time on formal greetings or chitchat before getting down to business.

Hello, Central

Now for the actual telephone itself. You'll want one line for handling phone calls and another for your fax machine and ISP (Internet service provider).

With three lines coming into your home, two will be for your office. Therefore, you'll want a two-line phone so you can put one on hold while you're answering the other. You can divide up the three lines any way you like. You might put your home line and your business line on the two-line phone, leaving the third line for your fax machine and modem. Or you might put the business and fax-modem line on the two-line phone, leaving your home line in the kitchen or den. The idea behind either of

All the Answers

If you choose not to go with voice mail from your local phone company, you'll need an answering machine. Unless you want to put your business greeting on your home machine and take the risk that your kids might erase messages to you, you should purchase a separate machine for your office.

The models on the market now are digital, which aside from the technical mumbo-jumbo means that they don't have audio tapes to get knotted or broken. There are also all sorts of fancy gizmos complete with caller ID, speakerphones, cordless phones, and 15 kinds of memos; but a good basic model capable of answering your business line can be had for less than $40. For a snazzier model that can answer two lines, you can expect to pay about $150.

these choices is that you can call out on your home or fax-modem line (when it's not in use) and leave the business line for in-coming calls.

Whichever option you choose, you will want the telephone itself to have two lines that can be put on hold. That way, business callers can't hear you explaining to your children why they can't have nose rings when they call you collect from the mall.

A speaker is also a nice feature, especially for all those on-hold forever calls to your banker, attorney, insurance company, or whoever. Your hands are free to work on financial data or your latest advertising materials, and your shoulder remains unhunched while you listen to Muzak and wait your turn. You can expect to pay about $70 to $80 for a two-line speaker phone with auto redial, memory dial, flashing lights, mute button, and other assorted goodies.

Take a Message

If you start off solo, a substitute you to answer the phone is a necessity. You won't be at your desk every minute or even every day. You'll be off on fam trips, leading tours, attending trade shows, delivering travel documents, or standing in line at the post office. If you hire a full-time secretary or receptionist, you'll still need a mechanical somebody to answer your office phone when he or she is off duty. A Murphy's Law of business life is that people most often call when a) you're not in your office, b) you're

Tip...

Smart Tip

In general, you will need one outgoing telephone line for every five employees, depending on your call volume.

Beware!
Don't "enhance" your answering machine message with background music or a cutesy script. It's not businesslike. Keep it simple. Give your business name—spoken clearly and carefully—and ask callers to leave a short message and a phone number. Thank them for calling and assure them that someone from your office will return their call as soon as possible.

sitting down to a meal, or c) you're in the bathroom. Another business law is that an unanswered phone is extremely unprofessional.

You'll need to think about who—or what—will act as your secretary when you're not available. One solution is voice mail, the phone company's answer to the answering machine, with a few nice twists. Like an answering machine, voice mail takes your messages when you're not in the office. If you have call waiting (a feature which discreetly beeps to announce an incoming call while you're already on the phone), and you choose not to answer that second call; voice mail will take a message for you. With voice mail, as with many answering machines, you can access your messages from a remote location. Voice mail costs depend on your local Ma Bell and the features you choose, but you can expect to pay in the range of $6 to $20 a month.

Cool and Calculating

What do calculators and telephones have in common? Besides a numbered keypad, they both have an important place on your desk. Even though your computer probably has an on-board calculator program, it helps to have the real thing close at hand. You can do quick calculations without zipping around through cyberspace, and you can check your work with the paper tape. Expect to pay under $15 for a battery-operated model and $25 to $50 for the electric variety.

Paper Cloning

The copier is an optional item; but as you grow, you may find it a necessary luxury for running off forms, brochures, fliers, and other goodies. It's far easier to run off one copy or 50 in your own office than to have to run down to the copy center every time the need arises. Copiers range from $250 to $600 and up.

Lightning Strikes Again

A surge protector safeguards your electronic equipment from power spikes during storms or outages. Your battery backup will double as a surge protector for your computer hard drive (or CPU) and monitor; but you'll also want protection for those other valuable office allies, your printer, fax machine, and copier. They don't need a battery backup because no data will be lost if the power goes out, and a surge protector will do the job for a lot less money. If you have a fax machine, be sure the surge protector also defends its phone line. You can expect to pay in the range of $15 to $60.

Take a Seat

Office furniture is another optional item. It's important that your work environment is comfortable and ergonomic; but if you are homebased, it is perfectly acceptable to start off with an old door set on cinder blocks for a desk and a milk crate for your files. When you are ready to go the big step toward real office furniture for that oh-so-professional look, you have a stunning array of possibilities to choose from.

We shopped the big office supply warehouse stores and found midrange desks from $200 to $300, a computer work center for $200, printer stands from $50 to $75, two-drawer letter-size file cabinets (which can double as your printer stand) from $25 to $100, and a four-shelf bookcase for $70.

Chairs are a very personal matter. Some people like the dainty secretary's chair for its economy of space, others want the high-back executive model for the tone it sets. There are chairs with kangaroo pockets and chairs with pneumatic height adjustments. Prices range from $60 to $250.

> ### Smart Tip
> **Tip...**
>
> You should never send a piece of paper out of your office unless you have kept a copy. You can always print two copies of every document you generate on your computer, keeping one as a file copy.

Laugh at Lightning

Y ou should invest in a UPS, or uninterruptible power supply (not to be confused with UPS, the package service), for your computer system. This is an especially good idea if you live in an area where lightning or power surges are frequent. You may not realize that even a flicker of power loss can shut down your computer, causing it to forget all the data you've carefully entered during your current work session, or—the ultimate horror—fry your computer's brains entirely. With a UPS in your arsenal, you won't lose power to your system when the house power fails or flickers. Instead, the unit flashes red and sounds a warning, giving you ample time to safely shut down your computer.

If you'll be spending a lot of time on the Internet, which accesses the World Wide Web through the telephone, you want to be sure that your UPS includes phone line protection. You can expect to pay $125 and up for one of these power pals.

Office Equipment Checklist

Use this handy list as a shopping guide for equipping your office. It's been designed with the one-person home office in mind. If you have partners, employees, or you just inherited a million dollars from a mysterious foundation with the stipulation that you spend at least half on office equipment, you may want to make modifications.

After you've done your shopping, fill in the purchase price next to each item, add up the total, and use this figure in the "Start-Up Costs" worksheet on page 85!

Items

❏ Windows-based Pentium-class PC with
   SVGA monitor, modem, and CD-ROM $_____

❏ Software:

   Word processing   _____

   Desktop publishing   _____

   Accounting   _____

   Mailing list management   _____

   Travel software   _____

❏ Laser or inkjet printer   _____

❏ Fax machine   _____

❏ Phones, two to three lines   _____

❏ Voice mail or answering machine   _____

❏ Uninterruptible power supply   _____

❏ Zip drive (if not included in computer)   _____

❏ Surge protector   _____

❏ Calculator   _____

❏ Reference materials   _____

Office Equipment Checklist, continued

❑ Office supplies: _____

   Printer/copier/fax paper _____

   Blank business cards _____

   Blank letterhead stationery _____

   Matching envelopes _____

   File folders _____

   Return address stamp or stickers _____

   Extra printer cartridge _____

   Mouse pad _____

   Miscellaneous office supplies (pencils, paper clips, etc.) _____

   Extra fax cartridge _____

Not on the critical list

❑ Digital camera _____

❑ Scanner _____

❑ Copier _____

❑ Desk _____

❑ Desk chair _____

❑ Filing cabinet _____

❑ Bookcase

Total Office Equipment and Furniture Expenditures

$_____

Special Travel Software

One of the big questions for newcomers to specialty travel is whether or not to purchase special software. If you're going the tour operator route, the answer is probably not, at least for the first few years. You may reach a point later in your company's career when you decide to offer a vast array of products and you'll want some CRS-type system to help you coordinate the air part of your air-inclusive packages. For starters, however, you'll probably do better to find a friendly travel agent to help arrange airfares, go through a consolidator, or—as Judy E., the cooking school agent, does—let your clients arrange their own airfares.

If you're going the travel agent route, the specialty software question is a matter of some debate. Some industry experts insist that you need nothing more complicated than the routine software any business office should have, while others advise getting hooked up to some sort of CRS-type program. Two of the three homebased agents that we interviewed for this book use *CruiseDirector* by Sabre, and one uses *Worldspan* (produced by Worldspan).

Cruise Directions

CruiseDirector is—as its name implies—software designed specifically for booking cruises. The program gives you top-secret type access to eight CLIA-affiliated cruise lines. You can check out scheduled sailings and cabin availability, compare rates among different lines and cruises, peer into pre- and post-cruise packages, and delve into group bookings. You can hunt around for online promotions, special incentives, and agency-specific fares.

You also get wait-list confirmations, cancellations, air assignments, pricing adjustments, upgrades, and payments due; this can save you time and effort calling and re-calling the cruise line. With all this intelligence at hand, you can print out itineraries, invoices, brochure materials, and other pertinent goodies for your clients.

According to the Sabre people, you can reduce your average booking time to less than five minutes by using the *CruiseDirector* software instead of calling the reservations agent. Of course, this magical speed is only an option if you want to book with one of the eight lines available through the software. You don't get that warm, fuzzy human-to-human interaction, but it's definitely worth considering.

Smart Tip

Tip...

No matter how user-friendly a software package is, there will still be times when you'll need hand-holding. So when you shop, be sure to ask what sort of technical support comes with the software.

What does it cost? You can pay $15 per month for six hours of access, with $2.50 per hour for overtime; this is how many new travel professionals start out. You can also elect to pay a flat fee of $175 per month.

Calendar Cruisin'

Another cruise-oriented subscription available on the Internet is *Cruise Calendar*. You don't get all the fun text and graphics stuff available with other programs; but for the nominal fee of $5 per day, or $25 per year, you can check out the site's list of 12,000 different passages. Search chronologically by date and length of cruise or alphabetically by cruise line. Once you have found a match for your clients' time frame, for instance, you can go to another venue for more information, or you can make a booking.

Planet Sabre

Planet Sabre is the fanciest new software on the block from the Sabre people. You get all the online goodies that come with *CruiseDirector*, plus you can book airline seats, hotels, car rentals, and hotels—with all the bells and whistles. Using *Planet Sabre*, you can shop for the lowest air fares; choose seat assignments from a floor plan of the plane (this is fun!); create and update customer profiles; shop for hotels and car rentals; or view and print itineraries, and even e-mail them to your clients.

You also get fun stuff with which to dazzle your customers, like destination information, weather updates, maps, and currency conversion rates. You can print out an entire Mission Possible-type dossier on their travel targets and shine like the pro that you'll be.

Planet Sabre has one significant twist—it's a dial-up system, meaning you must have a special modem to use it. The company has plans in the works to go the ISP (Internet service provider) route, which means eventually you won't need the special dial-up connection. If you choose to log onto *Planet Sabre*, you can expect to spend about $195.

Going Solo

Worldspan offers a similar product for independent travel agents called *Go! Solo*. With this ISP-based reservations system, you get basically the same goodies as with *Planet Sabre*, including travel-related weather data, destination activities, and mapping services. However, there's a significant twist. To use *Go! Solo*, your host agency must also have *Worldspan* software—this program sends your reservations information to the host for actual ticket printing!

Since *Go! Solo* is ISP-based, you can use it anytime, anywhere. Even if you're off on a fam trip to Thailand, you can still make bookings for your clients. The program is competitively priced. It's $50 per month with no initial or annual fees, and you can get it for free if you demonstrate a certain level of sales productivity. This price and the productivity level are subject to change; so if you plan to *Go! Solo*, be sure to discuss (and negotiate) with your sales representative.

The Profiler

While we're shopping for software, you might want to take a look at *Weissman Travel Reports*. This is not a reservation and booking system like *CruiseDirector* or *WorldSpan*, but instead spins out all sorts of relevant travel information on 10,000 different cities around the world. With this great product—which you update online monthly—you can generate brochures and reports tailored to specific clients and their particular travel destinations, or to your particular tours.

"It's very, very in-depth, like an almanac on computer," says Jim T. in Maryland, who recently added *Weissman Travel Reports* to his software library. "It gives you vast areas of information on each destination: background, crime, tourist locations, places to go, economics. You can get in there and commingle information, put together itineraries and print them out for your client. It's a really nice document. Our clients have been ecstatic about it because it gives them so much background on where they're going."

Choose from four types of *profiles*, or reports:

1. *International profiles.* These are reports on every country in the world. They include elements like "What to Do There," "Transportation," "Accommodations and Health Advisories," and also "What to Buy," "What to Eat" (which can be extremely entertaining), "Dos and Don'ts" and "Potpourri" (of fascinating tidbits about local customs).

2. *United States and Canadian Provinces.* These reports are similar in style and tone to the international profiles.

3. *City profiles.* These profiles include information for the city of your choice, including features such as Bird's-Eye View, Must See or Do, Especially for Kids, and Day Trips. You will also find CityScan, FAQs from average temperatures and rainfall to proper business attire, to areas in which to be on crime-guard, to city holidays.

4. *Ports of call.* This includes destination information geared for the cruise passenger voyaging the Americas and the Caribbean, with Fun Facts, Insider Tips (covering everything from whether the water is safe to drink to native slang), and a calendar of events.

You have lots of options with this information, and you can combine several profiles into a single report. Add your clients' itinerary or your own text into the report and even print the reports with your company name, contact information, and logo, and your clients' names on the cover page. This has a terrific, personalized impact and makes you look pretty darn slick!

How much should you expect to pay for all this? The basic package runs in the neighborhood of $75 per month. You may be able to wrangle a discount if you belong to NACTA or other groups, including some consortiums—be sure to ask when you call for a subscription. For an additional one-time fee of $40, you get the drop-in logo feature. And for an annual fee of $50, you can take advantage of Weissmann's Web Link service, which provides surfers of *Travelcorner* (Weismann's sister site geared to consumers) a direct Web link to your company site.

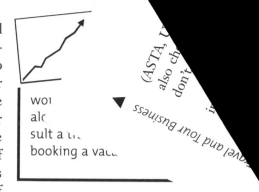

The Skinny on Consolidators

A spiffy way to get the skinny on which airline, hotel, and tour consolidators (over 300 of them) handle the products you need is with *Consolidator Profiles*. This is yet another online subscription; and it allows you to choose from a host of variables including the type of product, the destination, the consolidator's accreditations

---

Getting the Goods

You know what you'll need as far as office tools. Now think about what you might want to lease or purchase in the way of special equipment for running tours. Each specialty tour operation will log its own requirements. A white-water rafting supplier will have an entirely different list than a company that does walking tours.

Our purpose here is to get you started thinking about what you'll need and how much those items are likely to cost. Keep in mind that it's perfectly acceptable to lease or rent instead of purchase, and that this may actually be the smarter way to go until you're certain that you really want to invest thousands of purchase dollars on a dozen mountain bikes, for example. "You can lease equipment for a season," Jerry Mallett of the Adventure Travel Society advises. "That would be no problem and would lessen the expense."

Carefully think about everything you'll need to lead your tours, from big-ticket items like minivans or motor coaches—for getting your groups from place to place—to lightweight elements like food storage and preparation tools. Then make a detailed list of each element and its price.

STOA, etc.), and how many years the company's been in business. You can
ose to be snooty and exclude consolidators who sell to the general public,
print the price on the ticket, or who are not the issuing ticket agent.

After you've made your selections, the service spins out a list of consolidators
cluding their addresses, phone and fax numbers, Web site and e-mail links, the
mega-companies that own them, how many employees they have, their accreditations,
and the destinations or products they supply. All you have to do is contact them.
What's the price tag for all this insider information? It'll cost you $49.99 per year.

Freebie Alert

There are all sorts of travel resources available on the Internet for the asking. Since
they're largely consumer-oriented, you won't find as many insider fares, consolidators,
and other goodies as you will with the professionals-only, fee-based services.
However, with a fair amount of surfing, you can book hotels and airlines pretty much
as you would on a professionals-only site like *Planet Sabre*; but if you want to do cruises
or tours, you have to call the wholesaler.

It's up to you to sample the various sites and learn the navigation tricks (each has
its own endearing or frustrating quirks), but we suggest you check them out. For
starters, try:

- *Travelocity* at www.travelocity.com
- *Expedia* at www.expedia.com
- *Preview Travel* at www.previewtravel.com

The Travel Library

In addition to a selection of online goodies, you should begin building your very
own travel reference library. Most travel professionals go with *JAX FAX Travel
Marketing Magazine*, a paper (as opposed to online) magazine packed with articles,
editorials, ads, and other goodies, as well as scads of supplier listings. And we mean
scads! The magazine boasts over 5,200 air-only, tour, and hotel packages not available
in travel agency computers, with more than 450,000 flight departures in the following six months.

Each issue is divided into seven geographic regions of the world, which makes it
easier for you to get around within its pages. It supplies:

- Listings of over 5,000 specific scheduled flights and tours to over 100 destinations, including dates, prices, operators, hotels, and airlines.
- Directories containing contact information, commission rates, and other data
  for tour operators and passenger airline charter services as well.

JAX FAX also has a Web site with a sprinkling of all these offerings—enough to whet your appetite for more. You can check it out at www.jaxfax.com. What should you expect to pay for this publication? A one-year subscription runs $15.

Travel Weekly is another reference must-have for most travel professionals. This weekly magazine is packed with industry news updates as well as cruise and destination guides. You can have *Travel Weekly* mailed to you for an annual fee of $21.50. Or go online with *Crossroads*, the electronic version, which is free and also includes the fun of forums (interactive Internet message boards).

One more reference material that most travel specialists swear by is the *Official Tour Directory*, an annual tome that provides listings of more than 2,000 U.S. based tour operators specializing in over 700 worldwide destinations and more than 200 special interests and activities.

If that's not enough, *OTD*, is its fondly known, also gives you contact information for more than 1,500 travel-related companies. These include domestic and international tourist boards, airlines, insurance companies, credit card companies, and hotel chains. And it provides a brochure order hotline for tour operators (nice when your clients want that information *now*), as well as detailed area maps, destination information and travel tips.

> **Travel Weekly is another reference must-have for most travel professionals.**

The price for all this at-your-fingertips information is $48 per book. But it's free to IATAN agencies; so if your host is eligible for a freebie, you might ask for an extra copy.

Equipping for Success

On pages 145-146 we've provided "Office Set-Up Expenses" for our four hypothetical specialty travel companies. Our independent travel agents, as you remember, are Merry Makers Travel, which will target seniors with an emphasis on land-based tours, and After The Wedding, which will market cruises and land-based tours for newlyweds.

Merry Makers counts as its new equipment a color printer and *Go! Solo* booking software, which it will receive free because of its host agency's productivity. Its owner will use a computer already in the home. After The Wedding, on the other hand, will go with a top-of-the-line computer system, a color printer, *Planet Sabre* booking software, and a variety of other travel-oriented software packages.

Our tour operators are Magic Bay Adventures, which will provide walking tours of its owner's beach town, and Mysterious Journeys, which will offer a tour of ancient and arcane Britain, also led by the owner. Magic Bay and Mysterious Journeys are starting off with a low- and high-end computer system, respectively; the same color printers as their travel agent counterparts; and one type of special travel software, *Consolidator Profiles*.

To give you an idea of how much you can expect to budget, check out the costs of software, equipment, and supplies for these four travel companies. Review the high- and low-end estimates, and try to determine what your costs are likely to be for setting up your office and getting off to a good start.

Office Set-Up Expenses for Independent Travel Agents

Furniture, Equipment & Supplies	Merry Makers Travel	After the Wedding
Computer system (including printer)	$500	$4,000
Fax machine	250	350
Software	409	1,085
Reference materials	85	85
Phone system	50	180
Answering machine	40	0
Uninterruptible power supply	125	250
Surge protector	34	34
Calculator	50	160
Copier	0	500
Electronic credit card terminal	200	450
Desk	0	600
Desk chair	60	200
Printer stand	0	140
File cabinet	25	50
Bookcase	70	70
Printer/copier paper	25	50
Blank business cards	6	12
Letterhead paper	30	30
Matching envelopes	35	35
No. 10 blank envelopes	3	6
Address stamp or stickers	10	10
Extra printer cartridges	70	70
Extra fax cartridge	80	80
Mouse pad	10	20
Miscellaneous office supplies	50	100
Total Expenditures	**$2,217**	**$8,567**

Office Set-Up Expenses for Tour Operators

Furniture, Equipment & Supplies	Magic Bay Adventures	Mysterious Journeys
Computer system (including printer)	$1,500	$4,000
Fax machine	250	350
Software	409	534
Reference materials	85	85
Phone system	50	160
Answering machine	40	0
Uninterruptible power supply	125	250
Surge protector	34	34
Calculator	50	160
Copier	0	500
Electronic credit card terminal	200	450
Desk	0	600
Desk chair	60	200
Printer stand	0	140
File cabinet	25	50
Bookcase	70	70
Printer/copier paper	25	50
Blank business cards	6	12
Letterhead paper	30	30
Matching envelopes	35	35
No. 10 blank envelopes	3	6
Address stamp or stickers	10	10
Extra printer cartridges	70	70
Extra fax cartridge	80	80
Mouse pad	10	20
Miscellaneous office supplies	50	100
Total Expenditures	**$3,107**	**$7,996**

Your Ground Crew
Employees and Independent Operators

Depending on how much growth you envision for your business, you may never need employees. Or you may expand to the point where you can't do everything yourself—the point where you'll need to consider taking on assistance. Employees are another of those funny facts of life that seem to bring with them as many cons as pros. When you hire

Photo© Photo Disc Inc.

help, you are not a swinging single anymore. You have responsibilities. Suddenly there's payroll to meet, worker's compensation insurance to pay, state and federal employee taxes to pay, and work to delegate. Some people are born employers, finding it easy to teach someone else the ropes and then hand over the reins. Others never feel quite comfortable telling someone else what to do or how to do it.

One of the many perks of the specialty travel business is that you can accomplish a great deal without ever hiring anyone. You can start out as a one-person show, handling all the tasks of your fledgling company yourself. You won't need help immediately. But as your company flourishes, you may one day find that: a) you need more hours in a day, b) you need science to make great strides in the field of cloning, or c) you need to hire help.

Travel Agent Staff

As a homebased travel agent, your company will be structured differently than the traditional retail office, which is great! It gives you more freedom and more flexibility—even when it comes to hiring help.

Connie G. in Pennsylvania has four outside agents under her wing. And in true independent agent fashion, only one of them lives nearby, and each has his or her own specialties. The "neighbor" only books cruises through Connie's company; for the bulk of her business she works directly with land suppliers. Another of Connie's outside agents lives in Pittsburgh and heads up the company's Christian pilgrimages and tours. A third lives in Oregon and handles Christian and other cruises; and in addition, he caters to the company's blind clients. Since he himself is blind, he's the perfect agent for the job. "He can relate really well," Connie says. The firm's

> **Smart Tip**
>
> If your tour business will be a seasonal operation, like cross-country moose viewing trips, you and your guide staff should realize that they may have to find other employment during the off-season.

fourth agent lives in California and handles Connie's overflow of wheelchair and slow walker clients.

In addition to all of this, Connie is looking to take on a couple more top-notch, cruise-experienced agents. Is it hard to keep up with all this bi-coastal stuff? "Not at the moment," Connie says, "because I'm really cautious of who I'll take on and how much time I have. The only time I'll take on somebody with no industry experience is if I'm pretty sure I'll have time to properly train them. Which is more difficult than usual because I'm doing the training by phone and e-mail."

Specialty Tour Staff

As the owner of a specialty tour firm, you'll have a trunkful of responsibilities. You'll have to research potential tours to see if they'll work; locate guides and other permanent staff, or independent contractors; and handle the advertising, marketing, accounting, and record keeping. If your tours will be adventurous, you'll also need to screen potential tour participants to make sure they are hale and hearty enough to go the distance.

Out of Bounds

Outbound tour operators—especially those with more than one tour going at a time—often take on guides in the form of independent contractors hired on location. This is a boon for the new travel professional, who might not have enough scheduled trips or start-up capital to hire permanent, full-time guides. You can still meet your needs by working with freelance, professional guides that you hire at your destination, or by hiring a ground service operator to supply you with guides and other support personnel (as well as any transportation you need).

If you visit different countries at different times of the year, you may want to continue this type of arrangement as your business grows, working with operators you

The Second You

As your business grows, you may also want to hire an office manager or administrative assistant to be a sort of second you while you're out leading or investigating tours. This intrepid soul will answer calls from prospective tour participants, send out brochures, answer questions and correspondence, conduct direct-mail campaigns, and handle invoicing.

When you start seeking this "second self," look for someone who is capable of thinking on her feet, and who has a good sales instinct and terrific customer service sense. If she has all that, you can teach her the ropes of your business as you go along.

---

know and trust. However, if you operate a year-round tour to a particular foreign destination and find some sterling freelance guides, you may want to offer them permanent positions.

Before you send a group of your clients out on a tour with an unfamiliar ground operator or guide, take a tour with him yourself. This is the only sure-fire way to determine what his particular charms and capabilities are, which is crucial to the success of your operation. A guide should have a thorough knowledge of the region and activities on which you'll focus. He should also be able to educate the participants in an exciting and entertaining fashion, and ensure that everyone on the trip has fun.

When you start exploring a foreign country as a potential destination, you'll have to determine what services are available. You might be able to find domestic contacts who can refer you to terrific sources before you arrive in-country. Domestic tourism bureaus of foreign countries may also be helpful, along with publications and associations pertinent to your area of interest.

Besides professional guides, you might find guides among the academic community. As you read up on your country or activity of choice, stay alert to the mention of experts in the field, or try contacting colleges and universities. You just might find an engaging and experienced instructor who knows his or her subject inside and out, and who can lead people on tours.

Ground service operators usually offer more than guides, drivers, and porters—they have an entire office staff ready to meet any needs your clients might have. In case of emergency, a guide can contact his or her office, which will be a lot closer than you may be. Ground service operators can also help tour participants maintain communications with the "outside world" when necessary.

In Bounds

Inbound businesses, like outbound ones, can contract with outfitters, freelance guides and local experts in various fields. Inbound operators can also hire their own guides as permanent or part-time employees.

"Our company," says Savannah resident Karen A., "has five employees, two full-time and three part-time. Beth and I are full-time joint owners and we have three part-time guides. We are all variously certified as guides for historic Savannah and the U.S. Fish and Wildlife Service (Okefenokee Swamp). Any member of the company can escort a Girl Scout or school tour as long as they have a guide license that permits them to give tours in Savannah's Historic District. The package tours require an escort who has to be skilled in problem-solving and, on specific days, a biologist guide (we have two) or a licensed historic guide (we have four). Birding requires a specialist guide. We have one of these on staff and two others we can call on at need."

As with Karen's company, different types of tours will require different types of guides. You may need to hire guides with years of experience in a very specialized field. Or, you may be able to hire college students and train them yourself. If you have a river-rafting operation, for instance, you might take a few prospective college kids down the rapids to test their rafting, leading, and people-relating skills. You would hire the best of the lot, train them, and have them get their licenses. Then they can start leading groups.

The advantage to hiring students is that a) you don't have to pay them as much as you would pay older, experienced guides, and b) you can train them to your exact specifications. The disadvantage is that you may lose them to the "real" world when they graduate, leaving you to start afresh with a new batch of kids.

Meeters and Greeters

Just as there's more than one kind of tour operation, there's more than one kind of guide. Take a look at the various permutations:

- *Meet and greet guide.* This is the cheerful, chipper person who (you guessed it!) meets tour participants at the airport and greets them as a representative of the tour company. He makes sure all heads are present and accounted for and all luggage is rounded up; ushers everybody through customs; and sees them onto the shuttle bus or other transport and to the hotel, where the tour director takes over.
- *Tour director.* This is the counselor, confidante, shepherd, and baby-sitter all rolled into one. The tour director keeps everybody and everything running

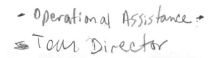

smoothly during the course of a multi-day tour. He is the one who offers commentary on the sights and sounds, acts as a cultural and linguistic interpreter, de-glitches any problems and—like any good host—makes sure all of his guests have a good time. A tour director can also be called a tour manager, tour escort, tour

Beware!
Foreign exchange rates can affect the amount you pay out-of-country guides and ground operators.

leader, or tour host or hostess. This is a 24-hour a day job for the length of the trip, and a good tour director can make a nice tour an outstanding one.

- *Step-on guide.* This term refers not to stepping on the other guide's toes, but to the fact that as a local guide, the step-on guide comes onto the motor coach and takes over the task of showing tour participants her particular city or area.

The Substitute

You'll want to base your own tour operation needs on the type of tours you're planning. A half-day city walking tour will have different requirements than a 14-day African safari. But even a one-person operation needs occasional assistance.

When we first spoke with Dr. Phil S. for this book, he was working solo. If he had two different tours requested at the same time, he would contact other New York tour guides and have them lead one of his tours. With an eye to that eventuality—or to the possibility that he might be sick on a tour day—Phil wrote up 50-page "scripts" on some of his tours to give to substitutes.

With three part-time guides to help with his booming workload already, Phil has also signed on one independent contractor to do tours on occasion. "She approached me," he says, "looking for work. She was persistent and a sharp negotiator." So much so that he started her off doing a few tours and liked the results. Among her stellar qualities, he lists her sense of humor—and just as important, if not more so—the fact that she always shows up for duty.

The Touring Incentive

Barry S., the car race tour packager, has an in-house staff of 12, who carry out most of the operations both on the road and in the office. "The people I hire start off by answering the phone, doing invoicing and itineraries, helping write the brochures, and selling the tours," Barry says. "Then staff are able to go on tour and gain expertise." This is a terrific way to gain staff loyalty. Everybody likes to go on the tours. "It's a learning curve," the former transit system manager says, "and it makes people happy that they're able to travel." How long a learning curve? "It takes a year or two before someone really becomes a help to us," Barry reports.

Most of the company's 52 annual tours are weekend events. Employees who work these minitours are given days off during the week, or are paid extra for their overtime efforts, which are considered a perk. Having an in-house staff work the actual tours has an additional benefit, Barry says. Staffers who have "been there and done that" on tours can sell products based on actual experience. Since they know firsthand the ups and the down of the tours, they don't inadvertently tell potential clients something's grander, easier, or more exciting than it really might be.

> **Bright Idea**
>
> If you feel you need help designing a brochure, catalog, or newsletter, how about taking on a college intern as an advertising whiz, copywriter, or graphic artist? You will benefit from the student's fresh ideas; the student will benefit from favorable on-the-job experience.

Some tour operators have a deep-seated fear that employees or independent contractors will absorb everything they learn about the business, then run off to start their own competitive operations. While this is always a possibility, it doesn't overly concern the tour operators we interviewed. Barry's staff has a shelf life of about five years, and they usually depart because of various life changes rather than to become competitors. On the contrary, two former employees now live in the South of France where, Barry says, he can call on them if the need arises.

You don't have to start out with a full house of 12 employees. When Barry started his company, he led some of the seven tour offerings, and his brother led the rest.

Family Affair

One cost-saving alternative to hiring employees is to put your family to work. We've already seen how some of the travel specialists we've interviewed use family computer gurus. Why not take your family operations even further? Judy E., the culinary vacation representative, has made her company a family affair. Daughter-in-law Amy is the office manager, son Craig acts as the company webmaster and computer guru, and husband Richard rounds out the team as the firm's business consultant.

But family affairs don't have to be exclusively for grown-up kids. Children can help out with preparing direct-mail products by folding newsletters and applying address labels and stamps. Older kids are often extremely capable when it comes to computer tasks, and so is a willing spouse—give them your data entry duties and let 'em roll. When you have on-call help in the family, you have the advantage of no employee taxes or insurance; although, at least in the case of teens, you'll probably still have to pay your workers. Helping mom, dad, or a spouse with the family business gives everybody a warm, fuzzy feeling of pitching in and can be a great togetherness booster.

Insuring Your Gems

Once you find those gems of employees for your travel agency or tour operation, you'll need to think about caring for them. Start off with workers' compensation insurance, which covers you for any illness or injury your employees might incur, everything from a back injury from lifting heavy equipment, to a paper cut gone septic, to radiation poisoning from close contact with the computer terminal. (People can come up with a lot of strange complaints when money is involved.) Workers' compensation insurance laws vary from state to state; check with your insurance agent for details in your area.

Although your employee may be working in your home, your homeowners' insurance probably won't pay for a problem incurred there, on the grounds that it's actually a workers' compensation case. Rather than making yourself a nervous wreck and creating your own mental health claim over all this, check with your insurance agent and then make an informed decision.

You don't need workers' comp for independent contractors, like outside travel agents or freelance tour guides, but you do need to make sure they are actually operating as independents. Check with your insurance agent and/or your accountant for guidance with your particular situation. Beyond the insurance issue, as your company grows, you may want to set up medical and dental plans for your employees, as well as some kind of 401(k) or other pension plan. These can be pricey for a start-up, so don't feel you have to jump into them immediately.

Bright Idea

Since every company will have computer problems at some point, look for an employee who can handle not only the "usual" role you're seeking to fill but who can also double as your resident computer guru.

Passport Pitching
Direct-Mail Advertising

n this chapter we explore one of the most fun, exciting, creative, and most demanding parts of the specialty travel business—advertising and promotion. After all, no matter how exciting, relaxing, informative, or entertaining your products are, nobody's going to know about them unless you advertise. As a travel professional, you will put a great deal of effort into designing and implementing advertising campaigns to take your sales to the limit and beyond.

Venues like radio, TV, and newspapers can work wonders for other types of entrepreneurs, but they don't make much of a dent on the psyches of potential travelers. Magazines work only for very specific types of tour operations. Your best bet for advertising your start-up travel business is direct mail, personal contact, and word-of-mouth. (You'll find information on personal contact and word-of-mouth advertising in Chapter 12). In this chapter, we'll tell you how to design a winning brochure for your direct-mail advertising campaign, and we'll explore the secrets of using mailing lists to your advantage.

Direct Mail

What exactly is direct mail? It's another way of saying *mail order*, and it can take the form of sales letters, fliers, brochures, postcards, or any other printed material you send winging into the mailboxes of previous and potential clients.

Direct-mail advertising can be extremely effective, but it's also expensive. By the time you pay for the paper, envelopes, printing, and postage for a major campaign, you've spent thousands of dollars. So before you decide to do a mailing to every potential traveler on the Eastern Seaboard, make sure you've thoroughly considered what your niche market wants and how your products will answer that desire or need.

The first thing to do when you start your advertising campaign is to take a figurative step back. Revisit your market research. Like a top-secret government organization targeting sectors of the public, you, too, have a "dossier" you have put together on your potential clients. Your dossier should include all the information that you gathered during your market research:

- Who are my potential customers? (Do they travel for business or pleasure? Are they hard or soft adventurers? Physically challenged? Desirous of mental challenge or simple relaxation? Are they students, families, or seniors?)
- How many are there?
- Where are they located?
- Where do they now find the travel products I want to provide?
- What can I offer that they're not already getting from this other source?
- How can I persuade them to purchase travel products from me or go on my tours?

Look over the answers to these questions—then ask yourself some more:
- What knowledge and skills do I offer?
- What image do I want to project?
- How do I compare with my competition and how can I be better?

Bright Idea

Try targeting SOHOs (small offices/home offices) in your community for their travel needs. They may be delighted to discover that—just like the mega-corporations—they can have their very own on-call travel agent.

Once you've answered these critical questions and you know exactly who you are targeting, with what and why; it's time to devise your direct-mail piece.

You can use any direct-mail format that works for you, from a letter introducing yourself and describing your products, to a one-page flier, to a multi-page brochure. Jim and Nancy T., the Maryland cruise specialists, send out quarterly newsletters as well as direct-mailing information on various specials throughout the year. Connie G., the tour and cruise agent in Pennsylvania, does an annual newsletter, lots of fliers, and a smattering of postcards. Harry G., the fishing tour operator, puts out a brochure once a year.

Experimentation, testing and—always, always—market research will give you the best idea of which format is the best for your company (look back over Chapter 4). We're going to talk here about brochures, but you can and should apply these same success secrets and tips to any other direct-mail pieces you design.

The Wow! Brochure

You'll definitely need a brochure if you'll go the tour operator route. And if you'll be acting as an independent agent, you may want to put one together, too. As you know, travel agents often purchase wholesale tours and then package them for resale. A brochure is a terrific way to pitch these products.

What should your brochure look like? That depends on your products and what will appeal to your target market. If your tours are aimed at the upper crust set and feature European five-star hotels and tea with Lord and Lady Whosit, your brochure will need to reflect this ambience. You would use high-quality paper, photographs, and perhaps castles, crests, and heraldry sprinkled about on the pages. If your tours are targeted toward budget travelers, you could emphasize your brown bag approach by printing your brochures on brown paper, with line drawings instead of graphics. And if you're doing city walking tours or other day tours, you can get creative

Smart Tip

Have a trusted friend or family member proofread your brochure. Sometimes it's almost impossible to detect minor typos in your own work; and while computer programs that check spelling and grammar are helpful, they can sometimes interpret things in strange fashion.

▲

The Participation Effect

Another of the quirky things about direct mail (which goes with another of the quirky things about human nature) is that people are far more likely to respond to an offer for which they have to actively do something. In other words, people like direct mail offers in which they're asked to paste a "yes" or "no" sticker on the reply card, or select an option. That's why all those Publishers Clearing House packets are full of stickers and reply cards and tear-offs; they work. Call it the participation effect.

Of course, these gimmicks cost money, but if you can afford them—and if they fit your company style—by all means use them. If not, think how else you might incorporate the same idea into your reservations form. For example, if you're offering an early booking discount, you might let your client "flag" the discount by checking a box on your form. Make sure your form is clear, easy to understand, and easy to fill out.

with a simple pamphlet that recreates the image you're selling, with whimsical line drawings of some of the high points of your tour.

Even though most people think high-gloss when they think brochure, you don't have to go with an expensive four-color masterpiece, especially not when you're starting out with just a few tour offerings. Use your imagination liberally, instead of your wallet. Choose a light-colored card stock and one or two bold, professional colors for your text. With the bounty of desktop publishing software out there, you can choose from a dazzling array of fonts, borders, and line art to jazz up your text. But don't sacrifice clarity for flashiness. A few graphics go a long way. For example, take a look at the brochure that Dr. Phil S. uses to advertise his walking tours of New York City (see page 164).

You can design your brochure so that—folded in thirds—it is the tidy size of a No. 10 (business-size) envelope. Or you can try a size that will make it stand out from all the other No. 10 envelopes in the mailbox. How about 8 inches by 5 inches? Choose whatever size works best with your layout and your budget. But think about how you feel when you see that odd-size envelope in your daily handful of mailbox bills and clutter. Don't you automatically think "Wow! Something special!" and turn to it first?

Brochure Brilliance

Once you have decided on the basics, take these tips into consideration:

- *Mug shot not.* People like to see who and what they're spending their money on, so it's okay to add a photo of yourself or your tour guides interacting with tour participants (not your driver's license mug shot, but a professional-quality picture). Make sure the photos are sharp and clear.

Beware!
Be sure to check with your friendly attorney to make sure your rules, regulations, and restrictions are properly presented.

- *Tempt with teasers.* Tease your potential customers with highlights of your tour's content, like this:

  - Take a ghostly walk through the most haunted hotel in Chicago.
  - Stroll our crystal shores and discover for yourself why Panama City Beach's Emerald Coast is called one of America's unsung scenic treasures.
  - Dine in candlelit splendor at a midnight supper with the master of the castle.
  - Relax, refresh, and revitalize your energies on our forest hikes for frazzled workaholics.

Think like a movie-theater coming attraction or the blurb on the back of a best-selling book. Leave your client eager to experience the details, which he can only do by booking a tour!

- *Be beneficial.* Explain the benefits of your tours, the harvest your customer will reap from participating. Try something like "Discover your artistic talents in the same sparkling air that captivated the Plein Aire painters of the last century as our guides, all professional art teachers, show you the secrets of seaside Impressionism."

- *Details, details.* Don't forget the details! Make sure you explain where and when your tours take place and how they're priced.

- *Discounts and freebies.* Tempt them further with discounts for seniors, spouses, students, or groups; or with freebies like special tour tote bags, T-shirts, memento ornaments (for Christmas tours) or some other giveaway.

- *Contact.* Put your address and phone number, along with your Web site and e-mail addresses, if you have them, where they're easily found and read. Make it easy for customers to contact you.

- *Drum roll to enroll.* Include your reservation form—the really important part!

- *Road rules.* Add in any regulations, restrictions and information about insurance, refunds, exchanges, single supplements, and other rules of the road.

The Hook

If this sounds daunting, try reading all those direct-mail pieces that come to your mailbox. The best ones to study are those that pitch tours, but carefully examine all of them, even those that are selling sandals or sweaters. What do they have in common? For one thing, they start off with something that immediately hooks your attention.

Maybe it's a description of the tour, enticing you to read on with tidbits of the sights, sounds, and scents you'll experience when you take that trip. Maybe it's a description of the benefits of having participated in the tour, like a more relaxed frame of mind and body, or terrific culinary skills, or a fishing story no one can top. Try the same approaches with your brochure. Experiment until you hit on something that sounds good to you and matches your particular niche.

Then go on to the body of the brochure. Again, analyze the ones you've received. What makes them work? Notice that they spend a lot of time describing the tour benefits. You'll want to do the same thing. Emphasize the

Smart Tip

Explain why you—or your guides—are superbly qualified to lead a particular tour. If you are doing prairie tours and you're a native Nebraskan with a college degree in prairie history, blow your horn. If your guides for nature walks are Nature Conservancy mavens, or your guides for cross-country ski tours are licensed ski instructors, point it out!

benefits of your programs throughout your body copy, repeating those benefits as often as you can using different descriptions so they stick in your customer's mind. If you have testimonials, use them too. They lend credibility to your tours and your company, and they add another dimension to your copy by showing that it's not just you who thinks your products are great—it's real people, just like your prospect.

After the main body of your brochure, tell your customer what she needs to do to book your tour. Put in a convenient order form that she can send back, or make your phone number large and legible so she can call and order if she'd prefer. If you've designed in a discount with a time element or a freebie, this is the place to mention it.

The Personal Touch

When preparing your brochure, try to incorporate these sales tips:

- *Grab that prospect's attention.* Remember to relate it directly to your tour and how it will benefit your client.

- *Use time-proven winning words like "secret" and "free."* Everybody wants to know a secret and everybody wants something for free! Like what? How about something like: "Discover the secret life of New York, the city that never sleeps!" or "Free fat-burning calculator when you enroll in our high-energy, low-fat cookery tour!"

- *Longer sells better than shorter.* Where you have space, try for headlines of ten or more words.

- *Don't write for thousands of prospective clients.* Write to just one, as though you're speaking to him personally.

- *Save the flowery prose for that poetry contest.* Instead, use everyday language for the average person.
- *Don't focus only on the features of your tours.* Be sure to describe the benefits, too.
- *Try indented paragraphs, underlined words and two colors.* These pack more of a punch and pull out plain text. But use gimmicks like boldface type, underlining, and italics sparingly. If you use them for no particular reason, or too often, they become annoying instead of intriguing.
- *Keep your materials clean and free of grammar and style errors.* Have someone you trust as a spelling, punctuation, and grammar star check your work before you commit to a print run.
- *Relax and enjoy yourself.* Creating your brochure can be one of the most creative and fun parts of advertising your travel business.

Penning for Profits

If you haven't already, check out the brochure used by Dr. Phil S., the New York City tour guide (see page 163). It's a brochure that's folded in thirds to the size of a No. 10 business envelope. We've included both sides of the brochure to demonstrate how Phil advertises the features and benefits of his tours, as well as the information

Accentuate the Positive

Don't get confused about the difference between the features and benefits of your tours—it's the latter you want to sell. The features of your program would be, for example, a romantic trip to the castles of Scotland combined with an intensive, two-day workshop with a leading romance writer. This is nice. But as far as your prospective customer is concerned, your workshop could be led by an auto mechanic and a dentist for all the good it will do—unless you stress the benefits.

As the old song says, accentuate the positive—the things that will make a significant, positive change in her life as a writer of romances. Emphasize that the tour is romantic in and of itself, and that it has the added benefit of teaching participants to sell winning romance novels, themselves. When you write your copy, you should describe the features, but just as important is telling your customers about the benefits. These, after all, are the reasons they buy.

> ## Bright Idea
>
> Describe any special features of your tour. If it's an aromatherapy program, explain your nose-on scenting session. For a soft-adventure hiking trip combined with a resume-writing workshop, explain that each participant will write an actual resume.

customers need to contact him and book the tours. Phil simply uses black text on white paper, along with a graphic of the statue of liberty—the quintessential symbol of New York. It's not flashy, but it effectively describes his operation, and this type of brochure is tailored to the start-up budget.

A sales letter can be just as effective as a brochure. Whether you choose one or the other is dependent only on your personal preference and your company ambiance. When you sit down to pen that sales letter, use the same techniques you use for the brochure—but with a special twist. Write that letter as if you're writing directly to your potential customer, not as if you're mailing the same piece to dozens or even hundreds of people. Take a look at the sample on page 164 for an idea of what a travel-oriented sales letter might look like. Yours should be tailored to your products and your target market. You might address it to honeymooners, golden-agers, or small office/home office business owners.

Surefire Techniques

OK, we've seen what direct mail looks like and how to design your own for optimum effect. Now let's review some sure-fire techniques for winning customers:

- *Give away freebies with prompt booking.* Remember, everybody likes to have something for free. Everybody likes a gift. Depending on your style, budget, and target market, you can give away something substantial (but still relatively inexpensive) or a mere trinket. If your tours focus on foreign travel, how about a money conversion table or a French phrase book? If you choose something your customers will use often and imprint it with your company name, you'll have given away not only a gift but free advertising for yourself.

- *Time-date your offers.* Say something like "If you respond within 30 days, you'll receive a free _____,"

> ## Bright Idea
>
> Try putting in a time element like "Order by June 14th to receive your 20 percent discount off the normal tour price of $999," or "Order by June 14th to receive your free companion guidebook." This lights a fire under your customer. She won't want to put off ordering because she'll lose out on the discount or freebie.

Direct-Mail Brochure

This is the brochure that Dr. Phil S. uses to advertise his "New York Talks & Walks" tours. The brochure is folded in thirds to the size of a business envelope.

About Our Founder

Philip E. Schoenberg, a professional speaker and a licensed New York City Tour Guide, received his PhD in history from New York University. He is a leading expert on the Big Apple. Dr. Phil has a special skill for entertaining and informing people about the Big Apple from its real life stories and folk tales.

About Our Company

Our company offers programs and walking tours to entertain and educate you about New York City. They may me customized to suit the needs of your association or group. We employ leading speakers, guides and experts on the Big Apple.

What People Say About Our Tours:

Touring the Lower East Side with Dr. Phil is not only like learning history again, it's like reliving it as well. Alas, if only more of our college history courses were as interesting - and offered as much useful exercise. – Mel Elfin, Editor, Emeritus, *U.S. News College Guides*

[Dr. Phil] takes on a fascinating trip in what really makes his historical and walking tours worthwhile and different is the joy with which he conducts them. - Albor Ruiz, *The New York Daily News*

Dr. Philip Schoenberg is delightful, informative, and friendly. His knowledge is tremendous and his anecdotes are charming. – Carol Fijian Starobin, Ruth Lipton and Leah Levitt of Great Neck, Long Island

Dr. Phil makes history come alive through his tours. - Jack Flynn, *Queens Chronicle*, N.Y.C.

A very enthusiastic New Yorker. – Elizabeth Neal, *Western Queens Gazette*, N.Y.C.

Philip E. Schoenberg, PhD, President
Dr. Phil & Associate: The NYC Experts
New York Talks & Walks™
P.O. Box 6780
Flushing, New York 11365
Toll Free: (888) DRPHIL5 (377-4455)
Tel: (718) 591-4741
Fax: (718) 380-7282
E-Mail: DrPhil1@aol.com
www.newyorktalksandwalks.com

ENJOY THE New York EXPERIENCE!

Reinforce Your Positive Expectations of the Big Apple!

Dr. Philip E. Schoenberg, President
NEW YORK TALKS & WALKS™

(718) 591-4741
(888) DRPHIL5 (377-4455)
www.newyorktalksandwalks.com

Outside

FOR A MOST MEMORABLE VISIT TO NYC, ENJOY NEW YORK TALKS AND WALKS™ WITH DR. PHIL AND HIS ASSOCIATES– THE NYC EXPERTS!

· Experience amusing tours by knowledgeable, passionate historians who loves NYC.

· Enjoy fun tours that are different from the run of the mill.

· Photograph memorable sites.

· Tour unusual museums and unique historic sites.

· Shop in New York bargain stores – no lower prices anywhere.

· Sample New York's exotic cuisines.

· Learn how to use public transit with confidence.

· Tour the nation's first capital – now the capital of Planet Earth.

WHO WILL ENJOY THESE TOURS?

· Tourists

· New Yorkers who love their city

· Senior citizens

· School groups

· Orientation for new-comers

· Convention-goers

· Corporate spouses

· Special occasions and celebrations

· Office parties and outings

· Family reunions

· College orientations

· Alumni reunions

MOST REQUESTED TALKS AND TOURS

· Brooklyn Bridge
· Jewish Lower East Side
· Hidden Treasures of Chinatown
· Kleinedeutschland: German East Village
· Multiethnic East Village
· Literary Garrets of Greenwich Village
· Luck of the Irish
· J.P. Morgan's Wall Street
· From Wampum to Wall Street: NYC's American Indian Heritage
· Dutch New Amsterdam
· Washington's New York
· Lincoln's New York
· Yiddish Theatrical Row
· Maritime New York
· Brooklyn Heights
· New York's World's Fairs

Call
New York Talks & Walks™
For a Tour at
(718) 591-4741
(888) DRPHIL5 (377-4455)

Inside

Sales Letter

Mysterious Journeys

Hi Susan!

I'd like to offer you a very special invitation to explore the ancient, arcane, and mysterious secrets of Britain with a very special tour company.

I've chosen you to receive this invitation because I know you've traveled a lot. You're not a tourist but a discriminating traveler who savors the unique and the extraordinary, the magical discoveries that make a trip abroad an adventure of the mind and heart.

So what is this is special invitation? It's the opportunity to explore the magic and mysteries of Britain, from Tintagel, site of King Arthur's castle in Cornwall, to the ancient stone henges at Avebury, to the mystical forces at work in Findhorn, Scotland. You'll experience sights most tourists never see: a secret circle of stones bathed in moonlight, a faerie grove in flickering sun, Celtic crags and crossroads veiled in mists, and magical lore, perhaps even the ghosts of those who once inhabited now-ruined castles! You'll come away from this trip with a sense of wonder along with the knowledge of how and why the mysteries of this ancient land still influence the world of today.

Who is offering this unique tour? *Mysterious Journeys*, a company designed specifically for you, the seasoned traveler seeking the adventures of learning for the heart and soul. I will personally guide you and a select few on this journey. As a university professor, now retired, I've spent a lifetime researching the secrets of Britain. And now I'll share them with you.

Because I'm so anxious for you to experience this new adventure, I'm inviting you to participate in my first Mysterious Journey, June 1st through 10th, for 20% off the normal tour price! It's a trip you won't want to miss.

I hope you'll take advantage of this special offer. I can't offer it for long. Space will fill up quickly, but I can promise that you'll come away from this Journey bewitched by the magic and mysteries you'll discover.

Call toll-free: (800) 000-1234. Or e-mail me at alix@mjourneys.com. *Please hurry! Because I must begin making arrangements for charter Journey participants soon, my offer must end December 1st.*

Very best,

Alix Arelson

Alix Arelson

123 King Arthur Court, Camelot, FL 30000   Tel: (800) 000-1234
www.mjourneys.com

or "This offer is good only through _____." This encourages your customers to book now instead of in the nebulous future.

- *Write riveting headlines.* Your brochure must compete with all the others crammed in your customers' mailboxes. Penning your headline before your text will help you to focus on what basic need or desire your product satisfies.

- *Offer testimonials from satisfied customers.* Use real first and last names and real hometowns. Remember that you must notify testimonial-givers that their names and hometowns will be used and get their permission.

Beware!
If you use testimonials, they must be from real people who have given their permission.

- *Accent with artwork.* Illustrations and photos attract attention. If you use a caption under a picture, make sure it has sales value. People will read captions even when they don't have time to read the rest of the piece.

- *Help customers respond quickly.* Accept credit cards and toll-free calls. It's much easier for your customer to fill in a credit card number on a form or call and give it to you over the phone, than to sit down and write out a check.

- *Remember the participation effect.* Give your customers plenty to look at and lots to read; and try to include something to stick, paste, tear off, or insert. If you can't afford these gimmicks, consider something like the seemingly handwritten note that implores the customer to "Read this only if you've decided not to participate."

I Love Mailing Lists

That said, let's look at mailing lists. You already know a bit, but there's more—lots more. A mailing list can make or break a direct-mail campaign, and a good list can be worth more than double your ad budget.

You can target your audience more effectively with a mailing list than with any other medium. Say you decide to go with an alternative and advertise on television—we don't recommend it, but for the sake of making a point, we will look at it, anyway. You might choose "I Love Lucy" reruns or "The X-Files" or the "Tonight Show." Although each will have its demographic profile, you will get a fairly indiscriminate selection of viewers. You

Smart Tip
Make it easy for prospects to order. Explain that they can reserve space by mail, phone, or fax (or your Web site, if you're set up for it), and that they can pay by check or credit card.

Tip...

It's a Fine Art

Connie G. in Pennsylvania has honed her mailing list to a fine art. "I've got clients broken down into three groups—all the 500 or so clients who've booked in the past few years are on a database," says the specialist in tours for the physically challenged. "Those folks get two to three mailings a year, one newsletter, and a couple of postcards. Many of them are people who only purchased airline tickets before, so the reason they're on the mailing list is to keep in touch for the time they're ready to start traveling and doing actual vacations." Connie keeps these folks on her list for another reason besides the fact that they may become cruise or tour participants. If they've got friends or neighbors planning a trip, her company will hopefully pop into their minds as a ready reference.

Connie has further refined her list into people who typically do tours or packages and those who do cruises. "This way," she explains, "I can streamline the mailings. If I want to do one to the top 100 people for a cruise, I can do that. The tour and cruise people get more mailings than others. When we've got some kind of cruise special going on, I can very quickly turn around and do a fast mailing that's more intensive, focusing on people who are likely to buy—which reduces my cost."

have no way of knowing if they are seniors on a limited budget, executives who travel overseas, families with children under ten years old, or maximum security prison inmates who couldn't attend one of your tours if they paid triple your asking price.

However, when you rent a mailing list, you have your audience targeted to a *T.* For those hiking and biking tours, you can choose Midwestern women who've bought health and fitness magazines. Or for those Maine sailing expeditions, you can get a listing of men in the New England area who buy marine equipment and earn over $50,000 per year.

Common Threads

In the mailing list world, there are two types of lists: the *compiled* list and the *buyer* or *response* list. A compiled list is made up of people with the common thread of a group or organization. For example, these could be members of alumnae organizations or car clubs; members of professional organizations from doctors to contractors; or even people who have attended different types of vacations, tours, seminars, or workshops. A compiled list can also be made up of people with certain demographic characteristics in common: those who live in Manhattan, make more than $30,000 a year, or are between 45 and 70 years old. You get the picture. The main point to remember with compiled lists is that unless you rent a list comprised of previous tour participants, you can't know that those doctors, contractors, or car aficionados have booked a tour or are likely to.

Now, the other type of list—the buyer list—is the one you want to shoot for. Why? Because the people on it are already known tour participants. They might be buyers of gourmet cooking tours, Amazon adventures, or Disney-mania programs. The main idea here is that since they've already booked a tour similar to yours, they're likely to book yours,

Smart Tip Tip...

What's a good response rate for a mailing? The answer is "it depends." Generally, 1.5 percent is considered a good, solid response. However, the higher your booking price, the lower the response is likely to be, which is not necessarily bad because your income potential is higher per response.

The Formula

Like any good mad scientist, the travel professional also has a magic formula for working with lists. That formula is RFM, with R for recency, F for frequency, and M for money. In other words, how recently have the people on the list booked a tour by mail, how frequently do they order, and how much money do they spend?

Besides the all-important RFM factor, demographics are crucial in choosing your list. You need to consider income, age, gender, education, type of residence, occupation, and use of credit cards in making purchases. If you're selling romance-writing seminars, you would probably choose a women-only list, because most men wouldn't be interested. Got it?

Another list selection factor is psychographics. This is the categorization of people by psychological profile. Political conservatives, for instance, are more likely to be hunters than those on the liberal left. So if you're selling duck-hunting tours, you might try mailing to Republicans. If a list owner or broker says he's got a psychographic profile, ask for it. Check out the ones listed to see if they match your prospective buyers.

Yet another factor to consider is who else has been renting the same list and how often. This can tell you who your competition is and how successful they've been with it. If you've got soft-adventure tours, and you find that another soft-adventure company has rented the same list four times in the past year, you can figure they're having good luck with it. This means you probably will, too.

which may not be the case with people on compiled lists. This doesn't mean you should never use compiled lists. It does mean, though, that you should use them carefully. List brokers are experienced at this sort of thing, so let them advise you on what's best for your particular situation.

Mailing List Fever

Where exactly do you get your mailing lists?

- Rent them from any number of list brokers, which you'll find in your local Yellow Pages under Advertising—Direct Mail or within the pages of direct-marketing magazines like *Catalog Age* and *Target Marketing*. (We've provided the names of a few list brokers in the Appendix to get you started.)

- Rent or swap lists directly from your competition, the other specialty tour companies engaged in selling programs to similar target markets. Yes, they'll often share!

- Rent directly from associations whose members fit your target market.

- Buy lists from a competitor who's gone out of business. This doesn't happen too often, but it is worth keeping an eye out for.

- Build up your own list in all the ways we've discussed so far (and any more you can devise) and use it often.

Salting the List

Notice we've referred to *renting* your lists, not buying them. This is how it's done in the direct-mail world. Unless you're swapping or purchasing outright, as we described above, you rent a one-time use of the list from the list broker. You're free to take any names that respond to your mailing and incorporate them into your very own house list, which you can use anytime you like. However, you can't use the rented list more than once, unless you rent it again.

How does the list broker or owner know if you decide to cheat? They salt in bogus names (for instance, their mother, brother, or dog) and addresses. Then, if Mom, Bubba, or Fido receives your mailing, you're caught. So don't try it.

The one-time rental fee for most lists runs from $100 to $150 per thousand names, and most list brokers insist you rent a minimum of 5,000 names. You'll also be charged $5 to $10 extra for each *select*, or special qualifier, that you choose (age, income, geographic region, etc.).

12

Media Time

Although unsolicited brochures can work wonders, they're not the only way to go. Some travel specialists don't use mailing lists at all, with the exception of their own in-house lists of present and previous clients. Instead, they rely on referrals from other satisfied clients and from their Web sites to garner initial interest.

In this chapter, we'll look at the other advertising methods you can choose from, including word-of-mouth, newsletters, Web site offerings, and print ads. We'll also discuss how to excel in the public relations arena.

The Golden Word

Independent travel agents, in particular, insist that word-of-mouth is their absolute best advertising source. "We do an awful lot of referral business from one client to another," says Jim T. in Maryland. "We deal mainly through word-of-mouth and our direct mailings."

If this sounds simple, you're right! But there's a catch. Like any other aspect of the travel business, you have to actively work at making those golden word-of-mouth contacts. Sitting home and hoping the phone will ring doesn't pay. What does is getting out in your community and letting people know about your business. For Jim and Nancy T., their business just sort of snowballed on its own. "One of the people we'd been cruising with became our first client, and it grew from there," Jim says. "And since both of us had worked in government agencies before, we had access to a large number of people."

Further south, in Atlanta, Roberta E. is working up a whole new set of contacts. "Within the last year, I've moved from where we lived for nine years," the cruise specialist says. "So I'm starting from ground zero as far as local business goes. I'm getting to know people in the local neighborhoods, finding out what groups are out here and becoming active in various clubs."

Wish You Were Here

Once you've made those contacts, a winning way to follow up is with postcards. "It's important to keep in touch with people," advises Connie G. "Even if you're not getting that call, you're still keeping your name in front of others." This is a terrific way to ensure that they call you when they're ready to roll out those travel plans.

Postcards get your message across quickly and efficiently. Even super-rushed, busy, and jangled types who might toss an advertising-suspect envelope will take the time to turn over a postcard and read the message. Everybody likes to receive personal mail; and as a travel specialist, you're in a position to provide postcards of a type few other businesses can match—greetings from a foreign destination, or at least about a foreign destination!

Get creative with those mini-mailings and design a piece that will have those prospects itching to read on and find out who it's from (you), and what it's about (your latest special). Forget the drab, boring sentences like "Call us for all your travel needs," or "Call about our exciting walking tours." This is not exciting prose. Instead, go for a variation on the same technique that works in brochures and send postcards that are time-specific. Try something like:

- *A photo of a cruise ship in turquoise waters mailed in January or February.* On the back write "Enough with snow! You could be sailing the sunny Caribbean. Book your cabin by February 10 and take advantage of our winter discount specials!"

- *A picture of happy tour participants gathered around a campfire or overlooking a scenic lake.* On the back write "Wish you were here? You could be—for less money than you think. Call us by May 15 to reserve a space on this summer's Sunsets & S'mores for Seniors Weekend, and get a 20 percent discount off the advertised price."

> **Bright Idea**
> Use those postcards to update people on news about your company. Judy E., the culinary whiz, sent out 5,000 postcards to past clients, travel agents, and other interested professionals to herald the advent of her new Web site.

Don't forget to put your contact information—phone number as well as Web site and e-mail address—clearly on the postcard. You've put forth the effort to intrigue your clients; now make it easy for them to reach you.

You can easily make your own postcards with your desktop publishing software. You can drop in clip-art photos (which means artwork ready-made for the public), photos you get from your suppliers (with their permission, of course), or your own pictures. Or go with elegant or whimsical line art. It doesn't matter, so long as it catches that client's attention.

What's News?

Another knock-out marketing tool is the company newsletter. Send these to your clients quarterly, as Jim and Nancy T. do, and you'll reap three benefits:

1. You keep your name and the delights of travel linked in your clients' minds.

2. You keep your clients up-to-date on your latest products and tempt them with any specials or discounts so you don't start fading into one of those once-upon-a-time, never-to-be-repeated memories.

3. You make your clients feel special! You've remembered them and added them onto your "exclusive" list.

> **Bright Idea**
> Add in a coupon to be redeemed for a discount. It's a cool way to keep your clients reading through your newsletter and eagerly anticipating the next one.

What do you put *inside* your newsletter? Use the space to tell your clients about those upcoming specials and discounts. Describe new and intriguing places to visit, or new and intriguing products (yours if you're a tour operator, or your suppliers' if you're an independent agent). You might pop in client-penned pieces about their adventures on tours or cruises you've provided. You can add in travel industry news that pertains to your products. If you are a cruise specialist, for instance, you could put in a piece about the newest "floating city" ships with some staggering fun facts highlighting things like the amount of food they carry per voyage. The main premise to keep in mind is that, like your postcard, your newsletter should be fun to read and should whet your clients' appetites for travel through your company.

Dollar Stretcher

It's fun and economical to publish your own desktop gems such as newsletters and postcards. But if you'll do more than 50 to 100 at a time, it may be cheaper to go to a printer like Kinko's. When you do, be sure to get several bids—printing costs can vary considerably.

Fold your newsletter in thirds, like a brochure, to give it that sleek No. 10 envelope look. Or fold it in half. If it's bigger and bulkier, it may command more attention in that stack of mail in the box. Get creative with something playful printed in a fun font above the client's name, like "Hot Tips for World Traveler (fill in the name and address)." Paste or stamp on a few travel stickers (something kids can do with delight) to make that piece look like an authentic travel missive. Who could resist opening it?

Robo-Marketing

A company Web site can act as your robotic (or maybe clone) marketing person, offering promotional materials to potential clients 24 hours a day, seven days a week. And you don't have to be anywhere near the office! People can read up on the products you have to offer, request brochures or other information, and "converse" with you via e-mail—even while you're out leading tours, narrowing down a travel wish list at a client's home or office, or delivering tickets.

For Judy, the culinary school representative, her Web site is a major part of her marketing effort and the success of her business. "My son came to me one day and said 'Mom, you need a Web site.' I said 'What in the world is it and why do I want one?' He explained, and sure enough, he was right," says Judy. "I've had that site for about seven years now, and I'm getting more and more people from it."

In Savannah, Georgia, Karen A. also believes her company Web site is one of her most cost-effective advertising venues. "We have spent a total of about $3,000 on this in two years, including photography, software, and Internet service provider—excluding our labor," she says. "We run it in-house, and it has undergone many revisions. It has generated most of our corporate business (corporations holding meetings in Savannah who want leisure-time activities for attendees), and some Girl Scout and school business, to the tune of around $20,000 in revenues."

Adventurous Web Shoppers

Web customers, by virtue of the fact that they are shopping online, tend to be more adventurous, more willing to try something new, and more interested in forging a relationship with the site (which is you).

What can you do to take advantage of these tendencies? Interact with your clients. Give them something new and exciting. Foster that relationship. This brings us to the

---

Agent or Consumer?

One of the biggest questions for specialty tour operators is whether to target your advertising toward travel agents or consumers. Like the old chicken or egg question, there is no one easy answer here.

"About a third of our business comes through travel agents," says Harry G., the fishing aficionado. "We advertise in consumer publications, and very extensively in the *Specialty Travel Index* and the *Official Tour Directory* (which are geared toward travel agents)."

"About 8 percent to 10 percent of our business comes from the travel industry," Barry, the race car enthusiast, agrees. "There are certain travel agents who have a following and are really good. Generally, though, most know nothing about motor racing. "I've had travel agents tell people that a race car driver will meet them at the airport. Drivers who are earning $3 million to $4 million a year don't meet people at the airport," Barry says. He explains that because travel agents may read something and not quite understand it, he's found that it's far better to deal with clients on a one-to-one basis and gear advertising to the consumer.

Harry G., the fishing tour operator echoes this sentiment. "The typical travel agent doesn't care about the moon phases and the techniques employed and the types of flies that are necessary. That's not their job description. Theirs is to sell cruises."

In Seattle, tour guide Terry S. says, "I target destination and event planners as well as individual consumers. Any marketing toward travel agents would be incidental. Besides, they would want a commission, and that's not what I am all about."

▲

> **Bright Idea**
>
> Treat your Web site like your newsletter; add in a few articles, as Judy E., the culinary representative, does. It makes your site more personal and lets you wax eloquent about your products without wearing that salesperson hat.

other big difference between Net and paper retailing—the way you interact with your customers. Clue them in to your travel philosophy. Are you a back-to-nature type tour guide? Do you specialize in cruises because you love the romance of the open seas? Give them the sense that they know who you are and what you're about. This is also a stellar spot to give Web visitors your credentials— your 25 years as an Audubon birder, your CLIA MCC (Master Cruise Counsellor) credentials, or your insider knowledge of your hometown.

Keep in mind, too, that shopping for travel is different than shopping for spaghetti sauce, a cotton sweater, or that Wayne Newton CD. Travel is a high-ticket item, which means your customers—especially those who have never before purchased from you—will need a certain amount of hand-holding. Travel shopping also differs in that there are many more variables to discuss than shopping for, say, an article of clothing. There are times, dates, cabin or room categories, airfares; and the list goes on and on.

"I'm getting more and more people from my Web site," Judy E., the cooking school agent, says. "But they'll look at the site, and then they'll want to talk to a person. They want the personal contact."

No Spamming

People who shop for travel or anything else the e-commerce way don't like hype. They expect to be informed and entertained; but they don't want to be electronically shouted at, patronized, or pandered to (which you shouldn't do to your paper customers, either). Sending requested e-mail updates is good business and fun interaction; but "spamming," or sending e-junk mail, is definitely poor Netiquette and will not win friends and influence customers. What will? The same elements that win you paper customers—honesty, integrity, fairness, service, and respect. Show your Web customers they are important by how you treat them. Offer discounts, freebies, and any other perks you can think up.

Try these tips for winning and keeping Internet mail order customers:

- *Give your customers easy access to you.* Don't force them to wade through page after page before finding your e-mail address and phone number.
- *Check and answer your e-mail on a daily basis.* Don't let virtual customers languish any more than you would phone or mail customers.
- *Update your site frequently.* If a cruise or tour is sold out, let people know. This way they don't get frustrated drooling for something that's not available, and

it shows them that your products are popular! They have to move on these things!

- *Add new information frequently.* This helps you market new products as soon as you have them available, and also keeps e-travelers coming back for more. If your site stagnates with the same material week after week and month after month, clients will get bored and stop visiting.

- *Don't frustrate customers with a site that's slow or difficult to figure out.* You'll quickly lose people this way. Keep your site user-friendly and easy to navigate.

> ### Smart Tip
>
> Web shoppers tend to go for the higher-end products, says Gregg Miller of the Hotel Metropole, an upscale resort on Catalina Island, California, with its own Web presence. Given the choice between a less-expensive room and a luxury suite, Web travelers will usually choose the suite.

- *Offer customers information and entertainment.* Use elements that will draw them in, hold their attention, and make them feel you're a part of their world and they're a part of yours. Post an article on the best vacation spots for the season, or ten tips for traveling with kids. Use the same mindset you'll use in your newsletters—tips, tricks, news, and even articles from fellow travelers (with their permission, of course).

- *Go easy on the graphics.* Pictures add impact to your site; but if your customers have to wait seemingly endless minutes for your page to become viewable because it's graphics-heavy, you're going to lose them. Make sure those photos are small enough to load quickly.

- *Check out competitors' sites.* Just as you check out competitors' other advertising materials, check out their Web sites. Borrow the best of what they're doing; then do it better.

Print Ads

For the travel professional, traditional print ads in newspapers and magazines usually do not pull in customers as well as direct mail—but not always! Barry S., the car race tour operator, and Harry G., the fishing tour operator, have found that advertising in magazines targeted to car and fishing buffs, respectively, works. Most industry insiders agree, however, that advertising in general consumer publications does not work. Why? Because, once again, you are not *targeting your market.*

If you have tours, or you are pitching a supplier's tours that have tight niche markets, the key is to find specialty magazines that will work for your particular products. Judy E., the culinary tour promoter, runs an ad in the *Shaw Guide to Cooking Schools.* You might pop a display ad for your tour for romance writers in *Romantic*

▲

Tupperware Travel

How about hosting a cruise celebration or travel soiree, a sort of Tupperware party of travel? Go through your mailing list and cull previous clients and those you think might be likely prospects; then invite them to an evening of virtual travel adventure at your home or at a hotel meeting room. Be sure to stress in the invitation that you'll be offering not only cruise or travel information, but also deep product discounts for these special invitees.

Set out party food and drinks along with the most important part of the evening—displays of your products including brochures, fliers, photos, testimonials, and lots of coupons for discounts. Offer deeper discounts if people sign up on the spot.

Some travel agents—particularly cruise-oriented agents—develop this theme into ambitious, full-blown events. They arrange for cruise suppliers to be on hand; coordinate booths for wedding planners, sportswear boutiques, luggage shops, and other purveyors of cruise-related gear; advertise in the local newspaper; and charge the public admission.

Times magazine, for instance, or plant an ad for your gardening tours in *Horticulture* magazine.

Karen A., who specializes in tours for Girl Scouts, finds that ads placed in one very closely targeted publication—*Birthplace Bound*, which is sent to Girl Scout troops by the Juliette Gordon Low Birthplace—are definitely worth the cost. "A $212 ad in 1998 almost single-handedly resulted in $101,000 in revenues in 1999," Karen reports.

You'll probably want to go with a *display ad*, the kind that usually features some sort of graphics combined with the printed word and is found throughout a publication—as opposed to classifieds which consist solely of the printed word and are found only in the classified section. Display ads can be very expensive (about $1,700 and up) and generally don't pull a significant response until they've run for several consecutive months. So think carefully before you buy that ad space, and as always, do your homework first.

Vampire Today

If you have done your homework and chosen a niche you are familiar with and enjoy, you probably already know which publications will work for you. They are the ones your target audience reads and the ones you probably read, too. These are the best places to start because you already understand at least part of the demographics and psychographics of their readers. If you are a vampire and your target market is vampires, for instance, you probably already know about *Country Vampire*, *Vampire Today*, and *Fashion Vamp* magazines.

Pick up those issues off your coffee table or nightstand. Study them carefully. Do you see any "mail order" travel ads, ones in which readers must contact the advertiser? Or are they "traditional" travel ads, like the ones trumpeting a splashy cruise line, that instruct you to "contact your travel agent for more information"? If mail order travel makes up a significant portion, you can figure that other companies like yours are experiencing success with the publication. In other words, the publication is a good fit for your ad.

Bright Idea
Can't afford that magazine advertising? Try a trade-out. Offer that publication a free product in exchange for advertising, for example, a three-day cruise or tour they can use as an incentive.

Passing You By

Newspapers, while a good read, and a good source of bin liners, creative wrapping paper, and packing material, do not make good travel advertising venues. The reason for this is a bit of a mystery but probably has to do with two factors: most newspapers have a very limited geographic range, and their readership is too broad to allow for target marketing.

Jim and Nancy T. do an occasional newspaper ad but use the daily rag as a minor player in their advertising program. "We've found newspaper ads to be not that fruitful, if fruitful at all," Jim says. "The problem with newspaper ads is that unless someone is particularly looking for you, they're going to pass you right by."

Local Listings

Don't let this turn you off newspapers, though. It all depends on what products you're pitching. Dr. Phil S., the New York City tour guide, has found his local papers to be an advertising treasure trove. "Getting into the newspapers on a regular basis," he says, "is my greatest asset."

Rather than buying advertising space, however, the Queens native sends listings about his tours to *The New York Times* and *Time Out New York* (which bills itself as the "obsessive guide to impulsive entertainment") as well as to a host of community newspapers. Since these publications tend to print entertainment listings based on available space, you can't count on your tours appearing in every edition. But when they do, they're absolutely free advertising that can work and be a boon to sales. "Usually when I make the *Times*, it is a feast; when I don't, it is a famine," says Phil. As an added bonus, the listings have more sticking power than you might think. "People will save those papers for months, weeks, and even years," the maven of walking guides explains. So readers who might not show up for tomorrow's tour may become die-hard groupies at a later date.

Phil advises compiling a slate of your local papers, then finding out who the editor is and submitting a listing every month. Make sure you check ahead to find out when they need the listing; it may be as much as two or three weeks before the date you want your material published. For instance, if you're doing special Halloween ghost walks, you may need to get your information in by early October.

And don't forget about those target markets. Phil says, "I do a German Heritage walking tour of downtown Manhattan and send a listing to German ethnic newspapers and magazines. Generally, they'll publish it because not too many people cover that particular heritage in New York City."

Terry S., in Washington state's Emerald City, got his company listed with the Seattle-King County Convention and Visitors Bureau. "When people ask, I get a good reference," he says. And he's listed as an attraction in the Automobile Association of America's TourBook. "Many individual walkers planning to visit Seattle find my business this way," he explains.

See and Be Seen

The place to be seen for specialty tours is *Specialty Travel Index*, a biannual magazine that, in addition to editorial features, allots space for hundreds of tour operators to strut their stuff. For a minimum of $400 per issue, you get a listing that includes your logo and your very own write-up of your products. The publication is mailed to more than 160,000 travel professionals and 6,000 consumer subscribers. This makes for a hefty slice of advertising. At no extra charge, you also get listed in *Specialty Travel Index Online*, which boasts 500,000 hits (or Web surfer drop-ins) a month. For another $25, your online listing can be linked to your own Web site and e-mail address so potential clients can contact you without lifting more than a mouse-click finger.

Specialty Travel Index lists tour operators by geographic destination—this includes everywhere from the Azores to Bulgaria to the Pribilof Islands to Vanuatu to Outer Space (yes! really!). As an advertiser, you get your first ten regions for free. If you're running tours that encompass Colorado, New Mexico, and Utah, for instance, you get a listing under each. If you go over 10 regions, each additional listing is $1. With each region, you also get to list an interest/activity category, and there are hundreds of these. You will find everything from brewery tours to cowboy skills to mushroom hunting.

The Automobile Association doesn't charge a fee for this listing, but they do come out and evaluate you before including you in their publication. Contact your local office for information on how to get listed.

Free Advertising

Yes, while in the words of the old cliché "There's no such thing as a free lunch," there are some terrific things you can do to get free advertising. Of course, you have to put forth effort, intelligence, and creativity; so it's not "free" as in easy—but the rewards are worth it.

The Magazine Expert

So what are these free advertising opportunities? One is word-of-mouth, which we have already covered. Another is print media. Take advantage of the thousands of magazines and journals out there by writing articles for publication. People do not always give ads a second glance, but they do read articles.

If you manage to get an article published, your credibility as a travel expert will soar along with the desirability of your products. If you're in a magazine, people think you must be a pro. And the benefits don't stop with the reader. People won't tear out an ad, but they'll tear out an article and pass it along to friends and relatives, so you get the word-of-mouth effect, even in print.

Gardening or Genealogy

What publications should you submit to? Take a look at your target audience, then go for the trade or professional journals they read, whether it's *Southern Gardener* or *Genealogy Today*. If you have an intriguing angle, say multigenerational travel, or travel for the disabled, you can also target general interest publications. These are the ones you find in the supermarket checkout lines, not *The National Enquirer*, but magazines like *Woman's Day* or *Self*. General interest magazines are much more difficult to get into than trade and professional publications; but if your topic and your writing skills are terrific, and if the editor's in the right frame of mind, you can do it.

> **Tip...**
>
> **Smart Tip**
> Make it easy for anyone who reads your article to contact you. Most publications will let you add an endnote that says: "For more information or for a free tip sheet, call or write to (fill in your name) at (fill in your address and phone), or e-mail her at (fill in your e-mail address)."

> **Tip...**
>
> **Smart Tip**
>
> You can also write articles for the in-house publications of client corporations and associations. You will get paid, and you will also keep your name uppermost in their minds.

The best way to approach the issue is to head down to your local public library and sit down with the latest copy of *The Writer's Market* (you can't usually check it out, so bring change for copying pages). Or if you prefer to have your own copy, you can buy it at your local bookstore for around $30. Thumb through this hefty volume and pick out the publications that might be good targets for your articles. You'll be amazed at the number of publications in every imaginable specialty.

Back at home, call the magazine or journal to find out which editor to send your piece to; then ask to speak to him *briefly* and find out if he'd be interested. Keep your conversation short and professional; editors are busy people. When you elicit interest, send a one-page query letter—written as temptingly as your direct-mail brochure or sales letter—describing the article you plan to write and asking the editor to contact you if he's interested. If so, then you write the article and there's your free advertising. As a bonus, you'll get paid for your piece. So not only is the advertising free, but they're paying you for the privilege!

Traveling Writers

Another terrific way to get your name out there in print at no cost is journalists who offer to write articles about your products in exchange for free tours. This is something Phil in New York has tried. This barter system can work wonderfully; but the world being what it is, you'll need to watch out for folks who claim they'll write those articles but never deliver the goods. "You can't beat free publicity, but you don't want to waste your time on something that will never see the light of day," Phil advises. To make sure you get that publicity, the former history professor offers the following hard-won suggestions.

"Interns who work for community newspapers should be charged nothing for a tour. My experience has been that they have always published something about me. Professional journalists who can show that they are not freelancers should be charged nothing if that is what they request—however, many have expense accounts.

"Student journalists at various colleges should be charged for any time before or after the tour, at $20 per half-hour rate. I 've worked with student journalists six times. I have never received a copy of the article or television production they did of me.

"People who claim they are 'travel writers' for newspapers [generally] go to their local newspaper and get a press pass and credentials on the promise they will send in articles. Just because they are writing something down does not mean they will write an article, or that the editor will actually print the article. Charge full price for your tours unless they can prove they will actually publish. Better yet, tell them they will get a refund when they send a copy of the actual article. They should also be charged $20 per half hour for any interviews they do before or after the tour."

Public Relations

In the travel industry, public relations is an important component of doing business successfully. Good public relations can accomplish two things:

1. It can put your company name out to people who may not otherwise have heard of you.
2. It can keep people who are already your customers thinking fondly of you and thus create repeat-bookings.

In other words, PR is another terrific source of free advertising. There are all sorts of low-cost techniques you can use. Try some of the following:

- *Find a local group looking for guest speakers.* Offer yourself on a free, or pro bono, basis to local associations or clubs that match your target audience. If you are selling local walking tours, you can talk to women's groups, men's clubs, business groups from the Jaycees to the chamber of commerce to various networking

Walking Ads

Those T-shirts imprinted with your company logo can also be a good source of advertising, especially if you're offering products like half-day tours in a tourist-heavy area. Potential customers will see other people walking around wearing your ads, and if they look trendy enough, some will simply have to have one, too. All this advertising will result in calls to inquire about your tours.

Before trying this one on for size, make sure you can buy the T-shirts inexpensively enough and—at least for starters—in small enough quantities that they don't break your piggybank. Dr. Phil S., in New York City, sells T-shirts for $6 each to go along with his Brooklyn Bridge walk. Since he pays $2.50 for them, it's a good deal—for his tourists and for him.

As always, do your homework. Take your own walk around town and scout out how many "walking ads" you see. Analyze what makes them work and what doesn't.

clubs, and even kids' clubs. Just be sure to tailor your topic to your particular audience. Remember that word-of-mouth is a powerful advertising tool and get creative!

- *Join any organizations that match your target audience.* Volunteer for things that will get you and your company recognized and thought well of. Most people respect volunteers within an organization and consider them experts in the organization's area of interest, which heightens your credibility.

- *Attend meetings of pertinent organizations.* Karen A. makes a point of participating in meetings of groups like the North Carolina Bus Association, American Bus Association, and nature-based tourism organizations. She says, "We attend these as cheaply as possible, and they usually generate business long after the event."

- *Go live on the air.* Volunteer yourself for a local radio station's chat show. You can discuss your niche, be it local walking tours, fun for the business traveler, or the new face of soft-adventure travel or cruising. Listeners can call in with questions. When they talk to you—on the air!—they'll be interested in booking your products. They may also tell their friends and relatives, which means more word-of-mouth advertising for you.

- *Offer a free booking.* Provide a free booking on one of your products as a prize for a charity event.

- *Get out and travel.* Karen A. says marketing trips to potential client-based areas (like North Carolina, Virginia, and Pennsylvania) that are organized by her local Convention and Visitors' Bureau are good, cost-effective marketing venues.

Traveler's Checks
Controlling Your Finances

Whether you're a chronic number cruncher or one of the finance-phobic, you will want to give your company periodic financial checkups. "Why?" you ask. "I already did all that math stuff in the start-up chapter." That was just the pre-natal exam for the precious baby that is your business. When you've gone through the birthing process and that precocious tot is toddling around, you will want periodic checks to make sure that your enfant terrible is as healthy as you have imagined. In this chapter, we will examine everything from pricing to income statements.

Crunching Those Numbers

Photo© Adobe Systems Inc.

Financial checkups don't have to be negative. They can give you a rosy glow by demonstrating how well you are doing, which might be even better than you expected. If you have been saving for a new printer or software upgrade, or if you are hoping to take on an employee, you can judge how close you are to achieving your goals. If there's a problem, you'll find out before it becomes critical. For instance, if you discover that your income barely covers your brochure-printing expenses, you can change gears and reduce the number of direct-mail pieces you send out.

"Crunch those numbers," urges Karen A. in Savannah, Georgia. "We do spreadsheets at the end of every month. You need to analyze *everything* to find out where you're making money, where you're losing it, and to answer questions [like]: What will our revenues be next year? Is this type of tour more profitable than that? What will happen to cash flow in February? What proportion of proposals actually convert into tours? Is the conversion rate of this type of tour higher than that? And don't just draw the conclusion: Act on it."

Making a Statement

An *income statement*, also called a *profit-and-loss statement*, charts the revenues and operating costs of your business over a specific period of time, usually a month. Go back to Chapter 6 and take another look at the income statements on pages 89–90 for our four hypothetical travel companies: travel agents, Merry Makers and After the Wedding; and tour operators, Magic Bay and Mysterious Journeys.

You'll want to tailor your income statement to your particular business. Remember that to make the statement really right, you'll need to pro-rate items that are paid

Remember that to make your income statement really right, you'll need to pro-rate items that are paid annually.

annually, such as business licenses and tax-time accounting fees, and pop those figures into your monthly statement. For example, if you pay annual insurance premiums of $600, divide this figure by 12 and add the resulting $50 to your insurance expense.

Use the worksheet on page 186 to chart your own income statement. You'll be surprised at how much fun doing your finances can be!

Figuring Profits

Let's look at how much you can expect to make, which means figuring out how to price your services. Warning: This section contains actual math problems. If you're one of us arithmetic-phobic types, you may be tempted at this point to take this book and toss it out the window. Please don't! There's a big difference between having to calculate when two trains traveling at different speeds on the same track will meet, and figuring out how much money you can actually make in your own travel business.

Travel Agency Pricing

As a specialty travel agent, you have two basic ways to determine how much revenue you'll earn:

1. Sell products for which the supplier has set a price already and for which you'll receive commissions.
2. Buy packaged tours at wholesale prices and then mark them up.

Put Yourself into Commission

The first method—selling pre-priced products for a commission—requires the least computing power and is pretty simple. Say you sell a "Mayan Magic" Mexican tour that's priced at $1,500 double occupancy and carries a 10 percent commission. Tours and cruises base their fees on *double occupancy* rates, which is another way of saying "times two." If the brochure says $1,500 per person, look for the small print that also says "double occupancy" and multiply that price by two. If your client is traveling alone, he or she must pay a *single supplement*, usually up to another 50 percent of the "per person" rate.

The price for your clients that bought the "Mayan Magic" tour is $3,000, and the tour operator pays a $300 commission (10 percent of the $3,000 price tag). Notice we

Your Monthly Income Statement

For the month of _____

Monthly Income

    Gross Monthly Income $_____

Monthly Expenses

    Rent $_____

    Phone/utilities _____

    Employees _____

    Postage _____

    Licenses _____

    Legal services _____

    Advertising/promotions _____

    Accounting services _____

    Office supplies _____

    Transportation & travel _____

    Insurance _____

    Subscriptions/dues _____

    Loan repayment _____

    Miscellaneous _____

    Total Monthly Expenses $_____

Net Monthly Profit $_____

didn't say the tour operator pays *you* $300. You have to split this with the host agency, remember? So if you've negotiated a 50/50 split with your host, you'll get 50 percent of this $300, or $150. If you've agreed on a 70/30 split, with the lion's share going to you, you'll receive $210.

Now, to determine what your annual income will be, we need to look at how many bookings you'll do in a year. In non-travel lingo, that means the number of tours, cruises, or other products you'll sell. As a newbie, this can be difficult. If you've never sold even one product, how can you know how many you'll do over the course of a year?

The answer lies in your market research. You go by what your homework has shown your prospective clients will be willing to purchase, and by what others with similar businesses are doing. You'll also need to base your figures on how hard you plan to work. The travel specialist who knocks herself out to identify clients, to make sales, and to satisfy her clients' needs, is going to earn a lot more in revenues than the one who dabbles.

Estimating Annual Gross Revenue for Commisionable Products

Take a look at the following breakdown of how to determine your annual gross revenue for pre-priced commissionable products.

1. Choose a product you think you'll sell fairly frequently. Let's go with the "Winter Sun" cruise which goes for $4,000 double-occupancy (double-occupancy means you double the quoted price).

   $4,000 x 2 = $8,000 price to client

2. Now take the commission from this $8,000 price tag. Most tour and cruise suppliers pay a 10 percent commission.

   $8,000 x 10% = $800 total commission

3. Determine what your commission split with your host agency will be. Most outside agents start off with a 50/50 split, so let's go with that. Now take your 50 percent of the total commission.

   $800 x 50% = $400 your commission

4. Estimate how many transactions of this type you'll do in a year. Let's say you figure on 200.

   $400 x 200 = $80,000 annual gross revenues

Connie G., the agent specializing in travel for Christians and the physically challenged, personally makes about 100 bookings (or reservations) per year. A booking is not necessarily per person—one booking can encompass a single traveler, a party of two, a party of five, or the entire cast and crew of a Broadway roadshow. When Connie adds in the bookings sold by her outside agents, she averages about 150 per year.

Let's say that, over the course of a year, you'll sell 200 "Mayan Magic" tours; and you'll earn a 5 percent commission (your half of the 10 percent), or $150, on each one. This means you will have an annual gross revenue of $30,000.

> **Smart Tip** Tip...
>
> Upscale hotels always boast a concierge—a sort of personal assistant for guests—to handle things like suggesting and making restaurant reservations, obtaining theater tickets, finding and ordering fresh peonies in February, or arranging for that chauffeured limousine stocked with root beer and cheese pizza.

However, if you decide to concentrate on higher-end products, such as the "Winter Sun" cruises that sell for $4,000 double occupancy, your gross annual revenue will tally in at $80,000. Not bad! Since each product will be priced at $8,000—considerably more per-booking revenue than $3,000 for "Mayan Magic" tours—you will earn $400 (your 5 percent commission) on each of the 200 cruises. Refer to the worksheet "Estimating Annual Gross Revenue for Commisionable Products" on page 187 to see a breakdown of the math involved in determining your annual revenue for this example.

Variations on a Theme

There are all sorts of variations on this theme. If you, like Roberta E., the cruise counselor in Georgia, decide to forgo the host relationship and sell a select sprinkling of products, you can double your commission structure since there's no host to split with.

And don't forget about overrides! When you and your host agency sell over a prescribed number of products, the supplier will pay an extra commission, usually 2 percent, which your host agency splits with you just like your regular commission. Since your host splits this commission with you, you'll end up with an extra one percent to add to your regular commission of 5 percent. So, that $150 for "Mayan Magic" can become $180 ($3,000 times 6 percent), and the upscale "Winter Sun" product selling at $8,000 can give you $480 ($8,000 times 6 percent). See the worksheet "Estimating Overrides" on page 190 for figuring the commission on the "Winter Sun" product, including the override.

Not everything you sell will be exactly the same, and that's good. Selling "Mayan Magic" over and over and over would lose its charm in a hurry. The great fun in selling travel is matching products to clients, which means lots of different packages and prices. You can specialize in either high- or low-end products, but there's still going to be a great deal of variety.

Bright Idea
Some travel agents supplement their earnings by selling travel-related products and services, like luggage and house-sitting.

One upscale client, for example, might opt for a seven-day New York City shopping package while another might go for a three-week Mediterranean cruise. Keep this in mind while estimating your earnings. You can make copies of the "Estimating Your Annual Gross Revenue" worksheet on page 191 and use them to figure earnings on various products you plan to sell.

Get It for Them Wholesale

The other method of earning revenue as a travel agent is to buy products from wholesalers and then sell them to your clients at a markup. When you sell a pre-priced, commissionable product, you send the client's payment directly to the supplier. Aside from expenses like advertising, it doesn't cost you anything to sell the product. But when you sell a wholesale product, you must first purchase the product yourself, then turn around and resell it to the client. This means that you'll need more money in the bank for this type of booking.

Something Fishy in Scotland

Let's say you've found a "Go Fish! Scotland" package that sounds like just the ticket for your clients, the fly fishing fiends. You can purchase it from the wholesaler for $980.

Now, here's how you figure out how much to mark it up. First, do a bit of reverse engineering and decide how much you need to make. At the very least, you've got to have $980 to pay yourself back for the price of the product. Then decide what other costs you'll incur. If you will send out a special mailing to your 100 fish-crazy clients that costs $250 for printing and postage, you will have to add in that expense. If you'll rack up another $50 in FedEx charges to deliver the tickets to your clients who buy the product, add that in. Now you have a total cost of $1,280, if you make just one sale.

If you add in a 50 percent markup (another $640), you'll charge your client $1,920, and pocket the $640. If you sell 20 packages at this price, you'll earn actual profits of $12,800 ($640 times 20). Or, you can lower your markup to 25 percent ($320), and sell each product for $1,600, which will earn you $6,400 in profit ($320 times 20).

As yet another variation, you could sell just one "Go Fish! Scotland" package to a single client who you know will snap it up. In this case, your only expense is the actual cost of the product or $980. You could apply a 50 percent markup ($490), which would give you a total price of $1,470. Alternatively, you could choose another markup of more or less, depending on what your research shows a comparable rate should be, or how low you want to go to reward a particularly good customer. It's up to you! Whatever you decide to do, and however you decide to do it, just remember to pencil the estimates into your projected earnings.

Travel Agent Perks

Travel agents get a lot of perks the rest of the working world can only dream about—"leisure" travel as a necessary part of business (fam trips), and the opportunity to meet fascinating people from all over the world. But that's not all. As an independent travel agent, you can direct your own income in a variety of ways. In this section, we'll explore how.

Estimating Overrides

Here's a breakdown of how to calculate the commission on the "Winter Sun" cruise—including an override for volume sales.

1. Let's take the "Winter Sun" cruise, which goes for $4,000 double-occupancy.

   $4,000 x 2 (double-occupancy means you double the quoted price)

   = $8,000 price to client

2. Figure the override. Most tour and cruise suppliers pay a 10 percent commission, with a 2 percent override for volume sales (for instance, if the host agency sells more than $800,000 in product in a year, which includes your sales).

   10% normal commission + 2% override = 12% commission

3. Now take the 12% commission from this $8,000 price tag and figure the total commission.

   $8,000 x 12% = $960 total commission

4. Determine what your commission split with your host agency will be. Most outside agents start off with a 50/50 split, so let's go with that. Now take your 50 percent of the total commission.

   $960 x 50% = $480 your commission

Note: You can take a shortcut on figuring your commission. Divide the total 12 percent commission by 2 (because it's 50 percent, or half to you).

Estimating Your Annual Gross Revenue

Use this worksheet to help you calculate your annual gross revenue for pre-priced commissionable products.

1. Choose a product you think you'll sell fairly frequently.

   $_____ Fill in the sales price of the product.

   _____ x 2 Multiply by two for double-occupancy

   $_____ This is the price your client will pay for this product.

2. Now take the client's price tag and multiply it by 10 percent, which is what most tour and cruise suppliers pay as a commission.

   $_____ Price to your client

   _____ x 10%

   $_____ This is the total commission on this product.

3. Determine what your commission split will be with your host agency. Most outside agents start off with a 50/50 split.

   $_____ Fill in the total commission on this product.

   _____ x ( )% Multiply by the split you expect to receive from your host agency.

   $_____ This is your commission on this product.

4. Estimate how many products of this type you'll sell in a year.

   $_____ Fill in your commission for this product.

   _____ x Multiply by the number of like products you expect to sell in a year.

   $_____ This is your annual gross revenue.

Go for the Gold

You know that domestic airlines pay low commissions (which you can generally figure at about 5 to 8 percent), and then there are those commission caps of $25 one-way and $50 round-trip. International airlines, however, will pay much higher commissions, sometimes up to 25 percent. Car rentals don't pay much—about 5 percent. And some budget-rate hotels don't pay any commissions at all.

On the other hand, most hotels pay 10 percent, with swankier properties checking in at up to 25 percent. Vacation condos can pay 20 percent commissions, and some preferred suppliers, like cruise lines and tour packagers, cheerfully hand over commissions of 12 percent to 20 percent, or more.

Smart Tip

Get your clients a better room rate by asking about discounts off the rack rate. Hotels often give discounts for corporate or other business travelers, seniors, military personnel, members of the Automobile Association of America, and even members of discount clubs like Sam's Club or Costco. But they won't offer the discount unless you ask!

What's a savvy travel agent to do? Sell those higher-ticket, higher-income products. It may take a bit more time and effort to send your clients off on a $10,000 tour of Tuscany, earning you a 15 percent commission, than to book them on a $2,000 fly/drive to Orlando that carries a 10 percent commission. But once you get the hang of it all, the difference in time and effort isn't all that great. Even reserving airline seats can involve a heck of a lot of checking back and forth and back again between your client and the supplier. So as long as you're putting forth that effort, you might as well work smart instead of just hard, and go for the gold.

The More the Merrier

Booking groups on tours and cruises makes your income merrier. You could send one couple on a Tahitian holiday cruise at $4,095 double occupancy, which would earn you in the neighborhood of $573 and would look like this:

$4,095 x 2 (1 couple double-occupancy)
= $8,190

$8,190 x 7 percent commission (your half of 14 percent) = $573.30

Or you could do the same amount of research for the cruise and book that couple, plus their road-rally club of 30 people. You would earn $9,172, figured like this:

$8,190 (one double-occupancy cabin) x 16 couples = $131,040

$131,040 x 7 percent commission
= $9,172.80

Of course, there are all sorts of permutations here. If everybody decides to go for the least expensive cabin category and the early booking fare, your per-couple price will drop considerably. And if your commission is only 5 percent, instead of 7, your commission will shrink even more. But do the math, and you will see that no matter the variables, booking groups is far more lucrative than booking a single cabin.

So encourage those group bookings. Ask your clients if they have friends or relatives who might like to go along. Point out that it's the perfect family reunion with all the togetherness time and none of the work—no potato and gelatin salads to prepare, no beds to make, no dishes to wash. Group bookings can be about more than just families, too. They can encompass sizes from three couples to clubs of 50 individuals or more. "We do a lot of group business that are repeat groups," says Jim T., the cruise specialist. "Each time we do one, we build a little more business for the next time."

Try it yourself. Actively solicit groups of all kinds—mystery or romance writers, bridge clubs, garden clubs, RV clubs, quilting circles, networking groups, weight-loss support groups (who may have to bolster each others' willpower on those eat-around-the-clock cruises), home-schooling circles, singles clubs, and parents of twins. Use your imagination and get those groups fired up!

Beware!
Most commissions are paid on base fares, which means the price less taxes and other fees. For a tour based on a $2,700 single supplement, for instance, the client might write a check for $3,000 or more when taxes and other goodies are added in. Your commission is based on the $2,700 price tag, not the final fee.

Halves with Your Host

You already know about splitting commissions with your host agency; you agree to share any commissions that you bring in. But what about those preferred supplier overrides? How do they get handled? The answer is: in a variety of ways.

Let's say you have a 50/50 split with your host. You're selling "Timber Tours," one of the agency's preferred suppliers; and the Timber people are paying the usual 10 percent commission, plus a 2 percent override once the agency (which includes you) books over $60,000 in annual sales. Now, between your efforts and those of your host (and her other outside agents, if she has them), the agency pushes the envelope and sells that $60,000 in bookings. This means that for the next "Timber Tour" you sell, you get a 6 percent commission (5 percent for your half of the usual commission, plus 1 percent for your half of the override). Right?

Beware!
A few host agencies out there only pay base commissions and don't share overrides of any kind. Make sure you have hammered all this out with your host before you sign on.

Not necessarily. The commission may be retroactive, which means that the Timber people step figuratively back in time and pay the host agency that extra 2 percent for everything it's done that year. This means you now get an extra 1 percent (your half of the override) for everything you've sold for Timber all year. The bottom line here is that you need to keep careful records of how much you've sold for which supplier and when. It can be difficult for the host agency to backtrack later and try to decide who gets how much of what, especially when it may receive a sudden "windfall" from the Timber people of $1,200 (2 percent of $60,000). The check doesn't say "Give $300 of this to Orville Outside Agent." So the easiest way for you to collect is to be able to show your earnings to your host at any time.

How do you know when the agency reaches that magic override collection mark? You don't. You'll have to count on your host sharing the bounty with you in an honest fashion. Most host agencies are perfectly happy to do so. But knowing that they hold the cards makes it even more imperative for you to go with a host that you've investigated and trust.

Commission Time

The other commission payment question, besides "how much," is "when?" What's the timetable for getting all those lovely, fat commission checks? Again, it

---

Greater Rewards

It's nice to sell your clients the highest-priced package on a tour or cruise—you reap higher revenues. But saving your clients money on a package can ultimately lead to far greater rewards.

"When a client does a booking," Jim T. says, "we don't forget about them until it's time for final payment. We continue to monitor all our bookings. If there's an unannounced special or a price reduction in some way, the client may never know, but we look for it and then pass it on.

"We had a client last summer who went on an Alaskan cruise. We found a special that ended up saving them $1,350 over what they thought they were going to pay. We didn't have to tell them, but we did. And it turned into a number of referrals from that client."

What more could a travel agent ask? When you pass along "windfall" cost savings, that original client is likely to be yours for life—and so are all those referrals.

Fun with Fees

Some travel agents charge their clients fees for certain kinds of projects. The whole fee-for-service shebang began when the airlines started tampering with commission structures. Traditional, commercially based agents who were suddenly on the wrong side of the commission tracks decided to take back some of their turf by charging their clients for writing airline tickets.

Today, some traditional and homebased agents still take this approach and have extended this thinking to include other services as well. Agents usually charge $10 to $25 per booking for airline seats, and as much as $75 for developing FIT (foreign independent travel) itineraries. Some agents also charge fees when a client cancels a booking, which is sort of adding insult to injury as the supplier demands cancellation fees as well. And some creative agents charge special fees for concierge-type requests, like making restaurant reservations or golf course tee-times, or redeeming frequent flier miles.

Whether you choose to go the fee-for-service route or not is up to you. If you do, make sure you spell out your policies at the outset of your relationship with your client, not halfway through, or after the fact.

depends on your host agency, on the supplier, and on how much effort you put into the mix.

The first thing to understand is that you don't get that check the second you give the supplier your client's credit card number. In the case of a hotel booking, the property doesn't count your commission until their guest (your client) has checked in and then checked out. So if you're sending someone on a FIT (foreign independent tour) of France three months from now, and you've booked her five nights at a hotel room in Nice where she'll arrive in three months, you don't enter the hotel commission picture until then. Tours and cruises don't generally pay commissions on bookings until after the final payment is received and the tour or cruise has been taken.

This may sound strange, but if you think about it, it makes sense. In the same way that a real estate agent doesn't get his commission until after the house has closed escrow and all monies have changed hands between buyer and seller, a travel agent doesn't get paid until the travel is a done deal. Otherwise, if the client backs out of the deal and the agent has already been paid, the supplier is going to have a hard time getting its money back. So they withhold it until they're assured they've been paid.

If you'll be acting as a tour operator, take heed! Make sure your travelers have followed through before you pay travel agents. But don't drag your feet, either.

Slow to Pay

Some suppliers are very slow payers. The hotel industry, in fact, had such a notorious reputation for "losing" commissions that many chains are now engaged in a hard-core effort to change their image. Look through the pages of agent-oriented magazines and you will see lots of hotel ads that proudly proclaim, "Agents Paid Promptly." Tour operators who are living on the financial edge may also have a difficult time coughing up the commissions. And sometimes, perfectly respectable suppliers honestly lose commissions in the maws of their computer systems, or in the mail.

> **K**nowing that they hold the cards makes it even more imperative for you to go with a host that you've investigated and trust.

Tour operators take heed again. If you drag out paying travel agents, sooner or later they'll stop sending business your way. Develop and maintain a reputation of paying commissions as promptly as possible, and they'll reward you with increased sales.

Dropping Everything

Now, assuming the supplier pays the commission in a reasonable length of time, it may not go to you anyway. If you're working with a host agency, that check will go to your host. And the host agency probably won't pay you the second the check arrives on their desk because:

- Host agencies often like to wait a period of time to make sure the supplier's check clears the bank before writing their own check to you. This is particularly true if the supplier is an unknown entity.

- It's far more efficient for your host to write a single check to you once or twice a month for all the commissions you've accrued in that period, than to drop everything and cut a check every time your commission lands on her desk.

So if we take that same scenario of the FIT to Nice with the hotel commission that you might not see for three months after you've made the booking, we now have to add on up to another month for you to get the check from your host agency. Of course, if you're fully independent—say a cruise-only CLIA affiliate—the cruise line's check will come straight to you, and you won't have to worry about this step in the process.

This is yet another reason why it is important for you to keep clear records of what you booked and when. In four months, you may have done so much additional business that you might not even clearly remember that Nice hotel reservation. So exactly what information should you track? Take a look at the tracking form on page 198. You can make copies and use it as is, or modify it with your company name and any other variables that custom-fit your operation.

Spiffy Promotions

The specialty travel world operates under the same laws of human behavior as the rest of the known universe. And one of those laws is that people perform better when given incentives. Understanding this, travel suppliers frequently offer bonuses, freebies, prizes, contests, sweepstakes, and whatever other perks they can dream up.

Just how spiffy are these *spiffs*, as they are often called? They can be mildly enticing or terrifically motivating, depending on the supplier, the promotion, and what you think is worth working for. Sometimes suppliers will offer a specific monetary bonus—say $10 or $50—for every booking made within a certain time period. Sometimes the spiff is an off-the-chart commission rate during a specific time period, as in 25 percent instead of 10 percent for each booking. Or, instead of monetary awards, a promotion might offer vouchers that you redeem for your own free travel.

You will also see contests, sweepstakes, and drawings for all sorts of goodies. Selling a certain number of hotel bookings might entitle you to a drawing for a free week at the chain's Cancun property. Selling a certain number of cruise bookings might qualify you for a drawing to win $10,000. You might be invited to submit stories about your clients' dream vacations on a supplier's tour (booked by you, of course), with the winning submission landing free travel for the agent and the clients. Or you might get points for every car rental you book that can be redeemed for everything from electronic gizmos, to toys, to airfare.

As a travel agent, suppliers' perks are worth checking out. You will still give your clients the same personalized service, while giving yourself an increased bottom line. As a tour operator, these kinds of perks are well-worth offering. You can attract agents who might otherwise pass you by and with whom you can develop a preferred relationship so that they sell your products on a regular basis. And you get those agents to introduce you to their clients, who, of course, will fall in love with you, too. Everybody wins!

Getting Familiar with Fans

Contrary to popular belief, travel specialists don't get to travel anywhere, anytime absolutely free. Fam trips generally have a price tag attached. True, they're far less expensive than what the average non-industry Joe pays. And it's also true that, like those Las Vegas high rollers, once you attain a reputation as a mega-seller with high productivity levels, you do get some complete freebies. But at the outset, you still have to fork over some funds.

Some hotels give travel professionals 50 percent discounts off the rack rate, while others quote a standard industry-affiliate room price. Attractions—everything from amusement parks to harbor cruises to museums to mystery theaters to rafting

▲

trips—operate on similar principles. Some allow professionals a free ride for the first visit, others offer 10 to 50 percent discounts, and some even give free admission to your guests.

Airlines often offer a 75 percent discount to you, and 50 percent to your travel companion, but they're extremely picky about what seats are available and on which days. Car rental companies usually spring for 15 percent to 20 percent discounts; and tour operators offer discounts of varying rates, generally 20 percent to 50 percent.

Some suppliers insist on seeing an IATAN card; others are happy with your business card and a photo ID. As with everything else in the industry, it's up to you to do your homework and check it out.

Payment Tracking Form

Date of booking: _____

Expected date payment is due:_____   Amount due:_____

Client:_____

Product:_____

Supplier:_____

Confirmation number:_____

Was host agency involved?_____

Date payment is received:_____   Amount paid:_____

Actions taken if not received:

_____

_____

_____

_____

Tour Operator Pricing

As a specialty tour operator, you'll be looking at pricing from a different perspective. One major factor is just what sort of tour you'll offer. A half-day walking tour of your hometown is much easier to price than an all-inclusive motor coach and museum extravaganza in a foreign country.

Pirates for Lunch

Let's start with the easy one and say you're doing a half-day tour of Panama City Beach, Florida, that you'll call "The Pirate Walk." It begins with an Alligator Breakfast in St. Andrews State Park, takes participants on a two-hour nature walk along the crystal sands, and concludes with a boat trip to Shell Island for a Pirate's Picnic Lunch. Take a look at "How to Price a Half-Day Tour" on page 203 for an idea of how to price your tour, and how much you can expect to make.

Keep in mind that the $43,584 you see at the bottom as annual revenue for "The Pirate Walk" represents an estimate. You are planning on 20 participants as your ideal number per tour. If you only get 10 people on some of your tours—or horrors, only five!—your bottom line will sink like Blackbeard stepping into quicksand.

You will also have to account for operating expenses, like advertising and insurance. What about special equipment, like a chest for the pirate's treasure, and food coolers and warmers? Since you'll buy those only once (or at least only once every few years), those go into your start-up costs. Keep in mind, too, that you may want to do more than "The Pirate's Walk." If you're a major go-getter, you might opt for an evening tour in season, something like a "Crystal Sands Sunset Walk and Fish Fry." This will add additional revenue to your annual income.

> ### Smart Tip Tip...
> A great place to start fam shopping is with FAMfacts, an annual directory packed with listings of suppliers and their fam price structures, categorized by type of supplier (tour operator, airline, etc.) and by region. Check out the Appendix for contact information.

Antarctic to Zimbabwe

If you do decide to go for the 14-day motor coach extravaganza—say, a game viewing safari in Zimbabwe, or a tour of the Falklands and the Antarctic, for example—your pricing strategy will be the same. Make sure you factor in every detail and get good solid price estimates. Small elements as well as large can throw off your profit margin if you ignore or forget about them.

You may need to add some of the following items to your price, depending on the type of tours you will be offering to your customers:

▲

Sparkling Sums

What's it like out there in the city walking-tour business? Like everything else in the specialty tour world, it depends on how hard you want to work, how many tourists your turf draws in, and how you entice them to your products.

Dr. Phil charges $8 to $15 per person for his New York rambles, depending on the complexity of the tour. He averages four tours a week in the warm season. In the first year, Dr. Phil made $100; in the second year, he made $1,000; and he brought in $8,000 in the third year—a steady increase in revenue.

Terry, the Seattle tour pro, averages 100 walking tours and 20 events per year. He charges $15 per person for half-day walking tours, $25 per person for a full-day tour, and a $200 minimum for groups. For his events—mystery and scavenger hunts built around Seattle sights—he charges $10 per person, with a $200 group minimum. Terry's gross income tallies in at around $25,000, a sparkling sum for a relative newbie showing off the Emerald City.

- *Net airfare per person.* Include any taxes, tariffs, or other goodies.
- *Transportation on the tour.* Whether it's motor coaches, land rovers, or zodiac boats, estimate the size or number of vehicles based on the number of participants you expect.
- *Parking fees or tolls.* Figure these in if you plan to stop at attractions along your route.
- *Hotel rooms.* Add accommodation costs for participants—don't forget to divide by two for double occupancy! You'll also need to figure in the cost of having rooms for your driver and tour conductor.
- *Luggage handling.* Find out what it will cost to transport your clients' personal belongings and your tour equipment, and figure this cost into your price.
- *Meals.* Multiply the number of meals by a single meal cost, by your number of participants; and don't forget to include your driver and tour conductor.
- *Parties.* Also account for the cost of hosting a welcome/reception party, or a farewell party for your participants.
- *Admission.* Be sure to include any admission fees (per person) for attractions that your tour may encompass.
- *Salary.* Figure in salaries for your driver and tour conductor—unless, of course, it's you.

Your particular tour may require these exact items or entirely different ones. Maybe, like Hannibal, you want to hire elephants to take your guests over the Alps! Whatever you decide to do, be sure you've done your research so you can arrive at a price that's good for you and your clients.

Dollar Stretcher
You may be able to get meals for your driver and tour conductor comped, which means the restaurant or hotel will feed them for free as thanks for the tour business you bring in.

The Tax Man Cometh

When you earn money from your wisely planned and brilliantly executed travel sales and products, someone will be queuing up for a piece of the action: Uncle Sam. If your budget allows, you should also engage an accountant. You probably won't need him or her for your daily or monthly concerns; but it is worth the expense to have someone in the know at the reins when it comes to April 15, or for those panicking questions that come up now and again.

Your tax deductions should be about the same as those for any other small or homebased business. You can deduct a percentage of your home office, so long as you are using it solely as an office. These deductions include all normal office expenses, plus interest, taxes, insurance, and depreciation (this is where the accountant comes in handy). The IRS has added in all sorts of permutations such as: The total amount of the deduction is limited by the gross income you derive from the business activity, minus all your other business expenses (apart from those related to the home office). And you thought that new board game you got for Christmas had complicated rules!

Basically, the IRS doesn't want you to come up with so many home office deductions that you end up paying no tax at all. If, after reading this lowdown, you are still confused, you should consult your accountant.

Driving Miss Travel Specialist

What else can you deduct? Business-related phone calls, the cost of business equipment and supplies (again, so long as you are truly using them solely for your business), subscriptions to professional and trade journals, and auto expenses are all fair game. Auto expenses accrue when you drive your trusty vehicle in the course of doing business or seeking business. In other words, you are chalking up deductible mileage every time you motor out to meet with clients, deliver tickets, give a travel talk or seminar, visit printers, or take a spin upstate to check out suppliers' products.

It's wise to keep a log of your business miles. You can buy one of several varieties at your local office supply or stationers, or you can make one yourself. Keep track as you go. It's no fun to have to backtrack at tax time and guesstimate how many miles you drove to which clients and when.

Let Me Entertain You

You can deduct entertainment expenses, such as wining and dining a client during the course of a meeting, or hosting potential clients at a coffee hour. Keep a log of all these expenses as well, especially if they come to under $75 a pop since you don't technically need to keep receipts for these. And if you're entertaining at home, have your clients or customers sign a guest book.

You must have a business-related purpose for entertaining, such as a sales presentation. General goodwill toward your potential customers or suppliers doesn't cut it, so be sure your log contains the reason for the partying.

Planes, Trains, and Automobiles

When you travel for business purposes, you can deduct airfares, train tickets, rental car mileage, and the like. You can also deduct hotels and meals. And under certain circumstances, you can even deduct recreational side trips you take with your family while you're traveling on business. Since the IRS allows deductions for any such trip you take to expand your awareness and expertise in your field of business, it makes sense to also take advantage of any conferences or seminars that you can attend.

How to Price a Half-Day Tour

Take a look at the following calculation of the price to charge for a half-day tour, and the projected gross annual revenue that will be earned.

1. Park entrance fee per person   *Dunn River* $2.25

2. Breakfast per person (provided by local restaurant) $5.00

3. Walk led by you $0.00

4. Boat trip per person (chartered by local outfitter) $8.00

5. Picnic lunch per person (provided by local restaurant) $7.00

6. Pirate's treasure (candy and trinkets) per person $5.00

    Total tour expenses per person $27.25

7. Add 50 percent markup $13.63

    Your price per person $40.88

8. Participants will perceive this as a "weird" price, so bump it up to $49.95, which people will perceive as "better" because it's less than $50.00.

9. Multiply your price per person by the number of expected participants.

    $49.95 x 20 = $999.00 (your gross earnings each time you run your tour)

10. Multiply your expenses per person by the number of expected participants.

    $27.75 x 20 = $545.00 (your costs each time you run your tour)

11. Subtract your costs from your gross earnings.

    $999.00 − $545.00 = $454.00 (your earnings per tour)

12. Multiply your earnings per tour by the number of days you expect to run it per week.

    $454.00 x 4 (you're accounting for rain days when you can't go out)

    = $1,816.00 (your earnings per week)

13. Multiply your earnings by the number of weeks you expect to run the tour per year.

    $1,816.00 x 24 (you're accounting for the seasonal nature of beach visitors)

    = $43,584.00 (your gross annual revenue from this tour)

Flying High or
Bailing Out

Most people succeed in the specialty
travel business by combining the tried-and-true business
methods of persistence and plain old-fashioned hard work,
with a healthy dose of optimism. If we've illustrated anything in
this book, we hope that it is this: Becoming a successful travel

professional involves lots of work. It is rewarding and sometimes exhilarating work, but hard work nonetheless.

We also hope we've managed to convey that becoming a travel professional is not the same as becoming an overnight success. It takes careful market research, loads of planning, and the abundant application of creativity to achieve those repeat and referral clients.

Love and Homework

When the travel professionals interviewed for this book were asked for some words of advice for beginners, they gave—not surprisingly—some very thoughtful responses. "Do your homework," says Jim T., the Maryland-based cruise specialist. "Set yourself up to be knowledgeable before you talk to your first client. Don't think you're going to start out, open your door, call yourself a travel agency, and then wait for people to come to you. Because it changes so rapidly, you have to go out and constantly upgrade your knowledge of the industry."

Roberta E., the Georgia-based cruise specialist, echoes this sentiment. "If you're going to have a host agency," she says, "research, research, and just keep learning and attending seminars. Keep up to date on everything that goes on in this particular industry. The more you know, the more it's going to help you."

Harry G., the fishing tour operator in California, agrees. "Investigate, investigate, investigate," he says. "Spend money wisely. Ask a lot of questions. Determine what exactly your needs and budget are, and don't get carried away with every vendor who wants to sell you advertising."

Karen A., the expert on Savannah, Georgia, also recommends carefully thinking out your funds. "Budget for three unprofitable years," she counsels. "Spend less money than we did in your first year. You may think you know what you should spend money on, but you don't, and you will waste a lot of it. Many small businesses change direction several times before finding their niches—you take advantage of the money-making opportunities that arise, so spending too much money on your first idea may just leave you short of cash when the great opportunity shows up.

"Find business advisors whether you have any previous business experience or not—not easy when you don't know the business community in town," Karen says. "But you can always go to the SBA [Small Business Administration] and get a SCORE advisor. [SCORE is composed of retired business professionals who volunteer to assist new business owners in their quest for success.] Join the Chamber of Commerce, or better yet, the Small Business Chamber, the Women's Business Group, or some other organization that will help you find people to advise you."

"Be creative," advises Connie G., the specialist in travel for the physically challenged. "Develop specialties. Take a look at what you're interested in and make a niche out of it."

"Get good advice on writing a business plan and figuring your taxes," counsels Judy, the cooking school rep. She also thinks it's crucial to screen "the people [cooking schools in Judy's case] you'll be representing very carefully to make sure they're good."

Beware!
The fear of failure prevents more would-be business owners from succeeding than just about any other factor. They are so afraid of failing that they never start. Don't let this be you!

Dr. Phil S., the New York tour guide, says you don't have to reinvent the wheel. You can join professional guide associations for help on developing tours. And remember that it's not what you know but how you come across that makes a good tour.

Barry S., the race car enthusiast based in Newport Beach, says, "Do something you love. If the profits aren't excessive, or [are] non-existent to start with, you'll still want to continue."

And in Seattle, walking tour and event expert Terry S. advises, "Do it because 1) you think you can do it well, and 2) you really would enjoy it. Don't do it to make big money. If it happens, great, but don't count on it. Be prepared to work hard and long at it to be successful in the sense of 'I'm glad I'm doing this!' As they say, don't quit your day job, unless you can afford it and you have tried it long enough to know it's really what you want to do."

Yin and Yang

If you're the type of person who can handle the ups and downs of entrepreneurship in general, and the yin and yang of creativity and number crunching that makes up the specialty travel world, you'll probably thrive. If not, you may discover during your company's first year of life, or beyond, that the business isn't for you. You may feel that instead of flying high, you're contemplating bailing out.

Whether or not you're earning money, the success of your business is contingent on a happiness factor. Because it's a lot of work and a lot of responsibility, you may discover that you'd be just as happy or more so working for someone else—and that's OK. With everything you'll have learned, you'll be a great job candidate.

However, none of the entrepreneurs interviewed for this book, from a relative newcomer to a veteran with 18 years' experience, seem to have any intention of packing it in. Rather, they seem to have a sense of delight in doing what they enjoy, helping others with the same interests, and being a part of the larger world.

▲

Bumps on the Road

But is it all sunshine and roses? Surely, we hear you asking, even the most successful travel specialists hit some bumps on the road to achievement. So we asked our interviewees about their best and worst experiences in the business.

The independent travel agents counted as their worst experiences scheduling or transit mishaps that were not of their making—and just as painfully—not in their control. "We've had a feeling of helplessness on two occasions in the air portion of cruise bookings," Jim T. relates. "One was a group going to San Juan, Puerto Rico, who got to Atlanta only to discover the airline claimed never to have heard of them or their reservations. Another experience was a sort of "Home Alone" misadventure when a woman missed a flight connection and had to spend an unexpected night in New York City worrying about her children. (Who actually were not home alone, but safely with their grandparents.) After a certain point, there's only so much you as the travel agent can do," Jim says. "It is up to the suppliers, who you hope can live up to the product you've sold on their behalf."

Judy E., the culinary school representative, tells a similar horror story. "A woman had paid for a trip through an auction, but when she arrived at the school in Italy, no one was there. We still don't know where the mix-up was. She came home, and the school apologized profusely. Luckily we didn't have any trouble from her."

"I can't really say there is a worst experience," says Harry G., the fishing aficionado. "The ones that hurt me the most are when clients come back from a trip and

---

Wheel and Deal

As a travel professional, you need to keep your costs pared to the bone to make a profit. So whether you're inquiring about special software, print advertising space, printing services, or suppliers' products, the key word is negotiate. Don't accept the first price anybody quotes you. Ask for a better deal, and surprisingly enough, you'll often get it.

Besides bargaining, shop around. Get quotes from several printers or list brokers. Evaluate not only price but factors like time estimated to complete a project and company qualifications. Talk to suppliers about discounts. Don't be afraid to ask questions. Nobody expects you to be an expert on everything, especially not immediately. If you don't ask, you don't learn.

they're disappointed. The fish were not cooperative, or the weather was not cooperative. One of my ground operators might have been having a bad day, or my operators were having an argument. Those are the things that literally kill me because I rely on comebacks and word-of-mouth. A bad trip is like ten bad trips in the hole, whereas a good trip is like 10 good trips in the bank for me."

Weather plays a major role in the business life of Barry S., the racing tour operator, too. "The worst experience," he says succinctly, "is something you can't control, like weather."

"Bad experiences fall into three categories, I think," says Karen in Savannah, Georgia. "One: Realizing you are going to lose lots of money this year—which has happened to us every October so far. Two: Discovering some horrid glitch in a tour that is your fault, like forgetting to tell the hotel that a group isn't arriving until 10 P.M. so they give the rooms away to someone else. Three: Things you have no control over."

Some Kind of Wonderful

Lest you decide to turn tail and run after these tales, Karen A. advises that the road to success is paved with far more good experiences than bad.

Model Employees

One good experience for Karen has been zero percent employee turnover. "No [company guide] has ever quit," she explains.

Another good experience for Karen has been realizing what competent employees she has, employees who can handle even the toughest situations on their own. Karen remembers, "There was the time Beth and I had gone to visit a barrier island—out of mobile phone range. Janis was in Savannah with a Girl Scout troop scheduled for outdoor activities, in what turned out to be ten inches of rain in seven hours." The group was scheduled for visits to "the Railroad Roundhouse (which was flooded); a walking tour; a program at the [Juliette Gordon Low] Birthplace, which [had] a flooded entrance and backed-up sewer; a picnic in Pulaski Square; and dinner at the Pirates House, which by midday [had] a ceiling from which tiles [were] falling."

Karen explains that her employee, Janis, was able to reschedule the events and bring the Scouts back to their hotel. Janis then arranged for their picnic supplier to bring the picnic to the hotel, which graciously offered the use of a breakfast room for the Scouts' meal. Karen recounts that dinner also had to be rerouted. Janis called a local café, covered the meal with her own credit card, and "subsequently [pointed] out to me that all this proved cheaper than several of the restaurants we regularly use," says Karen.

Reaping the Rewards

Also on Karen's list of good things about the business is the financial field. "It's realizing your revenues are going to be up 400 percent from the year before; receiving the contract and deposit on a $15,000 tour, feeling that you can look your bank and your SCORE counselor in the face," she says. "Our best experiences are yet to come: profitability and decent salaries."

Profitability is one sure measure of success, but it's not the only one. Terry S. in Seattle says, his success "is repeat business and referrals from clients who had a good experience with my company!"

Harry, the fishing guide, can relate. "The highlights of my business," he says, "are wonderful trips where clients write me glowing letters, and they send me Christmas cards. I'm the best guy on this planet. That makes me feel wonderful."

Barry, the car enthusiast, agrees. "We've had so many bests," he says. "We've had some wonderful occasions on tours, just magnificent. I look at some of the letters afterwards, and it makes me very happy."

And Connie, who enables those with disabilities to travel, voices much the same sentiment. "I've had so many bests in this industry," she explains. "Much as I hate issuing airline tickets, helping to get a runaway back home was one. Any time I talk to somebody after a trip, and they tell me what a fantastic time they had—how much they needed it, how it not only met their expectations but exceeded them—that's my best."

This seems to be the attitude of all the travel specialists who so generously helped with this book: the joy in a job well done and the desire to make a difference for others. If you go into this business with the right stuff—the willingness to work hard, to learn everything you can; the confidence to promote yourself and your business; and the drive to succeed—chances are you will!

Appendix
Specialty Travel Resources

They say you can never be rich enough or young enough. While this could be argued, we say "You can never have enough resources." Therefore, we present for your consideration a wealth of sources for you to check into, check out, and harness for your own personal information blitz.

These sources are tidbits, ideas to get you started on your research. They are by no means the only sources out there, and they should not be taken as the Ultimate Answer. We've done our research, but businesses—like people—do tend to move, change, fold, and expand. As we have repeatedly stressed, *do your homework.* Get out and start investigating.

As an additional tidbit to get you going, we strongly suggest the following: If you haven't joined the Internet Age, do it! Surfing the Net is like waltzing through the fabled Library at Alexandria, updated for the 21st century, with a breathtaking array of resources literally at your fingertips.

Associations

Airlines Reporting Corporation, ARC Corporate Communications, 1530 Wilson Blvd., #800, Arlington, VA 22209-2448, (703) 816-8525, www.arccorp.com

▲

Air Transport Association of America (ATA), 1301 Pennsylvania Ave. NW, #1100, Washington, DC 20004-1707, (202) 626-4000,www.air-transport.org

Adventure Travel Society (ATS), 228 N. F St., Salida, CO 81201, (719) 530-0171, www. adventuretravel.com

American Society of Travel Agents (ASTA), 1101 King St., #200, Alexandria, VA 22314, (800) 275-2782, www.astanet.com

Cruise Lines International Association (CLIA), 500 Fifth Ave., #1407, New York, NY 10110, (800) 372-CLIA (fax-on-demand for certification information), www.cruis ing.org

Institute of Certified Travel Agents (ICTA), 148 Linden St., P.O. Box 812059, Wellesley, MA 02482-0012, (800) 542-4282, www.icta.com

International Airlines Travel Agency Network, www.iatan.org

International Air Transport Association, www.iata.org

National Association of Commissioned Travel Agents (NACTA), P.O. Box 2398, Valley Center, CA 92082-2398, (760) 751-1197, www.nacta.com

National Association of Cruise Oriented Agencies (NACOA), 7600 Red Rd., #128, Miami, FL 33143, (305) 663-5626, www. nacoa.com

National Mail Order Association (NMOA), 2807 Polk St. NE, Minneapolis, MN 55418-2954, (888) 496-7337 (for ordering books and reports only), (612) 788-1673, www. nmoa.org

Travel Industry Association Of America, 1100 New York Ave. NW, #450, Washington, DC 20005-3934, (202) 408-8422, www.tia. org

United States Tour Operators Association (USTOA), 342 Madison Ave., #1522, New York, NY 10173, (212) 599-6599, www. ustoa.com

Books

Conducting Tours: A Practical Guide, Marc Mancini, Delmar Publishers

✳ *Home-Based Travel Agent: How to Cash in on the Exciting New World of Travel Marketing*, Kelly Monaghan, The Intrepid Traveler

✳ *How to Start a Home Based Travel Agency*, Tom and Joanie Ogg, Tom Ogg and Associates

Start and Run a Profitable Tour Guiding Business, Barbara Braidwood, Susan M. Boyce and Richard Cropp, Self-Counsel Press

Consortia

Cruise Shoppes America Ltd., www. cruiseshoppes.com

Vacation.com, (800) 843-0733, www.vacation.com

Helpful Government Agencies

Bureau of the Census, www.census.gov

U.S. Postal Service, (800) THE USPS, www.usps.gov, or www.usps.gov/business/ calcs.htm (for mail rate calculators)

Magazines and Publications

Catalog Age, Cowles Business Media, 11 River Bend Dr. S, Box 4949, Stamford, CT 06907-0949, (203) 358-9900 (editorial), (800) 775-3777 (subscriptions), www. catalogagemag.com

Cruise & Vacation Views, 25 Washington St., Morristown, NJ 07960, (973) 605-2443

FAMfacts, GTC FAMfacts, 717 St. Joseph Dr., St. Joseph, MI 49085, (800) 522-2093, www.famfacts.com

JAX FAX Travel Marketing Magazine, Circulation Dept., 397 Post Rd., Darien, CT 06820, www.jaxfax.com

Official Tour Directory, Thomas Travel Ventures, 5 Penn Plaza, New York, NY 10001, (212) 290-7355, www.vacationpackager.com

Specialty Travel Index, 305 San Anselmo Ave., #313, San Anselmo, CA 94960, (888) 624-4030, (415) 455-1643, www.specialty travel.com

Target Marketing, 401 N. Broad St., Philadelphia, PA 19108, (215) 238-5300, www.targetonline.com

Travel Agent, P.O. Box 6049, Duluth, MN 55806-6049, (888) 527-7008 (subscriptions)

Travel Age West, 9911 W. Pico Blvd., 11th Floor, Los Angeles, CA 90035, (310) 772-7430, subscriptions: (800) 446-6551, ext. 4445

Travel Counselor, One Penn Plaza, New York, NY 10119-1198, (212) 615-2635

Travel Weekly, 500 Plaza Dr., Secaucus, NJ 07094, (800) 360-0015

Note: Most magazines will send a sample issue free of charge if you call and ask. So be sure to!

Mailing Lists

Allmedia International, 17060 Dallas Pkwy., #105, Dallas, TX 75248-1905, (800) 466-4061, (972) 818-4060

American List Counsel, 88 Orchard Rd. CN-5219, Princeton, NJ 08543, (800) ALC-LIST, (908) 874-4300, www.amlist.com

Database America, 100 Paragon Dr., Montvale, NJ 07645, (800) 223-7777, (201) 476-2000, www.databaseamerica.com

Note: Check into any issue of magazines like *Catalog Age* or *Target Marketing*—advertisements for list brokers, managers, and owners abound.

Specialty Travel Software

Consolidator Profiles Inc., 1257 Worcester Rd., #269, Framingham, MA 01701-5217, www.consolidatorprofiles.com

CruiseDirector, Sabre Inc., www.sabre. com/travelagent/ta_desktop.html

Go! Solo, Worldspan, 300 Galleria Pkwy. NW, Atlanta, GA 30339, (800) 743-5781, www.worldspan.com

Planet Sabre, Sabre Inc., (888) 397-2273, www.sabre.com/travelagent/ta_desktop.html

Weissmann Travel Reports, P.O. Box 49279, Austin, TX 78765, (512) 320-8700, www.weissmann.com

Specialty Travel Web Sites

Crossroads, www.twcrossroads.com

Cruise Calendar, www.cruisecalendar. com

Expedia, www.expedia.com

Preview Travel, www.previewtravel.com

Travelocity, www.travelocity.com

Successful Specialty Travel Businesses

Karen Arms, President, Tootsy Tours Inc., 12½ W. State St., Savannah, GA 31401, (912) 232-0032, www.tootsytours. com

Judy Ebrey, Cuisine International, P.O. Box 25228, Dallas, TX 75225, (214) 373-1161, www.cuisineinternational.com

Roberta Elmhorst, Capri Cruises & Tours, P.O. Box 493, Brayson, GA 30017, (770) 985-4050, www.CapriCruisesandTours.com

Connie George, Connie George Travel Associates, P.O. Box 312, Glenolden, PA 19036, (888) 532-0989, (610) 532-0989, www. cgta.com

Harry Gualco, Rod and Reel Adventures, 566 Thomson Ln., Copperopolis, CA 95228, (800) 356-6982, www.rodreeladventures. com

Dr. Phil Schoenberg, New York Talks and Walks, P.O. Box 656780, Flushing, NY 11365, (888) 377-4455, www.newyorktalksandwalks.com

Terry D. Seidler, See Seattle Walking Tours & Events—Since 1993, 11980 SE 87th Ct., Newcastle, WA 98056-1743, (425) 226-7641, www.see-seattle.com

Barry Simpson, Grand Prix Tours, 1701 Camelback St., Newport Beach, CA 92660, (949) 717-3333, www.gptours.com

Jim and Nancy Terracciano, Cruises Come True LLC, (800) 365-9985, (301) 855-8777, www.cruisescometrue.com

Travel Agency Consultants

Dr. Robert W. Joselyn, CTC; Joselyn, Tepper & Associates Inc.; 8075 E. Morgan Trail, #1, Scottsdale, AZ 85258; (480) 443-0098; www.joselyntepper.com

Glossary

ACC: *see* Accredited Cruise Counsellor.

Accredited Cruise Counsellor (ACC): CLIA certification to sell its members' cruises.

Adventure travel: leisure vacations focusing on cultural or outdoor activities.

Adventure Travel Society (ATS): professional association of adventure travel tour operators.

Affinity group: tour group with a particular interest like genealogy or gardening.

Air-inclusive: tour package that includes airfare to the tour's origination city in the price.

Airlines Reporting Corporation (ARC): an industry association that appoints travel agents to write airline tickets and then administrates commissions.

Air Transport Association of America (ATA): an industry group made up of the major domestic airlines.

American Society of Travel Agents (ASTA): professional association of travel agents.

Appointment: designation to write airline or other travel product tickets.

ARC: *see* **Airlines Reporting Corporation.**

Assigned seating: cruise dining room plan in which passengers occupy the same table each night.

ASTA: *see* American Society of Travel Agents.

ATA: *see* Air Transport Association of America.

ATS: *see* Adventure Travel Society.

Base fare: air, cruise, or other fare excluding taxes and other fees.

Booking: a travel reservation.

Certified Travel Agent (CTA): certification available from the Institute of Certified Travel Agents.

CLIA: *see* Cruise Lines International Association.

Comp: abbreviation for complimentary; in this context a hotel room, meal, or other product given for free.

Computerized Reservation System (CRS): online system for booking airline and other travel product reservations.

Concierge: personal guest assistant on a hotel's staff.

Consolidator: a company that buys bulk airline tickets and resells them at discounted rates.

Consortium: a group of suppliers—like tour operators and cruise lines—that provides higher commissions to travel agents in exchange for doing a specific volume of business with them.

CRS: *see* Computerized Reservation System.

Cruise Lines International Association (CLIA): a marketing association made up of international cruise lines that accredits travel agents to sell cruises.

CTA: *see* Certified Travel Agent.

Deadheading: driving an empty bus from a passenger drop-off point back to a home base.

Double occupancy: tour or cruise term meaning that the price must be multiplied by two because it assumes two people will occupy a cabin or room.

Ecotour: tour focusing on ecologically or environmentally sensitive areas.

e-Ticket: electronic ticket issued by airlines instead of a paper ticket and boarding pass.

Fam trip: abbreviation for familiarization trip, which is a product offered by suppliers to travel sellers at a reduced price.

FIT: *see* foreign independent tour.

Focus group: a small group gathered for the purpose of conducting market research.

Foreign independent tour (FIT): a tour, generally of a foreign destination, in which the client explores on his own instead of with a group.

General seating: cruise dining room plan in which passengers do not occupy the same table each night.

GG Rates: *see* guaranteed group rates.

Guaranteed group rates: term meaning a supplier guarantees a booking agent will match any lower price quoted on the same product to a different agent.

Hard-adventure tours: high-energy, athletic-oriented activities like white-water rafting or mountain biking.

Host agency: travel agency (with appointments to write airfare, cruise, or other travel products) through which outside or independent agents sell products.

Hub-and-spoke concept: tour practice of lodging clients at a centrally located hotel and taking day trips to outlying areas.

IATA: *see* International Air Transport Association.

IATAN: *see* International Airlines Travel Agent Network.

ICTA: *see* Institute of Certified Travel Agents.

✳ **Inbound operator:** tour operator that brings in clients from abroad and takes them around the operator's home region.

✳ **Independent travel agent:** a travel agent who works alone or with a few associates or employees and is usually homebased.

Institute of Certified Travel Agents (ICTA): an international nonprofit educational association for travel agents.

International Airlines Travel Agent Network (IATAN): industry association that accredits travel agents to sell tickets for international air carriers.

International Air Transport Association (IATA): industry association of international airlines.

Land-only: tour package that does not include airfare to the tour's origination city in the price.

MAP: *see* Modified American Plan.

Master Cruise Counsellor (MCC): CLIA certification to sell its members' cruises.

MCC: *see* Master Cruise Counsellor.

Meet-and-greet guide: a tour representative who meets clients at the airport and escorts them to their hotel.

Modified American Plan (MAP): tour configuration in which clients are fed two out of three meals a day, usually breakfast and dinner, as part of the tour price.

Motor coach: tour bus.

NACOA: *see* National Association of Cruise Oriented Agencies.

NACTA: *see* National Association of Commissioned Travel Agents.

National Association of Commissioned Travel Agents (NACTA): a professional organization for independent travel agents.

National Association of Cruise Oriented Agencies (NACOA): professional association of travel agencies that specialize in selling cruises.

Option date: the date on which a tour or cruise deposit is due.

Outbound operator: tour operator that takes local clients abroad.

Outfitter: tour operator who provides trip-oriented gear like river rafts or bicycles.

Override: higher than average commission awarded by suppliers to highly productive sellers.

Preferred supplier: travel product supplier that rewards highly productive sellers with higher than average commissions.

Products: tours, cruises, hotels, and other elements sold by travel agents and tour operators.

Rack Rate: the regular rate hotels charge for rooms.

Seller of Travel Laws: state laws governing travel agents and tour operators.

Single supplement: extra price charged to tour or cruise clients who do not want to share a double-occupancy room or cabin.

Soft-adventure tours: culturally oriented activities like antiquing or gardening.

Spiff: an incentive offered by a supplier such as a bonus, an extremely high commission, or a free product.

Split itinerary: tour configuration in which clients are given a choice of activities on the same day.

Standard Ticket and Area Settlement Plan: an ARC-administered program to standardize airline tickets and also to mete out travel agent commissions.

Step-on guide: a local guide who steps onto the motor coach to show clients a particular city or area.

Supplier: companies such as air and cruise lines, tour operators and hotels that provide travel products.

Ticketless travel: *see* e-ticket.

Tour director: tour operator representative who shepherds clients throughout tour; also called tour manager, tour escort, tour leader, or tour host or hostess.

Tour operator: a company that designs, markets, and runs tours.

Traffic documents: airline tickets.

Travel Industry Association of America: an organization that works to meld the various elements of the U.S. travel industry into a cohesive group.

Trip cancellation insurance: insurance available to clients to protect against losing deposits or payments in the event of trip cancellation.

United States Tour Operators Association (USTOA): professional association of tour operators.

USTOA: *see* United States Tour Operators Association.

Africa First 651-646-4721

Index